231735

"Rabbi Spero is one of America's foremost authorities on the nexus of faith and freedom. Through an historic analysis of the founding of this nation and the intent of the forebearers, he offers a very thoughtful blueprint for the recovery of American pride and American exceptionalism. This book will give the reader hope for the future of our nation."
—Lieutenant General William G. Boykin, U.S. Army (Retired), author of *Never Surrender: A Soldier's Journey to the Crossroads of Faith and Freedom*, http://jerryboykin.com

"There are few activists with greater courage and conviction than Rabbi Aryeh Spero. His moral compass is a model of Judeo-Christian thought, and the clarity of his writing is superb. This book has the right message, and it certainly comes at the right time."
—Bill Donohue, President, Catholic League for Religious and Civil Rights, http://www.catholicleague.org

"Supreme Court Justice Benjamin Cardozo wrote, 'Danger invites rescue.' When the danger, as today, comes from multiple sources: from the Iranian threat of nuclear annihilation to the deliberate trashing of the Judeo-Christian ethos here at home, we have our champion in Rabbi Aryeh Spero whose courage drives the armor-piercing power of his words to inspire."
—Barry Farber, radio talk host, recipient of the "Radio Host of the Year" award

"With articulate precision Rabbi Aryeh Spero addresses the tension every conservative confronts in a nation driven by radical liberal ideology: 'Shall I remain silent and safe or lift up my voice in the arena of thoughts and ideas?' In a moment in history when truth has fallen silent in the streets of America, *Push Back* is a timely call to, in the words of Winston Churchill, 'Never give in to the overwhelming might of the enemy.' In reading Rabbi Spero's book, the words of the holocaust survivor Eli Wiesel come to mind, 'We must take sides. Neutrality helps the oppressor, never the victim. Silence encourages the tormenter, never the tormented. Sometimes we must interfere.' This book is a must read for every righteous American that wants to interfere."
—Aaron Fruh, Pastor, Knollwood Church, author of *The Forgotten Blessing* and coauthor of *Two Minute Warning*

"After a lifelong career in coaching college football and nineteen years as a television football analyst with ESPN, I know something about the importance of a strong offensive line. Rabbi Spero's book will challenge you to stand your ground in a day when the core values of Judeo-Christian faith are in jeopardy."
—Coach Mike Gottfried, former college football coach and commentator for ESPN, Founder of Team Focus, http://www.teamfocususa.org

"Rabbi Spero has been a leading and thoughtful voice in the ongoing Judeo-Christian conversation about how to confront the evil that confronts America. This book offers a valuable collection of his thoughts on the subject. It comes at a dark moment in our history and offers encouragement to all of us in the struggle. It is an eloquent statement of the truth that is the basis for all freedom and liberty."
—Andrea Lafferty, President, Traditional Values Coalition, http://www.traditionalvalues.org

"Rabbi Spero is an undeviating defender of the Judeo-Christian tradition that serves as the basis for our political and cultural institutions. This book addresses the radical secular view that this nation can prosper without its most basic principles. Rabbi Spero dispatches that argument along with other misguided notions that have gained traction in the cultural mist."
—Dr. Herb London, President Emeritus, Hudson Institute, http://www.hudson.org

"All who've been privileged to hear Rabbi Spero's inspiring words know he has the power to make us again feel we can cheer for America, even during these dark times. He champions the idea that the survival of liberty in our nation depends on following the virtues fostered by the traditional family and religious moral base. His clarion call to action and intelligent analysis of the issues, combined with keen insights into our social problems and a patriotic love of country make him a Tea Party favorite."
—Bob MacGuffie and Anthony Stark, Right Principles, http://rightprinciples.com

"In an increasingly dangerous, Alice-in-Wonderland, ethically challenged world, where bewildering problems of men in conflict with decency and with each other swirl all around us, on a planet colliding with its destiny, one need not imagine the wrath of God; we can hear His voice in the sound and fury and warnings of author Aryeh Spero whose voice resembles that of a brilliant, righteous, powerful, insightful, passionate, avenging angel."
—Michael Meyers, President and Executive Director, the New York Civil Rights Coalition (NYCRC), http://nycivilrights.org

"For nearly a generation Rabbi Aryeh Spero has tirelessly urged Americans to defend and nourish the Judeo-Christian roots of our civilization. In his new book he returns to this theme with the eloquence and candor that have marked his appearances in the nation's Public Square. *Push Back* is a timely book indeed."
—George H. Nash, author of *The Conservative Intellectual Movement in America Since 1945*

"*Push Back* is defined as 'the act of forcing the enemy to withdraw.' There is no better way to get our nation back and no one better to lead the charge than Rabbi Aryeh Spero."
—Janet L. Porter, President, Faith2Action, http://www.f2a.org

"Rabbi Aryeh Spero is a rare man of principle and courage who gets it! He understands that what has made this country the freest and most prosperous nation in history is the foundation that was laid by people who were empowered by their faith rooted in the Word of God. I am proud to call him friend."
—Dr. Rick Scarborough, Founder and President, Vision America, http://www.visionamerica.us

"Rabbi Spero's words will inspire you and make you cheer again for America. He combines soaring language with the need for action."
—Tim Sumner, Co-Founder, 9/11 Families for a Safe and Strong America, http://www.911familiesforamerica.org

"Aryeh Spero argues that Barack Obama meant it when he said his goal was 'fundamentally transforming America.' *Push Back* is a call to arms for those who would resist."
—James Taranto, *The Wall Street Journal*

"Rabbi Spero is one of our nation's most passionate spokesmen, continually championing our national identity and proclaiming confidence in the American spirit. He writes with courage and insight. Read this book, and you'll feel renewed about America's greatness and will be ready to act on her behalf."
—Major General Paul E. Vallely, U.S. Army (Retired), Chairman, Stand Up America, http://www.standupamericaus.org

PUSH

BACK

Reclaiming the American Judeo-Christian Spirit

Rabbi Aryeh Spero

Evergreen
PRESS

Mobile, Alabama

ISBN 978-1-58169-432-1
For Worldwide Distribution
Printed in the U.S.A.

Evergreen Press
P.O. Box 191540 • Mobile, AL 36619
800-367-8203

To my wife and family,
Marguerite,
and the courageous patriots
who fight for America

Contents

Introduction

Even before that historic and miraculous gathering in Philadelphia during the months preceding and after 1776, America had been animated by a soaring spirit that has continued to beat in the heart of its countrymen from generation to generation. For untold Americans, America is as personal and important as family and faith itself. And that is because America is more than a place where free elections take place; it is the *Land of the Majestic Idea*, where personal dreams and destinies are made possible precisely because of our founding idea and ethos.

Our Founders were men of serious scholarship, action, honor, and daring who culled their outlook from the Pilgrims who risked all to establish a New World, based on principles from the Bible, the classic philosophers of antiquity, and the natural law and common sense philosophers of the eighteenth century. They understood that the foundation of a fair, just, and productive society lay in liberty, not in a heavy-handed government imposing outcomes and stifling individual spirit. They declared their independence from Europe—with its aristocracies, monarchies, and government interference—so that a land of liberty could, for the first time in history, be given a chance to flower. This noble undertaking was called the United States of America, a singular beacon of liberty to those fortunate enough to be born or arrive here.

For liberty to work and endure, men must live by personal responsibility and a self-policing morality. Liberty for all is achieved when we are not classified according to the group we were born into but as individuals. Being an individual means not excusing your personal actions on the altar of group preference. Men have individual liberty when each person is provided equality. But our Founders stated, after much deliberation, that government cannot, nor should it attempt to, fashion equal material outcomes; rather it should guarantee equality—equal justice—under the law. It is treatment based, not outcome based.

Equal justice under the law, as well as men's other liberties, comes not from government but, as the Founders believed, is granted by God. Believing that rights and liberties come from God and not government is what distinguished the American Founding from the French Revolution and later European models. You see, our Founders were religious men who had abiding respect for the broad themes of the Bible.

In fact, the Founding of America was a moral enterprise, one based on five basic biblical principles: (1) personal responsibility, (2) seeing man as an individual as opposed to a member of a group, (3) rights from God, (4) moral conduct and moral clarity, and (5) the right of the individual to choose how he makes his living, what he owns, and the ability to aspire to be the best he can be. So as to secure these rights, a strong defense was proposed to protect against those who would jeopardize these liberties. This outlook is called the Judeo-Christian ethos, since its foundation and guiding lights are found in their fullness in the Old and New Testaments only.

The Judeo-Christian ethos does not suggest a particular mode of worship nor does it offer a specific religious creed. It is an attitude, a philosophy. It constitutes the historic American civilization and our ongoing identity. Until very recently, those who immigrated here became members of our civic identity through the "melting pot," and our children in school were taught our glorious civic heritage. Americanism was a crowning achievement and sought-after identity. Indeed, modern day political conservatism has as its goal the preservation and continuance of our cherished identity. This book is for all those who wish to learn about America as it was constituted, not those who are holding off their "love" until America becomes socialist Europe.

As *Push Back* will demonstrate, no country, even America, can endure without a specific identity; and identities are tied to nationhood, culture, and a particular religious moral outlook. Socialism and today's left liberalism come specifically to uproot and erase unique national identities. America's success has not come because it happens to be a land mass between the Atlantic and Pacific but is the direct byproduct of its Judeo-Christian ethos, an ethos and attitude not found similarly anywhere else. It is the engine, practically and morally, for our three hundred year success, and to the degree we allow it to be taken from us, we risk losing our liberty, prosperity, and national purpose.

We must *push back* against an unrelenting and programmed assault by liberal demagogues co-opting our schools and colleges, our media and entertainment, and much of our government and courts—national and local. Zealots are indoctrinating this generation, indeed our own children, to disdain what we love and to indict America. The liberal elite probably constitute but 10 percent of the population, but they have been successful because they invoke what they call morality, and we are too willing to grant them the moral high ground. But as readers will soon see, leftist morality is not classic morality at all, rather that which gives moral title to anything leading to socialism. I have known liberal movers and shakers firsthand for decades, and they are not more moral than you or I—perhaps the opposite. But they are making dangerous gains because we—both the religious and non-religious—have not fought back nearly enough.

For decades liberals have exploited American goodwill by demanding a superficial and simplistic notion of social justice. *Push Back* will demonstrate how this is but a disguise to enact a socialism that will ultimately impoverish the middle class and is hardly moral at all. Liberals have even begun targeting capitalism and free enterprise, but readers will see that capitalism is highly moral and the single greatest avenue for individuals to fairly reach their potential.

Leftist fanatics are feverishly dictating to our local schools, places of worship, and town halls, inundating us every moment with their propaganda, hijacking our moral language, and demonizing those who stand in their way. They have waged war against our historic American norms, beliefs, culture, and identity. Even the liberal clergy are pitifully engaged in what I call *religious correctness*. The Left will not stop by themselves. It is up to us to stop them, and after reading this book, I am convinced thousands will have the confidence and inner fortitude to take on the extremists who are today's liberal left.

The battle against mainstream America preceded President Obama, but there is no elected official more purposefully driven to transform America than he. It seems no week goes by without Mr. Obama quietly signing an Executive Order handing over American sovereignty to international agencies and, with it, liberties bequeathed this nation by God and our Founders. Tens of millions feel something terribly wrong is happening right in front of their eyes. In concert with self-centered elitists, who are often quite wealthy, Mr. Obama and a liberal ruling class see themselves as being above the people. Like the European aristocracies, they are working nonstop in every way they can to consolidate wealth and power, to the detriment of our historically robust middle class.

This is one battle that cannot be fought by our soldiers overseas: this battle is stateside, within our borders. We citizen patriots must now step forward resolutely and with courage. Fortunate are those who live in times where the battle is joined. My prayer is that after reading this book, we will all be strengthened and inspired to do the job of reclaiming America. Now is the time!

Aryeh Spero
July 4, 2012

★★★ ONE ★★★

Hearty Oaks

[*We are not tumbleweeds but hearty oaks firmly rooted.*]

Early last year, I was sitting in the lobby of a New Jersey hotel the morning after I had delivered a speech to a conservative group. The television was tuned to a CNN morning program showing a clip of Senator Mitch McConnell responding to the latest socialist-like stimulus package being presented by the Democrats. I cheered him on. I had spoken to Senator McConnell at length twice when he was in New York City and liked him not only as an honest and reliable man but also for his conservative principles and his follow-through in the Senate when standing up for those beliefs. No one else in the lobby, however, displayed any overt agreement with the senator's remarks. A few moments later, when President Barack Obama appeared on the TV screen, his supporters showed no hesitation in applauding him. I wondered if I was the only conservative in the lobby.

I was about to leave when two women came over, and seeing my yarmulke, beard, and suit, asked if I was a rabbi. "Yes, I am," I answered. They then proceeded to tell me of their admiration and love of Israel. One of the women pointed to two other friends nearby and remarked how they too prayed for Israel's security. I mentioned that Senator McConnell, who had just appeared on TV, was a great friend of Israel. I added, as I always do in these types of conversations, that he is conservative "just as I am."

A broad smile crossed her face—a smile of fraternity and relief.

"So are we," she said of herself and friends.

"I thought I was the only conservative in the room, since I was the only one who seemed to agree with the senator's remarks," I said.

I will never forget her answer: "When in public and among strangers, we keep our conservatism to ourselves. It's safer that way. We're real estate brokers and don't want to jeopardize our business; and even in social gatherings we keep our political beliefs to ourselves so as not to risk a friendship or upset anybody."

1

I didn't respond with a sermon, but simply said: "Liberals never seem to hold back from telling others of their liberal beliefs—not in private and not in public. Neither should we."

She hesitated and then very respectfully said: "I'm pleased to hear you're conservative. I figured all rabbis were liberals and Democrats. You know, so many clergymen preach that people of compassion should be liberal."

"I know, and it's one of the most misguided platitudes of our time," I answered. "The liberal agenda results in dependency, an ethos of victimization, and a loss of freedom. It gives control to those in charge of 'doing the compassion.'"

Later that day, I kept mulling over the irony of the lady's words. Here was a woman who was decent, compassionate, religious—and conservative—yet somehow assumed that others concerned with such sentiments as compassion were probably liberal. Who, I wondered, made her think this way? And why were she and her friends reluctant to publicly express their heartfelt conservative beliefs when liberals wear their liberalism as a public badge of honor? After all, today's conservatism embodies the historic belief and value system that constitutes Americanism, an Americanism rooted in the Judeo-Christian ethos. It has produced more across-the-board prosperity and freedom than the world has ever known, and within it lies decency, morality, blessing, and the seeds for human potential and accomplishment. It is remarkable, and every day I feel so fortunate, honored, and uplifted to be part of it.

It is we conservatives who should be announcing our conservatism—with great pride and enthusiasm—to all those we meet. It should be our badge of honor, worn with confidence.

★★★

As a political definition, conservatism means preserving classic and time tested principles born of past ancestors along with a wisdom that should be passed on to future generations, not only for their sake but also for the benefit of the country. In this way our country will blessedly endure. Conservatism is an outlook that exalts the notion of individuals getting up in the morning surrounded by a freedom that allows them to choose their personal way and become the best they can be, to fend for themselves and family, and to reach the potential implanted in them by God. This way of life eliminates any worries about an overreaching government or clique of elites micromanaging their lives and regulating their day-to-day activities so that they no longer are truly free.

But conservatism is more than a political outlook. In our day, it has become the repository for the profound moral truths and principles bequeathed to us by the Judeo-Christian ethos. It equips us with the necessary and fortifying tools to navigate the vicissitudes of life. Conservatism helps us distinguish between right and wrong, light and darkness; between that which is wholesome as opposed to that which is impure; and identifies evil for what it is and our ongoing mandate to crush it. Living by it is akin to wearing a pair of specially made moral glasses that allow us to see the world through a proper perspective. As such, it is a way of living and approaching life. What it is, really, is a *heritage*, a noble and inspired heritage.

It took thousands of years and untold sacrifice and heroism to fully develop this Judeo-Christian heritage that found its home and actualization in the unique mindset of America. If we lose it, nothing out there can match or replace it. It is worth conserving, worth fighting for. In fact, there is nothing more worthwhile and urgent than our battle for the soul of America so that we can preserve and perpetuate for our children and grandchildren that which we call Americanism. After all, don't we want them to have the blessings of freedom and prosperity we have had?

A majority of Americans feel as I do, and though they may not be able to express it in precise words, they know and feel in their hearts what I have just written. They love America—they love it for what it was and for what it is.

Unlike the political Left that wants to radically change America to become something entirely different, something like Norway or Belgium, we conservatives cherish our historic and unique American civilization. We are not withholding our love for her until such time that America forfeits its Americanism and morphs into a European socialist "utopia." Goosebumps rise as we hear the "Star Spangled Banner," and pride and awe fill our hearts when we think of the great men and women who founded this country and the soldiers who have defended it.

We look around and see how Americans, in each category, live better than do their counterparts anywhere else in the world. Those with an unblemished eye know, under our ethos of fair play for the individual, there is more opportunity and freedom in ten square miles of America for those willing to work hard or take risks than in entire continents in other parts of the globe. We don't spend our time always finding fault and announcing what is wrong with America, but instead we declare what is good about her. And that's because we love the ideal upon which this country was founded. We aren't out to change the Constitution because somehow it is outdated or flawed, but we revere it and feel fortunate to live under it. And in humility, we realize there are things greater in wisdom and morality—principles that preceded us—than the theories of the social engineers driven by their own self-worship.

★★★

For a nation or a people to survive it needs an identity, a specific cultural identity. Everyone in this country is free to practice any religious belief he wants so long as it does not harm others or force others to relinquish their civic rights and daily freedoms. But a nation needs to have an overarching cultural theme as to what makes it *this* nation and not another. It needs a certain ethic, a common sociology that embodies its value system and national character. For almost four hundred years in America it has been the Judeo-Christian ethos and outlook that has bonded us in nationhood and has served to create a transcendent fraternity among our citizens. And it has worked, as nowhere in time and place before.

Although Christian and Jewish in its religious origin, it does not demand public adherence to a specific religious dogma or ritual but supplies a set of moral and philosophic principles regarding economic, social, and political life.

The Judeo-Christian ethos should not be confused with theocracy or even a call to a meticulous religious life. Nor does it accept everything that is in the Bible. Rather, it's an outlook based on general themes of the Bible. But though general in nature, it remains singular and unique, for no other religious outlook sponsors and advocates these themes as does the Judeo-Christian outlook: not Islam, not Hinduism or Buddhism, not European Catholicism, nor earlier variants of high-end Protestantism, not even rabbinic Judaism as it has evolved. The Judeo-Christian ethos is a once-in-history Christian understanding and embrace of the Old and New Testaments. It is unique to America, and it is this ethos that has had more impact on America's vitality, growth, sense of fair play, justice, and success than any other philosophy. It constitutes our historic and ongoing identity. It's our civilization!

More than just an approach to governance and nationhood, it is the spirit of this nation—our moral outlook, one which shaped us domestically and impelled us to fight communism and Nazism. Because of it, we rejected the destructive welfare/entitlement state and knew not to appease terrorism and tin-pot dictators. It is a morality that has influenced our domestic and foreign policy and has been a blessing for those who see it as a paradigm for the personal decisions they make daily. Unlike any other national culture, the Judeo-Christian ethos is unique in that it supplies a personal day-to-day civic moral color to those who strive to live by it.

★★★

When my great grandfather came to this country, he could not wait until the day he received his citizenship papers and could boast of being an American. He was not on the lookout for the freebies he could demand and collect—there was no such aberration then—but for the sheer pride of knowing that he now belonged to something grand: the land of freedom and opportunity for those willing to persevere on behalf of those opportunities.

After he became a citizen, he knew he was then a member of a moral nation. He never pined for the Europe he left. He, of course, lived in a time before the liberal multiculturalists of the 1970s took hold and began counseling the newly arrived to retain their former national identities and become American to a hyphenated degree only. No, Samuel Victor Spero knew that America was an exceptional country, and he came here to be part of it and live by its laws and ethos—not to transform it.

The moment a nation or people forgets its identity or is too preoccupied or apathetic about it, is the moment it loses itself and decline sets in. It stops being what it was, and absent the breath that gave it life, it atrophies and becomes a confused and strange other entity altogether. Worse, it leaves a vacuum where other identities begin inserting themselves. Cultures and nations—identities—belong to those willing to vigorously assert them. In much of multicultural Europe today, their identity has become *no identity*. Some in America are pushing here for that same lack of national identity and are embarrassed by the whole concept of Americanism and the Judeo-Christian ethos.

Out of guilt or self-loathing over our own culture, many American multiculturalists see our historic American culture as inferior to almost everyone else's and seem intent on creating an homogenized transnational culture at odds with how we have lived here these last four hundred years. (I will address this topic at greater length in a later chapter.)

★★★

Multiculturalism is the term used by liberal elites to diminish the importance of a Western country's indigenous and historic culture. At first it was employed to assign equal credence to immigrant cultures and attitudes with that of the dominant culture of the Western host country. Over the last decade or two, it has gone much further and dangerously so. Multiculturalism is being used often to force the majority to abide by the cultural attitudes and sometimes the laws of outside, immigrant cultures.

As in so many places in Europe, England's Christian identity has been cast off, along with its specific culture and nationhood. England has so lost its identity and cultural will that elites within the government have enlisted the courts to forbid Christian women at work from wearing necklaces with a cross. At the same time they are demanding that Muslim women be free at work to wear their burka or hijab as their religious right. Too many Englishmen, cowed and subdued by multiculturalism, diminish the importance of their own history, religion, and culture.

A nation is defined either by its religion, culture, or sense of nationalism. Today too many consider their ancestral religion as passé or consisting of something so watered down and gelatin-like that it no longer provides special identity and purpose. It's become pop religion, a calling card for trendy feel-goodism. These people have allowed themselves to be browbeaten by Third World, United Nations' types to feel guilt over their culture having been built on colonialism and thus even question the validity of their own nationalism.

Much of the success Islam is having in transforming Europe to Islamic ways is due to Islam's belief in itself and its identity, and asserting that identity into the cultural vacuum opened up by nations tentative about their own identity and asleep as to who they are. Muslims seem to operate with no guilt over the things done in Islam's name, and thus we have this lopsided situation of those who feel guilt succumbing to those who never feel guilty. It is a formula for cultural suicide.

★★★

Since World War II, we Americans have had the luxury of coasting and not having to fight for the Judeo-Christian beliefs and Americanism we hold dear. But those days are certainly over. Too many powerful people wish to change America's historic identity. Those who push and urge others to assert all types of different identities and loyalties at the same time demonize those within the Judeo-Christian community who are proud of their unique American identity.

Too many find glee in maligning our Founding Fathers as either racists, homophobes, misogynists, imperialists, or Islamophobes, and desire to discredit them and thus the principles upon which this country was founded. We must push back…not only for the honor of those august men far more heroic and idealistic than those who sit in arrogant and mean-spirited judgment over them…not only in gratitude for the sacrifice, gift of nationhood, and treasured legacy they left us…we push back because they would want us to—so that their life's work and *self-evident truths* will, as they had intended and hoped, survive them. We push back because we won't allow ourselves to accept that which is disguised propaganda—it's an affront to our intellectual integrity.

Many of us have neglected the most important tool in preserving and promoting a culture, the most vital element in passing on a heritage—teaching it. We assumed our children would learn what we learned and live by it through some type of osmosis. But that's not how legacies and identities survive. That's not how the cherished things of one generation become the cherished things for the next.

One of my favorite biblical guideposts is found in Deuteronomy, and it speaks of what it takes to transmit a tradition and heritage:

> *And these words which I have bequeathed to you today should be set in your heart, so that you shall diligently teach them to your children, and you should converse about them, when in your home, and when on journeys, before you go to sleep, and when you arise* (Deuteronomy. 6:6-7).

Something important must be purposely taught and done so not haphazardly but with focus and diligence. There are simply too many cultural currents and distractions out there that compete for the minds and hearts of our young people. We can't assume that our children's hearts will be inspired and their minds filled by what we believe if we don't consciously teach them what we believe. It's our job to transmit to them the wisdom of the ages, our history, our Judeo-Christian beliefs, what this nation is, and the ideals that distinguish us from, for example, China, France, or Saudi Arabia.

During my years as a rabbi of a synagogue, I too often had parents come to me distraught over how their children were not following in their ways. The parents were good providers, but a father is not simply a provider of goods nor is a mother simply a facilitator for the social schedule. First and foremost, parents are teachers, the living link that transmits the wisdom they received to a new generation in need of that wisdom. In the past, these ideals and verities were taught at the dinner table or at the early afternoon Sabbath meal—be it on Sunday or Saturday. The Sabbath was not a day for sports talk but for serious, value-affirming conversations.

Each family should have a specific world outlook on religion, values, politics, and what constitutes fine character. Mine did. It represents the family's personal heritage of beliefs. The best way to impart and transmit this outlook—yes, it is a transmission—to children is through an ongoing, weekly conversation. Let us return to Deuteronomy where a formula for such conversation is presented:

> *And when your son shall ask you, saying: "What means this testimony, these laws, these judgments...?" And ye shall answer him thus...* (Deuteronomy 6:20-21).

Home life and parent-child relationships should consist of steady conversation—questions and answers about the important, enduring, classic elements of life. What a pity if a son knows which baseball team a father roots for but does not know his father's political and religious philosophy and how and why his parent reached those conclusions.

Sadly we can't rely on our public schools to teach America in the way my parents and I were taught it. Most of the educational establishment does not believe in it, and because school guidelines are coming out of Washington, D.C., as opposed to local school boards as was the country's original intention, those teachers who do believe in historic Americanism, free markets, a unique national identity, and biblical morality are stymied and endangered if they veer from liberal political correctness.

We should teach our children about America not only abstractly, but also with our heart, as something we deeply love: *and set in your heart.* "What comes from one's heart enters the heart of the other" is an old rabbinic maxim. We should teach our families the American way not once but steadily: *and converse with them, in your house...*

Our national identity and what constitutes historic Americanism is too important to yield before any man, certainly a man who has as his goal the radical transformation of America. Our rights do not come from President

Obama—that's not how it works here. Our country and our rights predate him. It's ludicrous for an American to give up rights he had before Barack Obama was even born. Americans whose family members served in the military and died for this country as far back as 150 years ago should not be so quick to give up their rights on the orders of any man, and especially to someone who recently came to these shores not to affirm its greatness but to question it. It is akin to someone showing up at the front door of your centuries old family home and telling you that he will decide what you may continue to possess and what no longer belongs to you.

It's not for Obamaites to reinterpret who we are or suggest what we are allowed to say or do. Nor is it for the President to tell us "America is not a Christian nation" or that "Islam has always been a part of America." For four hundred years we have defined ourselves as a Judeo-Christian country. No one has ever spoken of a Judeo-Christian-Islamic ethos, certainly not when it comes to defining what made America.

Jefferson, Washington, Adams, Madison, Witherspoon, and Hamilton did not look to the Koran or Islam for guidance when founding our Republic. We are not floating tumbleweeds to be pushed around by every new fad and ism, but hearty oaks grounded in an ancient soil that predates Karl Marx and his call for class warfare. Our biblical roots were robust and clarifying before there was a United Nations or a Barack Obama.

Every new Obama fiat or denial of rights is preceded weeks before by a moralizing and a rewriting of history designed to browbeat the public into ideological submission. So much of what Mr. Obama does, as well as his callousness and condescension toward mainstream Americans, reveals a man distant from basic American inclinations. It is not his liberalism that separates him from others, rather his Obamaism. I did not agree with much of President Clinton's outlook, but there never was a question as to his authentic American persona—he was the prototype "good ole boy." Obama does not fit into any American persona, white or black. Even at this point, who he is and what his background is remain murky and shrouded in mystery.

For the sake of our children apprehending the true history of America, when someone comes on TV and proclaims these things, it's best that we inform our children—and our friends—about the falsity of such agenda-driven, revisionist history, lest it begin to seep in, create a substitute for the truth, and transform our way of life.

When children come home from school echoing the lies they are taught about America, calling us a nation of racists or Islamophobes, or repeating the latest left-wing indictment of the American middle class, we must push back. It takes a little bit of spine to maintain an identity and stand up for what is true, especially when so many are zealously trying to undermine our beliefs. But courage is a great virtue—one to be cultivated—and is part of conservatism and being an American.

Most Americans would not stand for an outside force invading our country and taking away our liberties. Nor would we accept an outside force purposely social engineering our individual lives and national culture to force us to become who we are not and do not wish to be. Most of us would not accept an outside force coming to transform America and make it Sweden or Belgium. Why then do we accept it from those within who are attempting to do exactly that? It is not acceptable simply because they happen to live in this country as Americans. Unfortunately they are first and foremost ideological socialists and often cultural Marxists.

Our response cannot be tepid or based on some hope that the other side will back down and miraculously go away. For while we are immersed in raising our families and going to our houses of worship, the left-wing political and cultural class is strategizing and figuring out ways of how to run most aspects of our personal lives and take over all our public institutions, even the military. And they are doing so not simply for the government to have greater power but to personally imbue themselves with uncontestable power, the power that comes to those individuals running an entrenched socialist welfare state.

★★★

It seems that even America's free market system is now being questioned, though no liberal politician will admit to an underlying agenda to institute socialism. However, what can be more wonderful and moral than a man working hard for his family and being able to tell his son that he worked a little longer and can now buy him the bicycle his boy saw in the store window or can now send his daughter to summer camp for two weeks? It makes the son and daughter admire and feel pleased with their dad, not to mention the satisfaction and deep pride the dad feels for being able to provide. His work is being directly rewarded. Enjoying results born of personal effort is an essential moral paradigm. Even better, the importance of being part of a family is affirmed, as is its structure and relationships.

We Americans don't want to be wards of the state or live off the wealth redistributed to us from other people's hard work. Nor do we see any morality in making it difficult for parents to directly take care of their own family as a result of the government taxing their salaries on behalf of creating the welfare state and employees of a government utopia. That's never been the American way. There's something so cold about the socially engineered, top-down paradigm of the welfare state—it's unnatural and devoid of an understanding of what constitutes humanness.

If the New Jersey ladies I met in the hotel lobby almost two years ago were asked today, I'm sure they'd agree that America's free markets have produced not only prosperity but something more. They'd concur that it's not only pragmatically the best way to live but morally so as well.

I think that after witnessing three years of assault on Americanism by someone clearly not in love nor in sync with America, and certainly not humble before its history, the ladies from New Jersey would agree it's time to publicly make their conservative views known and become more feisty than their normal comfort zone would dictate. There is no political magician to do it for us. It is up to each person, in his locality and among his friends, to do the job. We simply cannot assume that our friends and associates know what we believe. A country's ethos is but the composite of public opinion, so it is vital that we actively participate and push within our national conversation.

We all know Americanism is more than eating hot dogs, barbecue, and ice cream cones or playing baseball or golf. Even Fidel Castro, an archcommunist, likes hot dogs and baseball. Those things are not in jeopardy. No one will die for them. People sacrifice their lives, their honor, and their fortune for things far greater and much more critical and timeless. If we don't want America to be taken from us, and if we don't want our children robbed of their heritage, conservative Americans will have to become much more active. It's our heritage—now is the time to fight for it!

★★★ TWO ★★★

Bigotry

[Accusations of bigotry: Thou shalt not bear false witness.]

Believing as we do, why aren't tens of millions of us out there every day vigorously promoting our conservatism and boldly making the case for it? Why aren't we announcing: "I'm conservative and proud of it"? Why don't we publicly and privately challenge liberals, including relatives and friends, who seem to relish challenging us? Why do we take a defensive posture when we should be asserting ourselves as if—and it does—the future of our country and children depends on it? And why do so many people of faith evade their responsibility to press for the conservative American values that constitute who they are, and instead, excuse and delude themselves by calling this "politics"?

Much of our lack of confidence comes from being told by the media that we conservatives are uneducated, simpleminded rednecks, and of course, their favorite charge, we are racists, mean-spirited, jingoistic, and too religious. For over fifty years the *New York Times* and its whole opinion-shaping crowd have castigated and browbeaten us over how guilty, unworthy, and unenlightened we are. It has been unrelenting and unfortunately effective. I would categorize its assault as cruel and unusual punishment. The media has initiated a war against true Americans—unfair and something we don't deserve. This constant harassment has eroded our confidence and made us tentative about our core beliefs.

When looking at the almost 150 million Americans who consider themselves conservative, it's obvious that such charges are false and, indeed, libelous. Over my forty years as an active conservative involved with thousands of individuals identifying themselves as true conservatives, I've never heard a racist remark against a black person because of his color. In fact, what matters to us conservatives is not one's color or race but one's political philosophy and love of country and love of God.

One certainly has the right to disagree on policy or attitude with, as I have, Jesse Jackson, Al Sharpton, Maxine Waters, or the Congressional Black Caucus. For example, I do not agree with an attitude that speaks of entitlement or reparations when, in my view, the fortune and blessing of living in the United States with all its freedoms is prize enough.

I have been critical regarding President Obama's healthcare mandate and published an article about it three years ago in *Townhall*. But I also was against national healthcare when Hillary Clinton was proposing it while her husband was President, and I was critical of it when Senator Russ Feingold was pushing it. Both are white and Feingold is Jewish. Yet we've heard many in the media charge that racism against Obama is behind our opposition to his healthcare reform. They make charges of racism in order to intimidate us into second-guessing ourselves and leaving the debate as a result. After all, no one enjoys being labeled a racist. But it is the socialism part of the plan and how it will diminish quality care and access to it that alarms me. Obamacare, as the media has dubbed it, will provide an excuse for government meddlers to intrude into so many private aspects of our lives. This is what makes us find this wholesale takeover of our lives so absolutely dangerous and immoral. It's intolerable to live under a system in which a bureaucrat from above will decide who shall live and who shall die.

Affirmative action is another hot topic among liberals. The media and liberal politicians enjoy telling us that opposition by white conservatives to affirmative action is based on racism. It is not. It is based on the fundamental and historical American value of meritocracy—the belief that position is earned not by color but through the merit of one's achievement borne of hard work and talent. It is really a moral issue, one rooted in the principle that an individual should be rewarded for what he does and not because of which group he comes from.

No doubt in the past there was discrimination, and many people were denied a job or opportunity, and their merit was not considered. But this country, like no other country in history, has turned itself inside out to remedy past discrimination. It is dishonest not to give our country credit and pretend things have not changed for the better. The year 2012 is not 1954. It is disingenuous and race baiting when professional race-mongers fabricate racism in matters and positions where any honest broker knows that it is not part of the transaction and does not exist. Nor can *reverse racism* be demanded in the name of remedying the past.

But the media and liberal politicians know the charge of racism is politically effective—a battle-proven tactic—and many Americans would prefer remaining quiet rather than risk being called a racist by a public whose definitions of who is good and who is bad is made for them by the mainstream media.

Most of us assume that any stranger we meet probably agrees with how the media portrays American life and how it defines the terms of our existence—and so we keep our inner beliefs to ourselves. We might find, however, that in not expressing what we believe, we have deprived a fellow citizen from coming out of the conservative closet, someone wishing to be an ambassador for our cause but afraid to do so. It's our job to speak up and thereby give confidence to others.

Unbelievably, some congressmen and some in the media have made the claim that white conservative opposition to higher taxes, redistribution of wealth, and the welfare state is rooted in racism, charging conservative whites with not wanting their money given over to minorities. Only a person obsessed with race, who sees everything in terms of race, could come to such a foolish and incendiary conclusion. People want to retain their earnings because they need it for themselves or family—that's why they work. It has nothing to do with race and everything to do with personal and familial economic survival.

The conservative viewpoint also has to do with our aversion to the socialist model, no matter who is the recipient. It is a moral issue. Having your earnings taken from you so as to be redistributed to others becomes a form of serfdom where the precious hours of your life, your lifeblood and energy, and the earnings that represent so much of who you are and what you do, are expended not for your own family but on behalf of those whom the state decides should receive the fruits of your labor.

In the American Judeo-Christian ethos, no group has the right to expropriate the body and soul of others for the purpose of fashioning a kingdom of soft tyranny. Claims of it merely being "democratic-socialism" are simply cover for what it really is: a permanent liberal ruling class determining our rights and values and the shrinking of a robust middle class wealthy enough to challenge the left-wing lords of the manor.

When the media or liberal politicians consistently, in knee-jerk fashion, charge us with racism over issues that have nothing to do with race but are concerned with philosophy and objective moral values, then we know that such accusations reflect more the mindset of those accusing than that of those being accused. It reveals the type of bigotry prevalent among those in the media and academia against a large swath of Americans simply because they are white, conservative Christians, and especially if they live in the South. Holding this low point of view against much of their own countrymen is the ticket needed to enter the "enlightened" liberal fraternity, to be a member of the "higher" judgmental class. It is itself a form of prejudice, snobbery, and classism. These are unsavory characteristics, and instead of being intimidated by the judgmental class, we should reject their accusations that represent deep character flaws these liberal elites need to overcome.

I'm personally aware of the bigotry and off-base assumptions against most white, conservative Christians common among the sit-in-judgment class. As a clergyman in Manhattan, I was frequently invited to dinner parties, art gallery cocktail events, and other get-togethers held by the Manhattan chattering class. I'm not from New York City but Ohio and was raised with very Midwestern values, especially since my family arrived in Ohio back in 1870. As a matter of fact, my grandfather, a second generation Buckeye, used to tell us of how he stood on Euclid Avenue watching the young soldiers in Cleveland march down the street in columns toward the train depot en route to being shipped off to fight in the Spanish American War. Imagine my surprise when, at these New York gatherings, I heard all these false and negative perceptions expressed about those Americans in the hinterlands, meaning those west of the Hudson River and south of Philadelphia. When I began writing my column for *Human Events* back in 2001, I coined a phrase, *the Salons of the Upper West Side*, to describe the meeting places of the radical Left and the *New York Times* crowd who sit in constant negative and smug judgment over fellow Americans. I call them *Smugsters*. I think they are the ones who could use some sensitivity training.

★★★

Let me give one more example of false accusations of bigotry, accusations designed to psych us out into retreat. Recently, a radical Muslim group called CAIR has been successful in demanding that state legislatures not pass legislation requiring that all cases coming before judges be decided according to U.S. Constitutional law as opposed to foreign law. Such legislation should be a slam dunk. Yet CAIR asserts—yes, that's why they've

15

been successful, because they are willing to be assertive and combative—that deciding only by Constitutional law impinges on their right to be judged by shariah law—Muslim law. Those legislators voting in favor of American law have been branded by CAIR and the media as Islamophobes. Again, the use of the race card.

It has nothing to do with bigotry, however, and everything to do with us living by the laws of our Constitution. Without the Constitution, Americans have no birthright. Absent the Constitution, we have no protection. If there's no absolute fidelity to the Constitution, judges can establish two sets of laws—one for most Americans and one preferred by Muslims. That's not how the United States works. That's a recipe for Balkanization and for separate legal precincts in America. It is contrary to the entire concept of having a common culture unified by our Constitution.

Are we, in the name of pleasing groups making destructive demands, supposed to throw out the Constitution simply because we're afraid of someone calling us a racist or Islamophobe? It is for us, with our own common sense, to decide if something is rooted in racism, not the group making the unreasonable demand and employing the word *racism* as an extortion tool. Opposing someone else because of his race is improper, but opposing an ideology is very American and proper.

Have we become a people so lacking in self-confidence as to who we are and what we stand for that we would timidly forfeit the concept of *all men living equally under one set of laws*, which is the moral bedrock and blessing upon which this nation was founded? Anything short of standing up for Constitutional law only is moral capitulation.

No group other than the Muslims has come to these shores with the demand that it live by its own set of laws. In England, there are now entire regions where Muslims are demanding that shariah law be applied to them rather than English law. The culturally confused and left-leaning Archbishop of Canterbury, now retiring, has opined that it may be a good thing. In some places, an Englishman can live by two sets of different laws and conduct if he walks from his home into a shariah zone.

In fact, it has begun to cross the Atlantic. In Ontario, Canada, they have suspended the decades old practice of placing Bibles in schools because it offends some Muslim parents, and one Ohio prison has banned pork because, you guessed it, it offends Muslim prisoners. When do we begin getting offended at them being offended by how life has been conducted here for centuries? Are we people with no beliefs of our own and more than willing to cancel out our own ways in order to fulfill the needs of those offended at those ways? This is not accommodation, but the *tyranny of a minority* over a majority who seem to lack the self-respect to assert their right to live as they did for centuries prior to the arrival of those who seem to be always offended and evoking their need for honor. People are leaving Belgium precisely because of this. Tell me: Where do *we* go?

America, in contrast, must believe in its laws. Our laws represent hundreds of years of collective wisdom rooted in the Judeo-Christian understanding of what constitutes justice, freedom, equality, and individual rights. It is our moral blueprint. Only those wishing to overturn the American system and ethos would advocate a right to live by a separate set of laws apart from their countrymen.

Only those gullible and weak-spined would acquiesce to that which will tear this country and its value system asunder, just so they won't be labeled Islamophobic. Aside from the Bible itself, the Constitution and Declaration of Independence represent the finest expressions and applications of the Judeo-Christian ethos anywhere. Failure to fight on its behalf is a failure of our faith obligation. Weakness, gullibility, or excuses of "not getting involved in politics" does not befit the spiritual progeny of Wycliffe, Tyndale, and Calvin, let alone Moses and Jesus, who both, as recorded in Scripture, were publicly brave in defending the law.

An important aspect of the Judeo-Christian ethos is moral bravery— being strong in defending the faith. Evading that responsibility by calling all this politics, or thinking we should leave the public domain and retreat to self-imposed ghettos of silence, isolation, and non-involvement, is simply too otherworldly. There will be time enough for the other world— an eternity's worth. But right now we live in this world, with an obligation to fight the good fight so that evil does not prevail. We become engaged in this fight for the sake of our children and neighbors so they can live with continued freedom and the blessings that grow from it.

It seems to me that active engagement of this sort is a religious duty. We are not some quaint religious remnant. Our mission is unfulfilled if we leave it for others to determine society's destiny. As I will show later, the Judeo-Christian ethos is action-oriented, something that makes it unique among religions.

A new set of laws, be it shariah or otherwise, is a repudiation of

America and the soaring Judeo-Christian values that constitute our building blocks and foundation. Therefore, it's personal to those of us who live by the Judeo-Christian ethos. Islamic law with its attitudes and values of preoccupation with men over women and believer over infidel, along with the cruel manner in which it punishes, differs dramatically from our Western Judeo-Christian culture. If it were the same, Mohammed would have stuck with the Bible that was already in existence and well known during his time. Unlike the New Testament, which gives credence to the Old by calling itself a companion, Koranic-based shariah rejects most of the Bible, except to lay claim to Jesus and Moses as somehow their own.

Look at the difference between the United States and Saudi Arabia, and therein you see a living model of the difference between the Judeo-Christian ethos and the Koran, the difference between our Constitution and their shariah. It is not racist to fight for the Constitution or for your own survival, which is dependent on the absolute primacy of the Constitution in our civic life. Let's not allow the judgmental class to bamboozle us again.

I am an Orthodox Jew who follows the Code of Jewish Law when it comes to private religious practice. Much of this code stems from the Talmud. But I know of no Orthodox community wishing to institute public zones of Talmudic law. Long ago in Babylonia (200 AD), Rabbi Samuel declared: "The law of the Land is the law." We abide by the same civic laws as do our fellow citizens. Nor would Rabbi Samuel countenance the subterfuge of declaring as religious law that which is really the province of civil law, the tactic of using freedom of religion as a cover to evade and be exempt from civic norms and authority.

★★★

The distinguished and courageous General Jerry Boykin has remarked about the nexus between faith and freedom. He is, of course, referring to the faith principles taught in America's Judeo-Christian outlook. We religious conservatives know that the freedom and rights we have under our Constitution are, as Jefferson wrote in the Declaration, endowed by our Creator. There is a direct relationship between God's Word in the Bible and the freedoms outlined in the Declaration and the Constitution. We wish to change neither.

It is precisely in our community where freedom and liberty are spoken of as the quintessential American ideals. We love America because she is the Land of the Free. The love of America and the patriotism we exhibit and feel for her derives from that relationship between faith and freedom. There is no greater community of patriots than that of the conservative religious community. It sends more soldiers to fight in our armed services than any other single group.

The politically liberal community, in contrast, does not wax about freedom and liberty but about redistribution of wealth, entitlements, social inequality, and the struggle between the classes. For them, it is not about freedom but government supplying the needs of the people—socialism. It is not about freedom but control, their "benevolent" management and control. They don't see rights as God-given but rather something for government to dispense. If the Judeo-Christian outlook was their guiding light, they'd be compelled to believe in God-given freedom as do we and be repelled by a philosophy advocating control.

There can't be that connection of faith and freedom for those who are essentially secular or live by a different set of religious values. And because freedom is not their highest ideal, as we too often see with President Obama, they do not imbibe the gut love and patriotism that comes from living in the Land of Freedom. Those in the salons of the Upper West Side rarely send their children to the military, though they are very quick to condemn our soldiers. When the day comes, God forbid, that Americans are no longer free as they once were but under greater state control, liberals will then love it, for it will have become the Land of Control—under *their* control.

Those of us who revere the words of the Bible revere the words of our Constitution as well. We don't arrogate to ourselves the mission of changing the Bible or the Constitution. We believe in original intent. It is no surprise, then, that the secular community, which sees the Bible as but literature and disregards vast sections of it that don't conform to its lifestyle or liberal views, has no problem changing the Constitution, dismissing it when it doesn't match its agenda for social engineering. Justices Breyer and Ginsberg want to interpret it sometimes according to foreign law and the understandings of different cultures. During his initial years in Chicago politics, a younger Barack Obama called our Constitution a "flawed document."

★★★

A recent ruling in Pennsylvania illustrates very well the exclusive tie between the Judeo-Christian faith and our freedoms. In Mechanicsburg, a local judge, ostensibly a convert to Islam, let a fellow Muslim (El-Bayomy) off scot-free even though there were tapes of that man physically assaulting another man. The one who was attacked was a non-Muslim man wearing a mask of Mohammed on Halloween and making remarks about it. The judge leveled his wrath not at the aggressor but at the one who was hit, exhorting: "Don't you know that Islamic people do not tolerate making fun of their prophet and that in Islamic countries you can be killed for this?" We already have here the application of shariah in an American court.

Now if a Christian was found beating up someone saying snide things about Jesus, he would be placed in jail for assault. He'd also be accused of five different isms. Yet in Mechanicsburg, because of the judge's "understanding" and application of the Islamic ethos, the Muslim man, the defendant, was free to simply get up and go home. But due process means equal application of the law in the same situations, not exemption from it due to Islamic cultural reasons.

This country has spent the last sixty years since *Brown v. Board of Education* (1954) making sure that every citizen is an equal recipient of the law, which is the intent of the due process clause. But due process is a two-way street. It is not simply there so that everyone receives rights equally but also so that everyone equally performs his obligations, to wit, not to hit your fellow man even though he is from a different religion and says things you don't like.

The judge further admonished the victim who was attacked "for being a poor role model for his son by jesting about Mohammed." To me, this is the most vital and illuminating part of this whole wretched decision, since it involves values and offers us a clear portrait of the difference between our values and those established in Muslim culture. In our culture, we would have admonished the father who did the beating as being a bad role model, for he taught his son violence and that one uses his fists when displeased. For the Pennsylvania Muslim judge and defendant, however, being a role model centers first around respect for Mohammed, not the need for holding back aggression or the requirement to live decently with your neighbor and fellow citizen.

This line of reasoning represents a completely different value system than our Judeo-Christian one, and since values determine law, the use in American courts of shariah cultural values will pervert our laws and justice.

And since laws teach values, the use of shariah law will slowly change our underlying values and morality.

Citing shariah and Islamic cultural norms, in 2008 a New Jersey judge dismissed charges by a wife against her husband over forced sex—something if done by any other American would have resulted in an assault and battery ruling. Fortunately, a higher court overturned the decision. But this line of reasoning, trendy among certain judges, is worrisome and adds to the need for decisions made according to our laws and cultural standards only.

As shown in the Pennsylvania and New Jersey cases, each culture has a different view on who is a victim. So often in Islam, right is determined not by neutral, objective standards of justice, but by who conforms more to Islamic law and who is higher up in the societal pecking order. That's not who we in America are! Ours is a system based on individual rights not group culture. That's what is meant by equality under the law. Just as freedom depends on our fighting for it, the retention of our moral code depends on us insisting on its unadulterated primacy.

Only a multiculturalist, who has no respect for our unique American culture and elevates other cultures over our own, would find shariah acceptable here. Indeed, these same multiculturalists remain quiet when Americans living in Saudi Arabia are required to suppress their Christianity—no Bibles, no crosses, no Christmas trees, no...

★★★

Diversity is a good thing; multiculturalism, however, is not. We Americans have always enjoyed the diversity of the different ethnicities that live here: the different foods, clothes, songs, holidays, parades, accents, and humor. But we always maintained an overriding common American culture—making our country a melting pot. Multiculturalism is an entirely different paradigm, made consciously by those on the left wishing to erase the unique American culture. It believes and says that there is nothing exceptional about our historic American culture, not even here in America. President Obama is in that camp. Worse, lately, multiculturalists have begun suggesting that other cultures may be *better* than our own, even here. In other cultures it finds no faults; while in ours, all it sees are warts and sins.

Those on the Left who insist every culture and religion be accorded great respect are the first to minimize Christian needs and, more often than not, condemn the assertion and expression of anything too Christian. It tells us where the Left stands regarding Christianity. As I will demonstrate later in the book, the whole agenda of the Left is primarily rooted in its war against serious, conservative Christianity and values.

Many on the Left who speak to us always of tolerance toward others dislike America—their own country—because of its unique Christian moorings, and in intolerance, disdain those fellow Americans for actually believing and practicing it. They label it *puritanical*. But to snuff out conservative Christianity, they must first demolish the historic American structure that is its home of homes. And to denude America and make it like a no identity Europe, they must demonize and expel the conservative Christianity that animates it and continues to supply and grace it with its special character. The Left wants us away from the corridors of power, the halls of public institutions, and microphones over the airways so they can change our national character.

Their disdain for Christianity explains the incomprehensible partnership we see between the Left and international Islam: both share the common goal of bringing down Christian America. The liberal Left views Rev. Pat Robertson as a greater danger than the Muslim Brotherhood. The Left thinks that after their mission is accomplished, they will live in harmony with Islam and in shared socialist bliss. After all, both Islam and socialism believe in a top-down societal arrangement and in submission of the people to the ruling order and ideology. Both hope to replace historic Americanism and the Judeo-Christian idea with a higher ideology.

★★★

Let us conclude this chapter by getting back to the names liberals love to call us, which proves their bigotry and not ours.

Jingoists: Love of country is not jingoism nor is it chauvinistic, except to those who do not love the country and are embarrassed by it. How long will we take our cue and allow ourselves to be ruled by those who can't seem to bring themselves to love America? Do we want to be ruled by elites who identify with Paris and Stockholm more than they do Dallas, Texas? By a haughty clique who, though preaching about egalitarianism, would be horrified if their daughter married a boy from Oklahoma State? Much of today's high-brow liberalism is rooted in a *classism*, the sense of being from a superior class. It is quite revealing that liberal elitists speaking for the "lower classes" are themselves steeped in haughty classism. They consider themselves the new aristocracy.

Mean-spirited: It is not mean-spirited to live by and apply timeworn standards, especially when those standards emanate from the most sublime and majestic ethos God and man has ever created. And, in contrast to almost everything else, these standards do work.

Let me tell you what mean-spirited is. It is what comes out of the mouth of elitist liberals maligning our soldiers by accusing them of having a blood lust or by diminishing their service by asserting that many enter the armed services from the South where there are no other available jobs. It is all born of jealousy, the jealousy of not having the physical bearing and inner courage as do our soldiers and the cynical disbelief that anyone would forgo a career or risk their life for country—sacrifices New York leftists would never make. Nobody can be everything, but we should have the grace to admire in others what we lack. Most of us do, but there is something within the personality of the Left that must denigrate and put down qualities found in others but lacking in themselves.

Rednecks: I attend numerous conservative conferences and rarely see what liberals call rednecks, and when I do see them, I often admire their ability to fend in the outdoors to a degree that those living in doorman operated Manhattan apartments are unable to do. I admire men who have physical strength and women who admire their men.

Uneducated: As to education, some of the greatest minds and experts today in classic knowledge reside among the conservative ranks. Liberal deconstruction of the classics may be trendy, but it is bogus scholarship and displays an inability to do the hard work and probe the deep mysteries of our great thinkers. Fashionable academic deconstruction is just another example of lack of reverence for those who came before. It is the epitome of self-worship, as well as obnoxious ingratitude to those who paved the way and made possible everything we have today.

I have known intellectuals in both the conservative camp and from left-wing circles. The difference I see between the two is humility. Conservative intellectuals are aware of their own expertise in a particular field but recognize that the strength of America lies in all its people. Left-wing intellectuals see themselves as *apart* and *above* the mainstream and cannot abide the fact that those people from Kansas have as much right as they in deciding the country's destiny. Due to their dismissal of the average Joe, they often feel impelled to reject the commonsense views of the average citizen, including the emotion of patriotism. They can't help it.

Left-wing intellectuals have often gravitated to authoritarian leaders who they think will listen to them and give them a hand in running the country top-down. After all, they are sure that they know better than the rest of us what is good for the people!

What liberals do have is a great facility for using language. Like Voltaire, theirs is sharp, facile, creative, biting, earthy, emotional, colorful, and personal. I concede that we conservatives can learn from them in this area. Stodgy language does not sell, and we must get into the business of selling our outlook.

Much of what animates liberals is a sense of moral and intellectual superiority, an overflow of self-righteousness. It is unbecoming and peculiar, especially here in America, and seems quite far removed from the egalitarianism they preach. In truth, America was made great by the spirit, entrepreneurship, values, and dedication of its people, people who believed in something transcendent and in something more important than their academic tenure. Yet exhibiting a sense of moral and intellectual superiority often works when wishing to make other people feel small or inadequate.

★★★

But after everything is said and done, nothing is more important than character. Character is the true measure of a man. Very often smart people base their outlook on life only after an initial emotional decision, and many of these emotional decisions are based on selfishness, anger, or rebellion. Their brain power goes into gear only after the emotions have chartered the course.

What we see and perceive depends, first, on what we feel. We see what our emotions want to see. Scripture states: "Do not go after the ways of your heart and the ways of your eyes" (Numbers 15:39). The eyes see what the heart first desires. We see only that which we desire to see. The ingratitude that causes no desire in the leftist heart to see how outstanding America is bespeaks of a terribly negative emotion. I cannot grasp how someone living here cannot love America.

What is the emotion that drives a person to such ingratitude? Much of leftism is based on the emotions of resentment, anger, and rebellion, which is why the theories and platitudes that grow from it are so repugnant and almost always leveled with scorn. I like to keep in mind what King David said in Psalms 1:1 about the scoffers: "Happy is the man…who sits not among the counsel or in the chamber of scoffers."

There is resentment from those not wealthy and resentment from the very wealthy Left who resent that others outside their circle still have some power. They wish to, once and for all, topple the existing social order and replace it with themselves. They invoke "civil rights" not out of moral concerns but as a tool to turn our society upside down and disenfranchise the conservative middle class. After all, some of the civil rights they are screaming for today are for terrorists!

If genuine civil rights were their concern, they would busy themselves with the horrendous abuses going on around the world. Instead, they ignore them and focus on the puniest infractions here as a way to convince us of our never-ending collective guilt and need for drastic transformation. The wealthy Left, their activists, and many in academia do not look at how wonderful our country is compared to others. They resent *this* country; since it is here, they want power and do not yet fully have it. They are not angry at Saudi Arabia or China—they aren't interested in other countries. They will resent and be angry at America until they *own* it.

Instead of looking at the real atrocities of the world that should grab their attention, they remain tunnel-visioned, focused on their selfish craving, jealousy, and anger at those in America who resist giving them total control. Liberalism represents tremendous personality and character flaws. Liberalism is a political outlet for a variety of personal, inner disorders, often bitter and vicious ones.

When I was a boy growing up in Cleveland, we had a saying: *Sticks and stones will break my bones, but names will never hurt me.* Growing up in the Midwest, it never seemed to me that the confident and rugged individuals of my grandfather's generation concerned themselves over what people would say. They said, rather, what they felt was right and called a spade a spade. What we need to do today on behalf of our country's future and destiny is far more important than concerning ourselves with someone calling us a name, especially when the accusations are being hurled by those who wish to stop us from getting in the way of their agenda of radically transforming the country. Besides, we know who we are. It's not their prerogative to define us.

Years of working in the conservative movement and among its religious people have brought me in contact with some of the most decent, warm, dedicated, kind, and loyal people I've ever met. That's not where the racism and prejudice is. I feel honored to have spoken at their events and have come face to face with genuine and open people. I can't say that for other arenas I've traveled in.

In fact, being the goodwilled people we are, we have spent the last fifty years in introspection and have made inner changes. The sit-in-judgment class and those always claiming victimhood and grievance, however, have felt *above* the need for any personal introspection over the prejudices they hold about us. It's about time they underwent the same social therapy they demand from us. And it's about time they acknowledged and recognized the good will and great strides Americans have made and stop pointing to a bygone past just so they can continue in their self-righteous war against other Americans. It's time for them to devise a new template, a new reason for getting up in the morning. Perhaps it is time they humbled themselves and asked our forgiveness for their continued false characterizations of us.

Let us finally free ourselves from this false accusation of racism and bigotry that has made many of our people hide. Let us declare that that day has come when all of us—black and white along with all other colors and races—can proclaim: *Free at last, free at last. Thank God Almighty, we're free at last!*

THREE

Hijacking Our Heritage

[A revolution by words]

Nothing is more important to an organized society than the words and language it uses to define itself and its aspirations. These definitions constitute a society's ethos and shape its political future. How leaders and opinion shapers define these terms animate society and determine the direction it will travel. Knowing this, the liberal Left is consciously redefining the historic terms and language of American society to provide credence and underpinning to its goal of remaking American life and transforming it politically, socially, and economically. To achieve this radical political transformation, the Left is increasingly co-opting our historic moral language through a *revolution by words.*

Whoever "owns" the language of a people owns its soul, its allegiance, and its future. How these terms are interpreted and understood will determine the goals of our longstanding institutions, our laws, and our courts— what we as a people stand for. What is at stake is our national character and what constitutes Americanism, and even the texture and personality of the individual American.

When pushing his agenda and commenting on current events, President Obama repeatedly refers to our values in an ongoing effort of trying to convince Americans that his brand of redistribution of wealth, radical multiculturalism, and transnationalism have always been part of the American perspective and landscape. But it has not. Instead, his viewpoint rejects the historic understanding of the crucial words that have defined us and our unique values and aspirations. It goes beyond relativism to an actual corruption of language, especially the moral language.

In a country such as America, founded on religious themes, and which prides itself on doing that which is moral, the Left has manipulated bedrock concepts such as justice, compassion, equality, fairness, and caring

27

about the poor to advance its political ideology manifested in the welfare state and transnationalism. Indeed, what the Left advocates resembles a cultural Marxism and socialism radically at odds with the principles bequeathed to us by our Founding Fathers and the Judeo-Christian ethos. This ethos spawned our country's extraordinary moral compass and resulting prosperity and has provided more justice and equality for its citizens than any other nation in the world. In fact, nothing more accounts for this country's *exceptionalism* than our historic Judeo-Christian foundation, which is relentlessly spurned and marginalized by those on the Left advocating transformation.

At the core of the Judeo-Christian philosophy is a belief in the integrity of the individual, his majestic aptitude for creativity and self-reliance, along with an accountability that comes from being an agent of free will. What on a religious level proffered man with a direct, personal relationship with his Creator extended to all areas of civic life, so that man, seen as an autonomous individual, was to directly chart his own course and responsibilities. To live by the ethic of personal responsibility shapes character, yields maturity, and fashions a strong individual—the goal for humans who are but "a little lower than angels" (Psalms 8:6). To live by free will requires the conditions of liberty and conscience, the cornerstone of Judeo-Christian thinking and the American ethos derived from it. As we have seen, this ethos is unique and is not now nor has it ever been the cultural and sociological norm of most societies. Indeed, it is America's civic heritage, and to the extent we transform and replace it by a non-American, leftist outlook, our unique heritage will be lost to us and our children.

Alexis de Tocqueville wrote that a corporate entity remains what it is only as long as it operates by the principles upon which it was founded. When it changes those principles, it becomes something entirely different and the success it had, based on its original formula, is uncertain and in jeopardy. He spoke not against periodic tinkering but warned against fundamental transformation. The success of America is a direct outgrowth of the foundational principle of individual responsibility and the need for volunteerism as opposed to statism. This has been our spirit.

America is not simply a land mass between the Atlantic and the Pacific; it is the Land of the Big Idea. It is that idea that has generated the idealism behind our outstanding success. Those engaged in redefining who we are and the language of who we are, hope to institute foundational changes. At peril is the Big Idea that brought us success. These redefinitions of core principles will most likely kill the goose that laid the golden egg. If that happens, the United States would be but another territory instead of what it has been—*America*.

★★★

Given the sensibleness of our historic ethos and the real-life blessings it has brought to hundreds of millions since our settlement here, how has the liberal left been so successful in shifting us away from it? They win by repeatedly using the term *social justice*. Precisely because we Americans relish the concept of justice and desire a society built upon it, we almost automatically defer to a paradigm labelled social justice and to those who speak in its name. As a result, a goodwilled public often thinks every program and piece of legislation liberals demand in justice's name must be moral. But their version of social justice is socialism, which brings about innumerable injustices to most of us. It is a *political* paradigm *not* a *moral* one.

There is the never-ending assertion by liberals that those who don't agree with and bow to their definition of justice are coldhearted, mean-spirited, racist, or phobic—something most people do not wish to be labeled. And it works. People want to do what opinion shapers tell them is right because they do not wish to feel guilty or be called names or maligned. Because the conservative side has neglected to engage vigorously in the battle over words and terms and has not couched its outlook in soaring moral language, the liberal side is crowned with representing the moral high ground, and what it espouses often goes unexamined.

Rarely do Republicans speak the moral language on Capitol Hill, preferring instead to focus on the overspending aspect of a Congressional Bill. They seem defensive, almost apologetic. Perhaps many do not really understand the profoundly noble and moral philosophy behind conservatism. As the forthcoming chapters unfold, it will become even more evident that the conservative position is the moral one, whereas liberalism offers in the short run what *appears* to show concern but is essentially a quick fix, electioneering, unjust to most, and militates against producing a citizen of strong and inspiring character. The liberalism of today is choosing the wrong side, and each day showing its moral bankruptcy.

Conservatives need to speak in language suffused with the splendid vocabulary of symbolism—a presentation less dependent on statistics and one more personal. Our candidates and spokespeople need to talk as *real* people and leaders, not like members of think tanks. We can convey our ideas and at the same time frame our outlook in an emotional language that *touches* people and their hearts. We should address the nation in the soaring and powerful language of *moral* narrative: our morality lies in living with liberty and not penalizing those who *daily live by active personal responsibility*. Those responsible people are society's heroes and role models. They are the ones who should be recognized and cherished.

Even in the prosaic practicalities of campaign messaging, Republican candidates for President seem timid and lack confidence. When vying against fellow Republicans during primaries, candidates are tough, audacious, and even ruthless; yet during the national campaign against the Democrat, they turn limp and cautious. John McCain, for example, said there was "nothing to fear about Barack Obama," so the public listened and voted for a younger, fresher candidate whom we had no reason to fear. Mitt Romney, a good man, repeatedly announces that Mr. Obama is "a nice guy," implying Obama has the best interests of the country at heart and is simply misguided. Well, the public likes nice guys. But Obama's policies are deliberate and, though probably a good family man with a nice smile, the following actions are not those of a nice guy: (1) his public humiliation of Supreme Court Justices; (2) his enemies' list; (3) his moves to curtail our liberties and legitimate choices; (4) his prosecution of interrogators doing their patriotic job of saving Americans from terrorism; and (5) his intentional lies to trick the American people into accepting national healthcare (knowingly reneging on promises made just to secure votes). We have heard his disparaging remarks about "Americans who cling to their guns and religion"; seen the intimidation and economic punishment of those who disagree with him and the rewards for those who support his policies; and observed the lack of graciousness and the absence of any humorous self-deprecation. Saying Mr. Obama is "a nice guy" or "represents nothing to fear" is akin to delivering the very image Mr. Obama wishes the public to believe about him. It constitutes a hand-delivered Republican gift to Mr. Obama, the opponent.

When liberals speak of social justice, what they really mean and want is social engineering. What happens to justice in a socially engineered society? Whereas justice should be a nonpreferential process whose purpose is to decide strictly on the merits of a case, applying across-the-board standards, many on the Left often rule according to "redistributive justice." It can result in an outcome that deprives the non-minority a right to justice. Liberalism's emphasis on group rights instead of individual rights is a consequence of left-liberalism seeing class struggle as the moral paradigm. Even when there is no evidence of any victimizing, liberals pronounce its existence. There is something un-American when injustice is called justice, when someone is denied his day in court on behalf of social justice or the greater good. It is justice for whom? Good for whom? Among the social justice clique, we conservatives simply don't count!

★ ★ ★

Redefining the moral language and what forms our values constitutes the full-throttle thrust of liberal activists for the past fifty years. But it accelerated during the Obama administration to unprecedented levels to keep pace with what the President is doing in actuality to remake our country. The Left enjoys using the language of morality to induce us to relinquish core freedoms, reduce our standard of living, and indict historic American power and leadership. It has discarded and replaced classical and traditional understandings of morality and justice with political correctness, repeatedly telling us these values constitute "who we are." But many Americans understand it is *not* who we are, rather what the Left wants us to become.

Because political leftism has a distinct world view, these national sensitivity training sessions from the bully pulpit do not stop at our shores. So much of the Obama foreign policy agenda is heralded as "acting in accordance with our historic values." These fabricated, radically new, supposedly historic values are evoked in order to shape our thinking toward a new set of values we have never lived by before—socialist ones.

These historic values are emphasized instead of our national interest because so much of the foreign policy is done on behalf of transnational interests and not America's interest. To be *transnational* is to make decisions not on what is best for one's country but on what is in the best interests of countries worldwide, specifically socialist countries. Mr. Obama goes even beyond that, seeing America as a sort of sacrificial lamb, even in the area of jobs, in service to Third World nations and other cultures. America is being exploited and *used* by him on behalf of overseas cultures, ideologies, and countries closer to his heart. For example, oil drilling leases in the Gulf of Mexico are not all renewed under environmental concerns, some have been canceled, and hardly any new ones have been authorized, yet the Obamaites have given $500 million for offshore drilling in Brazil, currently under socialist rule. The administration derides and threatens domestic drillers but facilitates drilling by Chinese companies. Domestic drillers capable of creating American energy independence are warned that routine deductions for drilling takes money from the government, yet the Obama administration gave billions of our stimulus money to projects overseas and billions more to political supporters engaged in unworkable, risky schemes, which are now bankrupt.

More examples: America is going bankrupt; yet against the voted-on wishes of Congress, Obama sent $1.5 billion in one fell swoop to Muslim Brotherhood-controlled Egypt. Energy independence for America can happen with the long-awaited Keystone Pipeline from Canadian oil fields to our ports in Texas, creating tens of thousands of jobs, yet he says no. He even decided the new mission of NASA would be "Muslim outreach" (July 2010) after Charles Bolden was confirmed as its administrator in 2009. He instructed Bolden of the new policy, and NASA is now withering in demoralization. So much of the glory and survival of America is being systematically destroyed, camouflaged under some higher calling. These are not simply mistakes in policy. My friends, there is something terribly wrong here. Something calculated and sinister is going on in front of our eyes.

The fact that foreign policy under this administration most often is directly opposite from previous Presidents proves that he is not acting in accordance with our historic values, rather repudiating them. In no way is this policy consistent with our values.

The American public finds it difficult to grasp the idea and accept the fact that many of its office holders and newsmakers have a Marxist definition of important terms and identify with its worldview and values. After all, Karl Marx is associated with communism, and America and its free market system has been directly opposed to it. But over time, while Americans were busy working and raising families, many of the premises upon which Marx built his Manifesto seeped into the liberal political class via the universities and those who fancy themselves intellectuals, Universalists, artists, and advocates for justice.

Back in my high school days, it was said to take fifty years for a theory to matriculate from inception to mainstream implementation. It is now a half century since the upending 60s. The result: Marxist notions of (1) class struggle, (2) reliance on the state instead of the individual, (3) exploiters vs. victims, (4) seeing a person not so much as a self-reliant individual but part of the great masses, and (5) the demonization of ownership, wealth, and capitalism have become ingrained in the outlook of many holding influential positions. Were they living in Europe, many liberal politicians would choose to be members of the Socialist or Labor Parties, neither of which are available here. But because here in America socialists are protected under the liberal label, too many Americans naively accept their definition of terms, not realizing how far removed these definitions and values are from historic Americanism and threaten the shining city on the hill—our American civilization.

The ideology of those spearheading today's liberalism is not your father's or grandfather's liberalism. It is actual leftism. This in contrast to the classic liberalism conceived in the eighteenth century, during the period of the Enlightenment, which was an admirable enterprise. It rested on the notion of judging a person as an individual as opposed to a member of a group, and on critical thinking, wherein the efficacy of a conclusion depended on objective reasoning and merit as opposed to dogma. In fact, much of today's conservatism lies in conserving the great ideals of eighteenth century Enlightenment.

Leftism, however, conducts a retrograde flow: it sees not the individual but membership in a particular group. It heralds not the native but whom it considers to be the outsider. It has become highly dogmatic and reeks of anti-Americanism, opposed to the land of the individual. It romanticizes those things that tear down the established order and traditional conventions. Any disagreement with its beliefs is scornfully condemned, and it demonizes those who do not conform to its leftist orthodoxy. To them, conservatives are society's criminals, instead of those who actually commit real crimes. Some professors are so doctrinaire that students must first *take off* their thinking caps prior to entering the classroom door. Leftism wishes to control and command as did the old European rightists it came to replace—it simply does so from the opposite pole.

The modern-day Left does not admire Adam Smith, the Scottish philosopher and advocate of capitalism who wrote *Wealth of Nations*; nor Edmund Burke, the English philosopher and father of political conservatism. Both greatly influenced our Founding Fathers. The Left venerates Jean-Jacques Rousseau, who claimed all men equally good and society at fault when men acted with evil or irresponsibly. In penance, Rousseau demanded that society transform itself and forever accommodate everyone.

Due to its guilt, he declared society had an obligation to guarantee everyone material equality. This was a political right, he wrote in *The Social Contract*, a later motif of the French Revolution. In contrast, the American Revolution rested on the premise that all men are created equal but are responsible for their own actions and welfare. Thus, America declared that society need not ensure equality of result, only equality of opportunity. There is no guarantee of happiness (property and cash), but there is a right to the pursuit of happiness.

The difference in how equality is defined and the importance one places on personal responsibility has great bearing on one's political outlook. During a speech in France (2009), President Obama seemed to opt for Rousseau's outlook. Many in the liberal camp have always identified with the European way of thinking regarding the position of the state above the individual. They are, in frenzied fashion, trying to recreate America in the image of Europe, be it regarding taxes, capital punishment, national healthcare, abortion, disarmament and appeasement, government control over business and speech, and Israel. There is no question in my mind that if a French socialist candidate, such as the late Francois Mitterand, would have been allowed to run in the U.S. for President, liberal elites would have been thrilled to vote for him.

The Left seems unmoved by the difference between our Revolution and that of Europe's transformation from monarchy to statism. Europe replaced its centuries-old monarchies with the State. It substituted one form of top-down authority with another, and traded oligarchs for bureaucrats. The benevolent state would now take care of the people. The French Revolution (1789), for example, was done in a rush, by the mob, and with violence. Our Founding came about through a protracted, *deliberative* process where it was decided the individual would rule over himself. The focus was on the individual not the state.

Our Founders looked to three men named John: Locke, Calvin, and Knox, and to Thomas Reid among others, as well as the Bible, in assessing man's nature and determining how he could best live in *responsible liberty*. No doubt, Aristotle's view of the virtuous man living by reason, conscience, and good citizenship borne of self-interest also had an impact. In his *Politics*, Aristotle wrote that happiness comes, ultimately, by living a virtuous life. Freely chosen virtue depends on an atmosphere of liberty.

Adams and Jefferson put the state in its place by trusting the individual to self-police by living according to the morality emblazoned in the Ten Commandments. James Madison, the pivotal force behind our Constitution, said: "Religion is the basis and foundation of government." Which religion? Madison's mentor, Dean of Princeton, John Witherspoon, told us: the Judeo-Christian, the Old and New Testament. The Founders were dramatically moved by Genesis' description of man, the individual, having been created in the image of God, a *servant to no one but Him*. Such thinking was absent in the French Revolution, which overthrew not only the detestable monarchs but, as Rousseau and Voltaire wrote earlier, the whole Catholic hierarchy that had given credence to the notion of a divine right of kings.

Present day liberalism's identification with European leftism is starkly different from the bygone American liberalism of Senators Scoop Jackson, Hubert Humphrey, John Kennedy, and Sam Nunn—all Democrats. In conversations with Congressmen Peter King of Long Island and Steve King of Council Bluffs, Iowa, I've heard of the wide chasm separating today's liberals from their predecessors of thirty years ago. Speaker of the House John Boehner feels likewise. This shift from liberalism to leftism revolves around the ever expanding welfare state and the newly fashionable belief in transnationalism.

To paraphrase James Carville, the Democrat strategist: *It's socialism, stupid!* Let us call this by its real name. Some Republican strategists say our candidates should not call it socialism, even though it is. They think by so doing, we will be branded extreme. I disagree. If we do not, many American people will continue thinking that what we are seeing today is simply a few Democrats engaged in a more liberal version of liberalism. Many Americans won't be alarmed, figuring that we have lived with liberalism for many years and are still functioning as Americans. But, if we refuse to call it socialism, it will continue under the radar screen and grow stronger as mere liberalism. We need to awaken the people to what is happening. People tend to accept what goes on unless they are rudely awakened and jolted. We need to supply that jolt. If we allow socialism to sneak by as liberalism, we will allow transnationalism to get by as nationalism too. It is our job to educate. Once we finally do, our election victories will become easier.

Why this fear among Republicans of being called extreme if one knows in his heart that what he is saying is not extreme at all but fact? Those who refuse to speak their heartfelt conviction of what the truth is out of fear of the other side labeling them an extremist are allowing the other side to control them and the debate. For some reason, liberals have the confidence to assert what they believe, while we have been spooked by them into not saying what we believe. Why? Because they will call us a name? They are *counting* precisely on that.

It is working for them. For example, they tell us we cannot call terrorism as Muslim or Islamic terrorism. We should call it "man-made disasters" or simply terrorism. But what is that which is done by a Muslim in the name of Islam as an act of jihad by the Koran, if not Islamic terrorism? Liberals do not want us to call it what it is because if we do, they know they will have to begin cracking down on many of our domestic Islamic groups whose leaders are preaching things bordering on the provocative. They do not wish to crack down on Muslims because Islam is now part of their political coalition.

Similarly the Left does not want us to call what they plan and are doing by its real name—socialism. They know that if we call it by its real name, the public will finally begin taking a much needed second look. Do we actually believe the Obamaites came to Washington, D.C. simply to implement Henry Jackson and John Kennedy's 1950s liberalism? The Obamaites came to seize power, dangerous and unchallengeable power. Something very un-American is taking shape right in front of our eyes. The Left do not want their intentions known, so they warn us not to tell the truth or else they will call us extreme. Do not let others spook you. Men who wish to retain their liberty and autonomy cannot allow themselves to be intimidated into silence or political correctness.

★★★

As the welfare state has expanded social engineering to preposterous levels defying common sense—against what early philosophers called natural law—it has become necessary for liberals to engineer our thinking and emotions so we will begin accepting their philosophy. Liberals are always telling us what to think, what to feel, and how to talk. Since a democracy cannot make rules by fiat, those wishing to transform society must first redefine the terms that historically guided the nation. We are now at the point where every moral category is being redefined to justify the domestic welfare state and the Left's transnational views. Instead of intrinsic morality dictating our political positions, the political positions of liberals are determining morality.

I'm reminded how during the administration of Mayor David Dinkins (early 1990s), New York City's police, fire, sanitation, and education departments were basically seen as conduits for social engineering. Their intrinsic purpose was sidetracked and diminished in service to "higher" liberal social goals, resulting in a glorious city bereft of decent city services and held in constant shakedowns by charlatans and provocateurs.

The purposeful re-engineering of morality is harmful not only to the country's historic ethos, its prosperity and security, and is a distortion of truth itself but harmful to the individual as well. Legions of people now think that morality or ethics is achieved simply by espousing liberal principles and supporting the welfare state concept: *I'm good not by virtue of what I do but by what I espouse.*

No matter how hard liberals try convincing us one is moral by subscribing to statist and politically correct policies, the fact is that morality and good character can only be realized by personally living and acting according to the classic understanding of moral categories. The Judeo-Christian ethic is action oriented and personal. What counts is *how you live your life.* Redefining moral imperatives so as to fit liberal paradigms reduces morality to a means to an end when moral imperatives should be inviolable ends in themselves. This travesty is the consequence of the Left's repeated mantra, originally coined by Carol Hanisch in the feminist movement of 1969, that "the personal is the political" with priority being given to the political.

★★★

With the Left's agenda moving beyond even welfare statism to multiculturalism and transnationalism, even more terms have been inverted and corrupted in order to justify its positions. So now,

- **Compassion** is reserved for those of the grievance communities and for preferential groups, while indifference is directed at those who work hard, the mainstream, and the middle class.

- **Equality**, as demonstrated in never-ending affirmative action, means that some are more equal than others.

- **Fairness (1)** means guaranteeing material equality on the backs of others.

- **Fairness (2)**: It is only fair for the majority to surrender to the wishes of minorities but unfair when the mainstream and majority ask that their considerations be equally honored.

- **Free speech** allows one to ridicule Christians, conservatives, or Tea Partiers, but it is deemed hate speech if it challenges liberal doctrine or disagrees with a position expressed by a minority or any of the grievance-preferred groups.

- **Greed** is assigned those who wish to retain more of what they earn so as to support their family; while those who demand the earnings of others for themselves, through redistribution of wealth, are not labeled greedy but entitled.

- **Investment:** While investing has always been understood as the parlaying of capital into business and enterprises to expand wealth creation, it now means a dead-end support of people through redistribution of money.

- **Lady Justice** has been forced to remove her blindfold.

- **Judgment** is a sin if done on behalf of upholding standards but is fine when directed at Christians for living according to standards.

- **Morality:** It is immoral to prescribe sexual morality, but moral to dismiss the whole notion of sexual immorality.

- **Multiculturalism** means that all cultures are equally good, except for historic Judeo-Christian Americanism, which is not.

- **Religion** has been the source of most of our wars and conflicts, unless that religion is Islam. "Loving the sinner" is worse than "hating the infidel."

- **Peace** is achieved by appeasing one's intransigent enemies and strongarming reasonable friends.

- **Pride**: The pride one has in his culture is admirable and beautiful if vaunted by a minority but racist and evil if expressed by a member of the majority regarding his own culture. Many on the Left believe pride shown by other nations is a wonderful thing but if done by Americans is chauvinism.

- **Racism:** Only the majority can harbor and be guilty of racism, not a minority. Thus a minority member is not culpable for the racism he espouses and even practices. It is racist for a member of the majority to disagree with a policy position expressed by a minority even though he would level that same policy disagreement if issued by a member of the majority. White, middle class Christians are assumed to be guilty of racism unless proven otherwise—but somehow that assertion is itself not racist.

- **Rights:** In the name of liberalism, fundamental Constitutional rights for law-abiding citizens, such as gun ownership and free speech, can be challenged; while Constitutional rights are extended by those same liberals to foreign terrorists who, through guns and propaganda, wish to destroy our Constitutional way of life.

- **Selfishness:** It is "selfish" to want to keep the fruits of your own labor, but someone else is not selfish for demanding it from you.

- **"The People"** are not those who silently work the hardest but are those who claim grievances against the society the loudest.

- **Tolerance** means abandoning standards and judgment, thereby tolerating the intolerable. Intolerance is pointing out the intolerance of those demanding tolerance from us, as well as the need for them to become tolerant. Tolerance has become a one-way street.

- **Understanding:** We must understand those who wish to upend or destroy our country but need not show understanding to those conservatives who love it.

For too long, many of us have attributed a "bleeding heart" to the motivation behind liberalism. Others, perceiving the word *liberal* as meaning "of generous spirit," assumed political liberalism was generated by a spirit of generosity. But as the above upside-down, inverted definitions indicate, there is nothing generous about these positions, nor even misguided. Indeed much of it is not compassionate toward large segments of our society and deliberately so. These attitudes are rooted not in morality but in politics, a mean-spirited political agenda to marginalize and disenfranchise mainstream America. Nothing here deserves to be credited with holding a moral high ground. The only moral aspect to it is its subscription to *moral relativism*, a moral relativism that does not differentiate between good conduct and bad, and often chooses and roots for the bad.

There is something nasty in the attitude and demeanor of today's elitist liberals. Instead of belief in our people, there is condescension toward them. Ed Koch, the former mayor of New York City, a patriotic American and, perhaps, the last of the old time liberals, said it best. Although he is a liberal, he said that he finds conversation with today's liberals to be distasteful due to an assertive nastiness, self-righteousness, and arrogance. He prefers the company of non-liberals. Based on what liberalism has classically meant, today's liberalism is quite *illiberal* and *intolerant* of that which it does not prefer. It could use a dose of humility and introspection and should stop feeling so self-righteous.

There is nothing honorable about pushing policies that hurt those who wish to make their way in life through self-reliance and steady, hard work, rather than relying on government programs made possible by squeezing those who are trying to do the right thing and achieve the American dream. There is nothing righteous about demonizing fellow Americans and pitting one group of Americans against each other—class warfare—and fabricating this notion that successful people "make it on the backs of others" and get up in the morning thinking how they can exploit their fellow American. I do not know anybody who thinks that way. Perhaps, the liberal Left thinks in those terms because that is what they wish to do to conservatives or those standing in their political way. It is quite dishonorable to appeal to the demons within human nature and sow hatred among people simply for political gain and to strip people of their innate spirit to succeed.

Nor is it admirable to be guided by snootiness born of one's feeling superior to fellow Americans not "smart" enough to "understand," as do the liberal *smugsters* who praise themselves. On the contrary, it is the average commonsense, hardworking American who has made this country into the rock solid middle class society it has been. America was built not by the politics of putting down, but by tens of millions looking up. The ideology and politics of envy used by the political Left ends up embittering the individual and corroding an entire society, often for generations. Knowing this, God calls envy sinful: "Thou shalt not envy your neighbor for his possessions, his house, and what he owns." Envy is a cursed thing, and those who gain power through the politics of envy bring this wretched curse upon a nation. Those, Mr. President, are *not* "our values." America deserves better, and we have it in our hands to, once again, make things better by reclaiming our values and our land.

★★★ FOUR ★★★

Morality

[*Doing what we ought to do because it is right.*]

We've addressed the importance of morality within the Judeo-Christian ethos. So, what does it mean? How do we of the American Judeo-Christian tradition define morality? *Moral* simply means "doing that which we ought to do because it is right." But what we do depends first on how we define what is right. It will take us a few steps to reach our answer, but it will help us get a handle on the animating principle behind Americanism.

First, morality is universal and not dependent on which group you come from. In other words, it is objective. Second, it should be fixed and not relative: what was wrong years ago remains so today and that which is right today had to be right before. The only condition that we all share today as before, and the only condition where there is no difference between individuals, is in our having been created by God and in His image. The Genesis story of the creation of man is so paramount because it lays out the precise common condition from which stems our obligation to live by a universal and fixed morality—not subjective morality, not moral relativism, but pure morality.

Now what are the singular features in man's creation? It is having been created as an individual and in the image of God: "In the image of God was human created." Since being human does not look like God, what does God's image represent? It means individuality, as in One God. It also means intelligence and with that intelligence the ability to choose. So as to choose wisely, man has the power of discernment. Guided by his Creator, man's possibilities are endless. God made man with intelligence and said that His creation was good.

Man's individuality, intelligence, and ability to choose with discernment make him human. This distinguishes him from an animal. Our mind

41

allows us to discern and our soul provides us conscience to do that *which we ought*, i.e., that which is moral.

This specific account of man's creation is in the Old Testament only. From it derives our entire understanding of man as a free moral agent. It is the philosophical underpinning of the Judeo-Christian view of man's identity and obligations. It is crucial to how man is viewed within society and what we can demand of him and what demands he can make of us. Other religions, as we will show in later chapters, do not share this exact view.

Being an individual means to be autonomous. Having autonomy means taking care of oneself and being accountable for one's actions and choices. It means the right to set one's own personal boundaries, which is the definition of liberty. An accountable being is obligated to fulfill his responsibilities. And what are we responsible for? We are responsible to fulfill the obligations which, with liberty, *we have freely chosen*.

Our original question was: What is morality? It is that which we *ought to do*. And what is it we ought to do? Take care of ourselves and assume the responsibilities that we have chosen. Our accountability lies in these two things. Moreover, moral responsibility, according to the Genesis Creation account, resides not in and for groups but in and for the individual. It is personal. *Personal responsibility* is what is meant when talking of moral responsibility. It involves living by the choices we make. There is more to life of course, but at the most basic level it is precisely this.

Choosing correctly is central to the biblical motif. "Therefore choose life" reminds us that what our life becomes (barring circumstances beyond our control) is tied to the personal choices we make. We are responsible to choose correctly. God would not demand that we choose if He thought we were incapable of making good choices. He knows we have a mind capable of discernment and a conscience to do what is right.

What I have just proposed has nothing to do with the realm of creed or dogma. This book is not about the theology of religion, salvation, redemption, or the end of days. I wish to focus only on the philosophy of religion, the Judeo-Christian philosophy, as it relates to man as a mortal individual and as a member of society. Naturally, for the religious person, taking care of oneself goes beyond the physical and material and extends to the religious and spiritual as well.

★★★

Fending and supporting oneself is our first human obligation. Because it is right, it is the moral thing to do. We have no moral right to expect others to do it for us. Once we are capable adults, we cannot demand that others support us. We have no entitlement or claim to it. A capable adult demanding, under some claim of entitlement, to be supported by others is shirking his first moral responsibility.

If morality is doing that which ought to be done, then demanding that which ought not be done is an act of immorality. One specific morality is not to steal another's money, his time, or his energy. Demanding from another human that which does not belong to you is robbery.

The welfare state advances the notion that simply because one lives, he is entitled to that which belongs to others, is not accountable for his choices or obligated to fend for himself. It is disguised thievery and immoral. The radical welfare state gives entitlement status to those making claims on other people's earnings and property and makes them indirect overlords of the time, energy, and talents of others. The phrase "investing in people" is an appealing but clever twist of words used to promote redistribution of wealth, which squeezes those who have risked and worked hard in fending for themselves. It is for this reason the famed economic philosopher Frederick Hayek declared the welfare state as a *Road to Serfdom*. It is a social and political paradigm that ought not be, not only for what it does but for the destructive values it teaches.

The Creation of man by God is the foundation of the Judeo-Christian outlook regarding the role of the individual and society. The destiny and freedom of any given society depends on personal responsibility being its national motif. Nothing is more efficacious to society than each individual assuming his own personal responsibilities. America has been successful because it has followed this specific ethos, and all who subscribe to it can achieve some form of success. Without this ethos, all sorts of sloth and social anarchy take root, forcing tyranny to ride in as the saving knight in shining armor.

★★★

Those countries that are perennially unsuccessful—and have been for ages—are those that do not have as their guiding motif the ethos of personal responsibility. Had America not lived by the ethos of personal responsibility, it would have never become the land of prosperity we behold and enjoy today.

Some countries like to claim that their failure is due to colonialism. But these countries did not thrive even before colonialism. They like to blame America, though America wasn't even involved in colonialism. In fact, America's involvement with these countries has been to send aid and food and, very often, the blood of our young soldiers. But all the aid and food have not changed the ongoing dreadful condition of these countries because they seem unable or unwilling to live by the theme of personal responsibility. And it is not always due to a lack of money. The regular people of Egypt, Iraq, Libya, most of Saudi Arabia, and many parts of present day Iran, have a very low standard of living despite the fact that these countries have oodles of money from the oil they sell—oil they did not create or invent but is simply there. They live by a cultural and religious ethos where personal responsibility is a foreign and often rejected idea.

What it really boils down to is this: The "sin" of America (and now Israel) that much of the Third World, the United Nations, and fervent Islam (Death to America!) declare we are guilty of is our sin of *success*. Their unwillingness to accept that our adherence to the Judeo-Christian ethos of personal responsibility is the root of our success leads them to all sorts of creative reasons over why they are mired in poverty: "It is America's fault"—because we exist. "We have taken the resources that belong to them"—as if we stole it and didn't pay for it! They will never admit to the efficacy and blessings that rise from the Judeo-Christian ethos since they wish to remain with the system and approach to life they have had for hundreds of years.

Many on the Left who can't bring themselves to credit Americanism and have an inner aversion to our Judeo-Christian ethos, dismiss the pivotal role it has played in bringing economic blessing. Instead of lauding our American ethos, they indict us for it. The guilt trip never ends. President Obama continually blames America for many of the world's woes because, as he says, "we use too much of the world's resources." On the contrary, it is our payment for those resources that provide those countries the little bit of cash they have. Are the nations of the world, then, equally sinful and guilty because they buy too many of our iPods and too much Coca Cola? And if to be successful, according to Mr. Obama, a nation needs all the natural resources it can extract, why has he done more to stop domestic oil drilling here in America than any president on record? He's a bundle of contradictions that can only be explained by a deeper inner identification with the world outside America than the people, ethos, and land of America itself.

★ ★ ★

We would all agree that, beyond ourselves, our first responsibility and obligation is to our spouse and children since they are relationships we have freely chosen—by marrying and begetting children. No obligation is more important. We, of course, also have an obligation to do good, honest work for those we have chosen to be our employer and pay us for our work. Any relationship freely chosen brings with it accountability and obligation—*reciprocity*.

Included in responsibility is to give to those who have given to us. While we did not choose our parents, it is a relationship that demands responsibility out of reciprocity. They gave us life and the many support structures we need to survive and grow. We may not have chosen them, but we accepted what they provided. Honoring thy father and thy mother is so important that the commandment is placed in the very middle of the *Ten Commandments*, God's great treasure to us.

When we look at our primary personal responsibilities, which are to ourselves, spouse, children, and parents, what we have is *family*. In the Judeo-Christian outlook, responsibility to family comes first. Out of family comes responsibility to our brothers and sisters. Helping our siblings is part of honoring our parents who bore them. Friendship also entails responsibility and a degree of obligation. Only after those responsibilities can be adequately taken care of can we move on to other things.

The more *direct* the relationship, the greater priority it has over our basket of responsibilities. The neighborhood and locality where we choose to live bring to us greater obligations than places where we do not live. Deuteronomy 15:7, Exodus 22:24, and Leviticus 25:39 tell us that donations to the poor should go first to those local and nearby. (The word in Hebrew for poor is *ani,* which means those afflicted by unfortunate circumstances.)

Beyond the responsibility inherent in every freely chosen relationship is the need to give back to that which has been given to us (the message of the fifth commandment). In the moral world of reciprocity, we cannot take from something without giving back to it.

After locality comes country. Every moment we live here is a moment in which we are freely choosing to live here. We have chosen this relationship. We fulfill our responsibility through such things as military service, civic projects, and other forms of good citizenship. If we were never to get a penny from the U.S. Treasury, we would still be responsible to our country since we have freely chosen our relationship to her.

But beyond that, we have a *moral* obligation to give to our country because she has given to us—reciprocity—not because we are a recipient of a government program, but because the United States gives us something far greater. It gives us freedom to live our lives as we choose and provides us with the protection to do so. Because each citizen lives in freely chosen relationship to this country and receives freedom and protection from it, each citizen is obligated to do something on her behalf, be he rich or poor. The quid-pro-quo of being in America, our relationship and obligations to it, has nothing to do with whether it is paying for our rent or food, but whether it continues to protect us from outside enemies and allows us to be free.

Furthermore, America allows us to do what an individual was created to do: live by personal responsibility. Because of all this we give America our loyalty and patriotism. Patriotism is gratitude to America. Those that are not patriotic are guilty of ingratitude and cynicism. Loyalty and gratitude are core conservative and religious virtues.

Because our relationship to America has nothing to do with what she gives us monetarily, our obligations to her have nothing to do with money per se, but in doing those things that make it possible for her to maintain her purpose of defending and providing freedom to her citizens. After all, this nation was not founded by people so that a government would supply them with food, rent, housing, contraceptives, and insurance payments for cosmetic enhancements—government handouts—but by people in need of defense from common outside enemies and by people wishing to live free. We were founded in liberty not dependency, as a republic, not as a welfare state. The only entitlement claim one can make on America is to be defended and granted freedom. One cannot morally make a claim against America for not taking care of one's economic needs. That was never the original contract between America and her people.

What we pay in taxes should be for those things our government needs to defend us and maintain our liberty. Those who are able-bodied enough to work have a moral obligation to take care of themselves. Failure to do so is a rejection of personal responsibility and morality. Demanding that others put at risk their ability to perform and discharge their primary obligations to family and the defense and freedom needs of the country is an act of immorality and far removed from the vision of man portrayed by God in Genesis. Immorality on a grand scale leads to national bankruptcy, poverty, and disease.

★ ★ ★

After responsibility comes the need for generosity. First is generosity of spirit and action. The other form of generosity involves giving some of our money to others—charity. The sick, many of the elderly, and the truly needy require our help. Many people do generously contribute to charity. Knowing full well the heavy requirements we have to our primary obligations, the Bible was mindful not to stress us and kept our obligation to a reasonable level. For example, many of us tithe 10 percent. But charity was never meant to be punitive.

Charity is important for two reasons. It helps the person in need of it, and it helps the person who gives it. "God's kindness fills the world" (Psalms 33:5) the psalmist sings. When we give in charity, we open up to others and we ponder our need to share with others from that with which God has blessed us. God made a world where charity is needed and by so doing brings kindness into the world through those who give it.

But while good for our soul by instilling in us kindness, and while necessary if a society is to be healthy and sound, charity is not an entitlement. One cannot demand it. The charity we give, as with everything else in the Judeo-Christian ethos, is personal and given by the individual. It is not something that government can tax away from us in order to establish the welfare state or for the purpose of distributing money to causes and charities it prefers and deems politically correct. Let us be forthright about what redistribution is—it is not charity but politics and a reordering of the country's values.

Charity must remain a relationship between a benefactor and a recipient. Those who receive should feel grateful to those who have given to them. Feelings of gratitude swell the heart and allow love to flow in—love for the provider and, ultimately, love for God, the greatest Provider of all.

Charity is not good when the receiver feels entitled to it, and no longer agrees to the necessity for personal responsibility, accountability, or reciprocity. The redistributed largess of the welfare state cannot be characterized as charity when it engenders the corrosive notion of entitlement, sanctifies dependency, and subverts our moral ethos of individual autonomy. Such brings about not felt kindness, but the opposite—ingratitude. "The government wouldn't be sending me this money every month unless I was entitled, would they?"

Ingratitude begets a stingy soul. Ingratitude is the opposite of generosity of spirit and is a form of human numbness. As will be shown throughout this book, ingratitude is, in the eyes of God, a most grievous sin. Charity needs to be good for the soul of the recipient, just as it was intended to be good for the soul of the benefactor. We need to do that which causes in people thanksgiving and instills in them the quality of appreciation. In charity, we must also differentiate between real needs as opposed to wants. (We'll address more about charity in future chapters.)

★★★

Besides the moral aspect, a society under heavy taxation cannot create wealth. Without money for investment, an economy and country shrink. The working middle class suffers and upward mobility stops. Those who wish to fend for themselves and make a better life are penalized and deprived from doing so. Imposing an economic model that subsidizes one segment of society on the backs of those eager to work and better themselves is cruel and immoral.

Furthermore, every citizen should pay something in taxes or in service. Reciprocity demands it, and it creates an attachment. Generally we are more attached to something to which we have contributed. Something of us is now invested in it, and giving to it cements within us its importance. Why be grateful for something if told that what you receive is not a gift but an entitlement? It is not a coincidence that love for America and patriotism is generally far greater among those who give to this country than those who live a lifetime receiving and give nothing. I have seen this occur hundreds of times.

A society that stops creating wealth is a society that no longer has individuals with the financial wherewithal to give substantial charity. Our country has always been charitable because so many have earned sufficiently so that money has been available for charity. Our museums, orchestras, hospitals, and so many more institutions have flourished due to contributions from people with the financial means and heart to do so. Look at England. As it began sliding into welfare-statism, its people no longer had the financial resources to contribute as they once did when they were the world's leading mercantile society. I have no doubt there are those on the Left displeased by the charities and causes to which we conservatives donate. They'd rather have the government, which is their treasure chest, decide which are the "worthy" causes and charities.

Americans of all economic stripes donate more than any other population in the world. It is a direct consequence not only of our generosity of spirit but grows out of our Judeo-Christian ethos instructing the individual to give of himself through action and charity.

We are also generous because we live in a land where we think that we will always be able to earn yet more tomorrow. We have felt that way because we have lived under a free market system, not one in name only, but in robust reality. The implementation of the welfare state puts all that in jeopardy. The cheerfulness that comes to a society that sees tomorrow as better than today, as has been the case here, happens when freedom, not government regulations, reigns. What is at stake is the sweetness of American life: the more socialist a state, the dourer its people.

The American Judeo-Christian ethos, centered on the individual, has given rise to *action* as a mode of operation. We don't rely on others to do that which we as individuals are expected to do. We don't rely on government. This ethos fashioned a unique American characteristic and personality. Alexis de Tocqueville saw it on his journey to America before the Civil War. He labeled it *Volunteerism*. He saw in America that which he had not seen in Europe, the continent of kings, behemoth governments, and bureaucracies. He saw a people, a religious people, who had churches, clubs, guilds, societies—all local—taking care of their own legitimate needs and those of their neighbors. He saw people take into their own hands the health and welfare of their communities.

America is a land where the good ladies in town busy themselves with volunteer projects. Ask anyone who has come here, and they will admit to this remarkable American phenomenon. One sees it in Israel too but not as pronounced. The welfare state is a poison against it. Looking elsewhere in the world, one hardly sees this at all.

This action-oriented ethos and the freedom to act, lead to that quintessential American trait—rugged individualism. Combined with generosity of spirit, the American personality was formed. The rugged individual imbued with generosity of spirit is a man of *character*.

★★★

Let us contrast this value from those who live by the values of the welfare state. A people taken care of from cradle to grave, womb to tomb, on the domestic side is one that becomes incapable of defending itself, inside or outside. The people no longer have steel and true grit. Lacking that rugged individualism, Europe did not battle communism. And today it is not battling the Islam that is slowly taking over their continent. "Here's my country—take it, please!" seems to be their sentiment.

Furthermore, necessary military spending steadily declines as more is spent on domestic welfare state programs. In fact, as the U.K.'s *Daily Mail* (April 30, 2012) states, Britain as a country and Britons as individuals are using a significant portion of their money to subsidize Muslim immigrants who have discovered a free lunch by simply moving to England. Even more punishing to the taxpaying English worker: although England does not allow polygamous marriages to take place within the country, it will grant marriage status to the three or four wives concurrently married to one man when those polygamous marriages were performed in Muslim countries, since Muslim law allows polygamy up to four wives per man. A non-working wife is supported by the state to the tune of around $15,000 per year for the two of them, plus additional payments for each child, plus housing. A man with three or four wives has many children being supported by Englishmen who, due to high taxes, find it difficult for themselves to have more than one or two children.

People are remarking how the generosity of the English state encourages immigration by those wishing to live a Western life for free and creates many schemes for enlarging one's family and relatives to receive more subsidies. It is a rip-off on a grand scale. This is not the kindness the Psalms had in mind. Distressingly, it shows a craven and pitiful lack of conviction by the English of their historic Christian and Western standards regarding marriage. Evidently, the new god is multiculturalism and cultural sensitivity.

A nation of self-reliant individuals, who daily wrestle with the challenges of life, is a nation with the mindset and strategy to fight forces that must be fought. It's not soft but strong. It has developed the inner strength that comes out of the crucible of going up against the odds, of competing. It is a nation that leads because its people know how to take care of things. It remains free.

In the end, that which is immoral causes weakness. In individuals, immorality often leads to disease. In nations, it leads to weakness, then rot, and finally, loss of freedom. Living by what is moral is not just so that we can be goody-goodies. It is so that we can continue living. For four hundred years we lived under the moral vision of the Judeo-Christian ethos. I urge Americans not to give it up for the bowl of porridge called entitlements. In return for being taken care of, we will have, like Esau, given up our birthright.

To paraphrase Thomas Jefferson: The more we rely on government the more we forfeit our liberty, and with it our individual and national strength. Benjamin Franklin warned: Those that trade liberty for (government) security end up with neither liberty nor security.

We Americans need to choose to continue to live by the Judeo-Christian moral heritage that preceded Obamaism by thousands of years. *Yes, we can.*

FIVE

Morality vs. Sentiments

[*A crucial difference exists between sentiments and morality.*]

Sentiments often make us feel good about ourselves and allow us to feel we are nice. As we have seen, morality is doing what ought to be done and what needs to be done for the sake of society's preservation so that the individual chooses correctly.

The blurring of the two—thinking that what is nice and what makes us feel good about ourselves constitutes morality—is the single greatest confusion besetting our Western societies today. Left to sentiments alone, we risk economic meltdown, social disintegration, and national suicide, especially in light of the forces out to destroy us by exploiting our obsession over being nice to all.

The purpose of religion, and the Judeo-Christian philosophic ethos that arose from it, is to make us people of *discernment* so we can know what is the correct thing to do. It often seems contrary to what is nice, but religion, through its moral code, teaches far more important lessons than being a perpetual *Barney*, the fuzzy pink dinosaur mindlessly singing that he loves us and we are one happy family. Religion wishes to foster strong individuals and nations that can discern right from wrong so that they can survive and flourish. Morality is not found in a type of endless appeasement or passivity that not only fails to fight evil but also can end with society committing slow suicide on the altar of niceness.

Often what we must do is hard on the stomach and contrary to feel-good sentiments. But choosing correctly, though often difficult, makes us mature and inculcates within us an inner strength. This strength within the millions of individuals comprising society creates an overall strong society, one that is self-reliant, confident, and willing to act. Sticking always to immovable platitudes about love and peace means we are but robots on cruise control. Nobility of spirit comes through individuals struggling through the tough decisions necessary to grow and mature. To be noble is to rise above the commonplace. A noble person is guided by inner strength, not fear and faddishness. Individuals able to discern and choose that which is specifically right for a specific situation—and eschew the easy, cruise-control platitudes—become candidates for leadership in their community and the nation.

Nobility of spirit, inner strength, and intellectual maturity is the hope religion has for human created in the image of God. One-size-fits-all platitudes end up being excuses for not discerning and making necessary judgments. It is but moral escapism. It falls short of the biblical concept of man, being created in His image, who is to embody discernment and action. God Himself is at once a God of compassion (Exodus 34:6) and a God of war (Exodus 15:3). He is a God of peace, but a God who knows when avenging is necessary—never war or vengeance as a delight or sport or as ends in themselves (as with the pagan gods), but traits often necessary to protect the innocent. When done within the proper context it is called justice.

Too many stuck in permanent Barneyism interpret being a *light unto the nations* (Isaiah 42:6) as disarmament, naively thinking that simply promoting love and understanding will bring to heel those out to destroy us. But, in fact, being a light of the world means choosing the proper moral approach when confronting evil—vanquishing it. When confronting evil, the light we shine must reflect our mandate to fight it. "And thou shalt eradicate the evil" is mentioned no less than six times in the Old Testament. Treating evil as we do everything else manifests a woeful inability to see and discern evil. It leads not to light but darkness. Illumination is achieved through discernment, not escapism, and certainly not by a moral relativism unable to see the difference between good and bad.

Moral relativism is the opposite of morality. Not only does it not see and apprehend evil, but it tries to understand and even justify it by providing all types of excuses on its behalf. Too often, moral relativists put the onus of restraint and peace not on those committing the evil but on the victims of it. Moral relativists sometimes begin identifying with the forces of evil they try so hard to understand. What any man with common sense understands as evil, the moral relativist begins calling a ray of light. Being a light unto the nations cannot be left to those who no longer know what light is and who have lost their moral compass.

Quite often, moral relativism is simply a manifestation of cowardice. As an approach, it lacks nobility; and as a policy, it endangers the peace loving nations. When people begin rejecting historic Judeo-Christian morality, they are unlikely to have the courage to defend it or offer the sacrifices necessary to preserve it.

Moral relativists like to describe their understanding and pre-occupation with these detestable forces as a sign of their moral superiority. In other words, they think of a personal morality so above the common man, they are impelled to defend that which the common man seems unable to do. But what this really constitutes is either amorality or, worse, immorality. This sense of moral superiority over the rest of us represents, in actuality, a code of inferior morality. As we will highlight in later chapters, more than any time in our history, or perhaps even in Western history, a dangerously large amount on the Left are engaging in a self-aggrandizing moral superiority. The result is putting us in the West in tremendous peril.

This type of amoral "light" coming from the moral relativists of the American and European Left is simply enabling the forces of darkness. The Left's unwillingness to see the source of today's evil and identify and call it by its specific name is making it more difficult for us to immediately stop the escalating evil. We see, for example, little Jewish children being murdered in French schools in Toulouse, France, as a seeming desire to avenge French participation in the Afghan war; the barbaric oppression of Coptic Christians in Egypt; and the genocide of Sudanese and other Christians all across Africa. Instead of naming the ideological source behind all the terrorism we see unfolding before our eyes, the current administration labels it but "man-made disasters" and foolishly wastes its time, and our time, at airports checking grandmothers in wheelchairs and babies in strollers.

Too many who spurn our historic Judeo-Christian understanding of right vs. wrong engage in moral relativism, the opposite of a well-worked-out moral code calling us to our mission of acting correctly. In fact, being loving and kind where one should not is a gross abdication of morality. Ecclesiastics 3:1-8 teaches us of our need to distinguish and discern: "To everything there is a season, and a time to every purpose...under the Heaven" (yes, with Heaven's endorsement). "A time to plant, a time to uproot; a time to embrace and a time not to embrace; a time to keep, and a time to cast out; a time for silence, a time to speak; a time to love, a time to hate…a time for war and a time for peace; a time to kill and a time to heal."

★★★

This ability to discern is *wisdom*. God wants us to grow in wisdom and inner strength. Ecclesiastics was written by Solomon, the wisest of all men. But only those with a real attachment to the Old Testament live under the influence of this sacred calling for discernment born of distinctions and real life application. Discernment is a lifetime process that leads to *personal growth*, as opposed to what happens when neat, absolutist platitudes keep us mentally stuck in the days of childish *Barney* simplicity. Herein lies the big difference between moral wisdom and feel-good sentiment.

Our need to distinguish is often rebuffed by those wishing to hear and live by simplistic notions that free them from making difficult judgments and allow them to parade as moral paragons who do not get their hands dirty. Those concerned more about their image or in being purists of "love and understanding only" are being morally and intellectually irresponsible. But the payoff for discernment and moral courage is grand, for it provides maturity of thought, inner strength, and valor. It imparts confidence to a nation forever having to answer those who exploit such good things as love, tolerance, and peace in pushing their moral relativism and appeasement.

The Bible could have been limited to ten pages if it was only meant to impart thirty or so iron-tight platitudes. But it came also to teach discernment for a real life where, as Solomon writes, there is a time for and a time against, a time to and a time not to. It provides dozens of real life stories and narratives—of heroes not angels—striving to teach us when to and when not to, and especially how the failure to fight evil has led to the death of millions who were innocent but whose leaders could not muster the courage to fight evil—not to placate it, accept it, or live with it—and expunge it. Such constitutes necessary light and why the Old Testament was forced to retell the stories of gore and battles against evil, and of God's assistance and miracles when heroic men and women rose against it and fought it.

As important as it is for us to rise in righteous anger against those afflicting the widow and orphan, or those taking advantage of the poor, it is equally important that we stand up in righteous anger against those engaged in evil against our civilization. We need to take a stand for *justice* because it is the moral thing to do. It is as necessary to defend humanity from evil and not accept justifications by those who have become inured to evil as it is to heal the sick, visit the bereaved, and care for the needy. Eradicating evil shows love of God's moral code and is our biblical mandate. Failure to do so will eventually lead to a condition of untold new widows, orphans, poor, sick, and bereaved, as well as a replacement of the good society by the soldiers of evil.

★★★

The biblical coin of morality has two sides: one imprinted with mercy, the other emblazed with justice. Both are needed for individual and societal preservation. The moral individual must live by both and know when to choose which. When he chooses a war for justice, war is no longer a misdeed but becomes a *virtue*.

In fact, God showed the way. Though He created the world, He demarcated between light and darkness, "And He separated the darkness from the light." Being able to first accept the notion of distinctions and afterward discern accordingly, brings moral clarity and the wisdom and genuine understanding so vital to one's personal inner growth and maturity, and society's survival. It fosters *active* responsibility.

This application of morality based on discernment is crucial; civilizations rise and fall on it. Aside from being a Book about spiritual salvation, the Bible is a document given to mortals who must be able to make distinctions. In Leviticus 10:10 God tells us: "And that ye may put differences between the holy and unholy," referring to lifestyles, especially regarding the sexual. Further in that same verse, He speaks of the "difference between the clean and unclean," meaning that which is acceptable and worthy and that which is unacceptable and unworthy. Discernment as an ongoing process is the Almighty's charge to us. Further in Leviticus 11:47, God says that we "make a difference between the pure and the impure," including ideologies.

God intentionally made this a hazy, beclouded world requiring us to make distinctions within it. Through that process we becomes agents of understanding and wisdom, so as to fend for and protect ourselves. It is a religious obligation and part of the ongoing religious experience, and reflects our partnership with Him. It includes choosing not only among things that exist but within characteristics and virtues such as love, compassion, tolerance, and peace. No one can be complete simply by subscribing at age ten to a set of predetermined categories that need no further investigation or specific application. It is as theologian Edward Plumptre said, while commenting on Ecclesiastes: "It is wisdom to do the right thing at the right time." Only those choices that have proven effective remain inviolate.

That we must choose and choose correctly is announced one final time toward the end of Deuteronomy where we read: "Behold, see, I have placed in front of you the life and the good, the death and the bad. Therefore, choose life" (Deuteronomy 30:19). Choice comes from discernment and not as a result of our feelings. God gave us brains to be used, as opposed to feel-good sentiments that appeal to our emotions only and fail to nourish moral clarity and engineer active responsibility.

Any ideology that has death at its core is characterized in that scriptural passage as being *bad*. It is anti-life. Any ideology that extols suicide bombing or the constant jihad of death against those considered infidels is, as the Bible says, "the dead and the bad" (Deuteronomy 30:15). The same with any cult of death, such as those who see anytime, anywhere, for whatever reason abortion as an expression of "the right to control one's body." It must be rejected, especially for those who believe in "Therefore choose life." It is not a coincidence that fervent "abortion anytimers" can often be found among those advocating for the rights of captured terrorists. Such are the natural offspring of moral relativism.

★★★

Those mired in the intellectual laziness that refuses to distinguish, and those dedicated to making whatever they choose as moral equivalents, too often endlessly offer peace when what is needed is war, and end up waging war on those who deserve peace. In her bending over backwards not to offend in the war on terror, Janet Napolitano, Secretary of Homeland Security, has instead warned us about and profiled (April 2009) a different group of possible terrorists: "disgruntled American servicemen coming home, and others with guns, 'right wing extremists,' and those unwilling to accept the election of a black President." Hollywood types obsessed by a superior sense of tolerance (a situation we will write about in later chapters) seem ever ready to wage a war of intolerance against those advocating a wholesome life.

Similarly, one must be guided by a common sense that distinguishes between unnecessary anger vs. righteous anger born of respect for life and justice and as a necessary emotion to defend one's life, family, and country. Love is not an absolute that is always good, nor is anger an absolute that is always bad. In normal life and circumstances, for the most part one chooses to extend love and forgo anger, especially with family and friends and those who have simply slighted us. However, in particular circumstances, anger is the emotion implanted in us by God to spur necessary action to redress a terrible wrong and make sure it does not occur again.

On cue, after each new act of terrorism, America and the West are too often preached to by political and religious leaders telling us not to feel or "give in to anger." These acts of horror are deliberately planned acts of terror aimed at killing our loved ones and executed to make us afraid and bow to terrorism. These exhortations against anger are an attempt to squelch and social-engineer our emotions so that political leaders are not put in the uncomfortable position of having to, once and for all, root out the source of terror. It is also done by some religious leaders who find it easier to talk of love than undertake the task of explaining the religious duty of self-defense and vanquishing people of evil. By so doing they are denuding the human being of his full array of God-given emotions, one of which is using anger at the right time for the right purpose. Absent the full employment of our emotions, we end up being stunted, instead of beings composed of real flesh and blood.

We are to control our anger, not renounce it completely. If there is no condition under which anger is appropriate, God would have not placed it in us. Stifling basic human emotions and forbidding our need to act upon it when necessary block inner growth and maturity. It is automaton living. Anger can be like an allergy, whose symptoms warn us of something bad for the system. Indeed, righteous anger was legitimized as an appropriate human feeling against racism. Anger is not to be characterized as always unreligious. Jeremiah, Moses, Elijah, Samuel, and Jesus all showed necessary anger at the appropriate time.

We should feel anger after jihadists enter the home of a Jewish family at the Sabbath table and gleefully murder father and mother and each of the children by cutting their throats in ritual slaughter. Anger is the appropriate reaction to a man yelling *"Allah Akbar"* at Fort Hood while mowing down dozens of innocent people. Anger is the called-for response against Mideast terrorists who bomb innocent people at a train station in Europe. Our failure to feel and express justifiable anger renders us only partially human. Suppressing legitimate anger after such incidents inures one to murder and death. Failure to feel anger is to numb us to the sanctity of life. It is that warranted anger which spurs people to rise up and say: *Enough.*

★★★

It is our moral obligation to do whatever is necessary to save ourselves and family. In my view, profiling, a routine investigative technique used by law enforcement in countless other situations, is not as grievous as allowing people to die. We must love our children more than we love political correctness and its outrageous obsession with sensitivity. Actually, profiling is the name liberals deliberately call it in order to give it a negative connotation, instead of how law enforcement for fifty years used it as part of the science of "highest probability to…"

I am reminded of the declaration of the creature known as Adam created by Dr. Frankenstein. He turns to Dr. Frankenstein and announces: "You created me, but I have become your master." Political correctness was created by liberals but now controls them. Now in the name of fairness and sensitivity, innocent Americans, even children, are often subjected to humiliating searches at airline checkpoints while people more inclined toward terrorism are not checked at the gate if they don't happen to be from whatever random, passenger slot used that day by inspectors. Though unconcerned about the humiliations of ordinary, innocent Americans, politically correct liberals denounce the use of checkpoints by Israeli border guards inspecting incoming Arabs for suicide bomb devices. Many suicide bomb packages have indeed been found at these border checkpoints. But to the politically correct, Muslim honor is more important than Jewish life.

God Himself spoke of anger—not mere disappointment or vexation, but anger—so as to let us know that anger is the legitimate response to repeated injustice and barbarism. Throughout the Bible we read: "And God's anger was kindled." "And God became angry" (Exodus 32:10). His anger is not like that of a pagan god angry over trivial and sensual issues or as a god of permanent anger, but One illustrating an appropriate time and condition for anger. There's an old Yiddish expression: "If it really hurts, you cry out in pain, anger." We aren't to live by a duality of polar opposites but by discernment from within. Like God, we can be aroused by anger, though we do not act *in* anger. Renouncing anger completely is emotional passivity and escapism, unbefitting humans who were called to act as people of destiny.

Leaders warning us not to feel anger are often those unwilling to act on behalf of a nation's legitimate anger. I view such platitudes as their talking down to us, as if citizens are children. Religious leaders who admonish us to accept and feel love and not anger are taking the easy way out both philosophically and socially. It is but sentiment.

I know the American people. Most of them will not take their anger beyond its appropriate measure. They will be impelled by it to do that which is necessary for defending hearth and home and will go no further. Perhaps those wishing to stifle our basic human emotions have little trust in fellow Americans. But Americans have shown themselves to be much more civilized than their terrorist tormentors, frenzied people relishing retribution and rejoicing in the slaughter of children. Perhaps we know how to manage anger on a national scale precisely because we were historically taught, in our Judeo-Christian ethos, when to choose anger. Social historians have written how societies renouncing anger on purely religious grounds have succumbed to uncontrollable anger when mob sentiment took over. Living by choices and demarcations facilitate mature individuals and responsible societies.

There is a moral right and obligation to get angry when anger is called for. When called for it is a *virtue*. Knowing when to be angry and when not constitutes moral clarity. No nation has been guided by moral clarity as has America. The casting aside of our Judeo-Christian heritage imperils that clarity and will usher in its harmful opposite, that which ultimately crumbles nations and brings darkness—moral relativism.

★★★ SIX ★★★

Responsibility and Reciprocity

[*Both giving and receiving are based on a moral reciprocity.*]

The whole philosophical contest between liberals and conservatives boils down to the fundamental and essential questions of: What is man, who is the individual, how do we define his responsibilities, and do we exempt certain subcultures from acting properly due to their role as players in the liberal paradigm of class warfare?

Central to the Judeo-Christian ethos and historic Americanism that grew from it are the facts that we were created as individuals, are moral agents capable of free choice, and live with personal responsibility and accountability. It is that which makes us *actively* human and created in the image of God. This paradigm is incumbent not only on he who acts and gives but also for those who receive.

No one can place himself in a receivership category that places him beyond, or exempts him from, living by a moral code requiring that he live and choose correctly. To do so would be a personal statement undermining one's own status as a moral agent and an announcement of his inability to act as an accountable being. Personal responsibility is the quintessential definition of what it means to be an *active* being. Whatever our situation, be it as giver or receiver, we are expected to do our moral part within any relationship.

Obligation to give and allowance to receive within nonbinding relationships (those beyond family and other freely chosen relationships) is based on a moral reciprocity between giver and receiver. The giver gives of his money or time and energy and the receiver reciprocates through *conduct*, moral conduct. The receiver need not pay back with money or with an energy or time equal to that offered by the giver. A relationship based on moral conduct is good and is made for the sake of society. When, however, the receiver acts in ways that are immoral, the axis between the two is broken and the relationship morally dissolved.

Furthermore, one should not expend resources for that which enables the continuation of something immoral and certainly not to that which threatens the survival of the giver. Self-defense and self-preservation are cardinal obligations, especially since God fashioned a world where much of our fate lies in our own active responsibility to protect ourselves, family, and society.

Compassion, love, tolerance, and peace are all virtues. But too often—especially in today's ethos of sentimentality, entitlement, and guilt—far too many exploit these concepts for their own benefit. Out of a sense of entitlement, many continue to demand that society underwrite their behavior even though it is destructive not only to themselves but the very society they demand support them. The ethos of *entitlement* works against the need for those who feel entitled to understand they must live by a moral code and choose correctly, especially if they wish to be recipients.

Liberalism has created this sense of entitlement and freedom from moral responsibility by claiming that society's obligation is tied not to reciprocal moral conduct but is a result of society's *guilt*. Liberals claim that society is at fault for the condition of the taker—and society must make a type of financial reparation for its guilt. Worse, in some cases, the Left says that society must also forfeit some of its freedoms as expiation. This ends up punishing the givers and frees the taker from moral responsibility and choosing correctly, and has reduced some recipients, as we have seen, to acting as if they are without conscience. A conscience can hardly be developed when a person is freed from making proper choices under a false belief that he is but a victim, a passive human being from whom we expect nothing.

But no man should be allowed to excuse himself from having to act according to the moral code implanted within our conscience by God. Each human possesses an intuitive conscience. After Cain killed his brother Abel, God confronted him over the murder and indicted him by saying: "What hast thou done?" Cain could not exonerate himself by claiming he had not learned a commandment forbidding murder. Both Cain and God knew that within man lies an intuitive understanding, a conscience, which requires moral conduct and a responsibility to choose correctly. Cain was culpable and had to change his ways.

No matter how many times it is shown that not all people in similar circumstances act brutally, or how people in similar or worse situations have risen above their circumstances, liberals always find another reason to blame society and free too many people of the need to act correctly. They continue supplying these excuses so as to give legitimacy to the entitlement state and *guiltify* taxpayers into accepting higher taxes and funding failed social programs. (Some see redistribution as a pay-for-peace extortion formula.)

Many liberals actually believe that mainstream America is oppressive and phobic (excluding them, of course). Some get an inner satisfaction seeing fellow Americans squirm in guilt.

Conservatives' expectation of proper conduct is dismissed as reflecting middle class values or the morality of *Dead White Males*. Dead White Males is the term those who wish to impugn our Constitution use to refer to our Founding Fathers. Professor Derrick Bell, a black professor at Harvard and a mentor of Barack Obama, often used this phrase in his "Critical Race Theory" that basically rejects our entire society as having been founded in racism. If, as the theory goes, the Founders are irrelevant Dead White Males, then by implication our Constitution and our entire society built upon is dead and irrelevant. I remember how a borough president in Brooklyn, New York, years ago tried to take down a centuries-old picture in Borough Hall of one of Brooklyn's founders. After all, he said, he is just a dead white male. This is blatant anti-white racism, made acceptable because it is fashionable and correct today to malign anyone who is white. Why do we accept this malicious double standard?

Ironically, the multiculturalists who preach that everybody wants the same things in life end up telling us that our endorsement of *achievement* is a middle class value we dare not foist onto others.

The liberal mantra of "it is society's fault" results in people acting without conscience and obligation—without soul. It deadens the soul. As maturity grows so does the soul, but maturity is cultivated only when we believe we must choose and live correctly through discernment. Aristotle meant this when he spoke of living the virtuous life. But we live in times of sentiment as opposed to morality, so that those who speak of morality are called mean-spirited.

★★★

Despite today's climate, a Judeo-Christian society must continue asserting that individuals act correctly. We cannot become a society that keeps enlarging the circle of people from whom we expect nothing.

Demanding nothing leads to worse than nothing. It leads to soullessness and the ugly and terrible acts that come from humans who no longer live with a conscience. Absent a sense of responsibility, a would-be conscience has nothing to feed it.

Unlike any other outlook, Genesis twice emphasizes the *majesty* of man by characterizing him as a being morally obligated to conduct himself with active responsibility. To the extent we replace our Judeo-Christian ethos with one socialist or secular, or according to the readings and values found in other ideologies called religion, we are diminishing man's majesty and reducing him.

Nations and societies can be compared to computers. What we see on the screen is a reflection of the software within the computer's monitor. If we change the software—the ideology—behind our society, so that it no longer runs by our Judeo-Christian imprint, our streets, institutions, and children will reflect that. Sadly we are already seeing the effects of a society run by liberal elites using the software program of liberalism, transnationalism, and multiculturalism. We see decay, decline, national weakness, and a society where only half of the populace pays taxes.

England may never recover from its decades of dispiriting socialism and calls for multiculturalism. It is not a laughing matter when people begin speaking of Londonistan. Multiculturalism is a harmless sounding phrase that has as its goal the brutal toppling of the Judeo-Christian culture and its offshoot, the historic American civilization.

The liberal view of the individual is dramatically different than what we in America have historically believed. Liberals differ from us profoundly in how they define the terms that animate our morality.

Leftists are guided not by the biblical vision of man as the noble and majestic agent of free will and moral responsibility, rather by the banality of man as *sameness*. Such an outlook strips man of his individual uniqueness and makes him but a member of the great masses, akin to the position animals hold within their species. Sameness equals indistinguishability. It strips man of spirit and soul.

Secularists do not bother with such trifles as soul, nor subscribe to a God creating man in His own image. Many in left-wing religious circles have replaced Scripture with Marxism and liberation theology and see man as someone who simply submits.

It is incredulous how so many look at liberalism as a panacea for man when it only reduces man. Perhaps people come to that conclusion because they think in terms of mankind instead of the individual. Liberals are so preoccupied in their mad rush to save mankind that the individual better get out of the way. Indeed, the individual is the first one run over by the liberal mob rushing to rescue mankind.

★★★

As we have seen, morality involves acts not sentiments. We must, therefore, first determine if an act or gesture is morally warranted. Acts of morality sometimes involve tough love, what our fathers did to make us responsible people who would, later in life, choose correctly, take care of ourselves, and fulfill our obligations to those relationships we would one day freely choose. Most of us now appreciate the tough love we previously disliked.

So much of morality centers on assuming personal responsibility. Let's return again to Genesis and the garden of Eden. What is the primary lesson of the story of Adam and Eve eating from the fruit of the forbidden tree? It is personal responsibility and accountability for our actions. Adam claimed he was not responsible because he listened to Eve, who comprised Adam's entire society. In other words, Adam said it was society's fault. Eve blamed the serpent. It was not her fault; she was lured. The penchant for humans to absolve themselves from accountability is more than ages old; it is primordial.

God did not exempt them from personal responsibility. He held them accountable. No, they weren't sentenced to death after all. But God, our moral Teacher, threw them out of the garden. There would be no more freebies for them. They had to make a living for themselves by the sweat of their brow. The carefree life may have undermined their understanding for living by personal responsibility. They learned the game of excuse making; now they would learn responsibility by being personally responsible for their own food and welfare. Thus human civilization began on the rock of personal responsibility. Personal responsibility is the cannon from which was shot man's moral destiny.

★★★ SEVEN ★★★

Direct to God

[*Religious and political life are direct, personal, and involve accountability.*]

The idea of personal responsibility and the need for the individual to take care of his personal obligations, so central to the historic American ethos, did not happen by accident. So much of what is part of a nation's culture is rooted in the original religious beliefs of that society. Even when, years later, a society no longer consciously does things out of a religious directive, its culture and ethos function on an autopilot that arose out of specific religious beliefs.

Our belief in direct responsibility to fend for ourselves grew out of a belief that our relationship to God is direct, that the way to God is not through clergy or institutions, but by man praying directly to Him and by man being answerable to Him and not others administering on His behalf.

The translation of Scripture into English allowed men to read for themselves what God wanted and obviated the religious man from relying on intermediates telling him what the Bible in unfamiliar Latin said. Furthermore, if men could by themselves directly read God's Word, then God Himself was directly speaking to them. If He was speaking to them directly, then He is a personal God, One that we as persons, individuals, pray to directly. "God is nigh [close]; as the Lord is nigh to whenever we call upon Him" (Deuteronomy 4:7).

With the invention of the printing press, hundreds of thousands of people previously not in direct contact with the Bible could now read it, and did so as a personal document and in personal relationship with its Author. They could discern for themselves what God had written and not live their religious life by the oral transmission from others. All this was a great liberation for the religious man; a type of theological civil right for the religious individual who was now free to worship God directly and understand His Word personally. "The law is not hidden from you, nor far away or out of your reach" (Deuteronomy 30:11).

Similarly, man was to live his political life directly, neither through the State nor answerable to it, but by electing those who would represent him. As free moral agents, men choose their form of government. A government is moral only when freely chosen. Men could no longer live in philosophic and moral comfort under a political system unless the people had direct control over their political life.

Calvin, Knox, Zwingli, and others went further. Man's direct relationship to God went beyond prayer and encompassed what he daily did. What man did on a daily basis was part of man's service to God. That service lay not necessarily in becoming clergy, but in the everyday things man did in his dealings and in providing for his own upkeep. Service to God was not limited to prayer and worship nor specific rituals and scriptural mandates, but in how man actually lived out and approached his daily routines.

More than anything else, the daily life of man is involved in work. Thus, work itself is part of the religious paradigm and a form of worship if done with honesty and diligence. As a means of taking care of personal responsibilities, work is virtuous. That an individual's work or craft is a form of service to God is possible only if one has a direct relationship with God. Work is a virtue; and its opposite, slothfulness, was considered sinful. Whatever facilitated honest work and taking care of oneself was also virtuous, such as thrift, industriousness, sacrifice, and saving. That which militated against work and a productive life was considered errant, such as, laziness, indulgence, and immediate gratification. Later, the renowned sociologist, Max Weber, would label this the Protestant Work Ethic.

Doing good deeds such as visiting the sick, giving charity, or feeding a hungry person was always considered service to God. But to turn work itself and a productive life into actual religious virtue and service is possible only when a theology of direct relationship to God is primal. Because work as a form of service and worship is done outside the confines of the church and synagogue building, and is separate from the relationship between parishioner and clergy, work is personal service.

In the Old Testament, God charges the individual with all sorts of daily responsibilities. They are not secondary among the things constituting a relationship with God. They are personal and were addressed to him in the personal "you," not the collective "you" of mankind in general. So much of the Old Testament tells *you*, the individual, to make sure that your daily dealings be done with honest weights and measures, to pay laborers on time, to allow paid fruit pickers to eat of the grapes while working, not to lend with interest, not to keep the borrower's collateral (if a needed garment) overnight, and not to muzzle the working ox. "Six days shall ye work" (Exodus 20:9). There is dignity in work, and human *dignity* is achieved through it. God is ever concerned with that which brings about human dignity. He would not have emphasized work unless it was a pathway to dignity.

Though the New Testament was open and explicit in the need for a salvation that comes singularly and only through faith and acceptance in Christ, the Pilgrims that settled America embraced the personal and direct emphasis of the religious dimension, beyond ritual and ceremony, of daily productive life. American Catholicism, in contrast to European and medieval Catholicism, eventually to a discernible degree, incorporated much of this theme. Sanctifying the routine of life is the goal of the Old Testament and is that which brings earthly redemption and heavenly reward.

This form of Judeo-Christianism sees virtue in things that we do, not simply in our holding particular theological creeds. Thus, it is *action* oriented. It is not a coincidence that it is in America, and today in Israel—societies that are action oriented—where we find more accomplishments born of human activity than is found in other societies. Both America and Israel are at the center of breakthroughs in science, technology, medicine, and other inventions.

If there is in work something divine and good, then that which comes from it must also be good, namely wealth and prosperity. This contrasts strongly with other religious outlooks that have viewed wealth and prosperity with a jaundiced eye as something impure and to be accepted as a compromise to human ambition, something beyond the spiritual. But since God loves man, wouldn't He desire for him that which brings about man's greatest chance for health, dignity, and welfare, which is prosperity? God's concern for us goes beyond the soul and includes our physical well-being as well; after all, He fashioned us as flesh and blood with specific physical requirements. God could not possibly want mankind to permanently live in poverty with all its distressing effects. That would not be a loving God.

Throughout the Old Testament, God speaks of the physical and material blessings that will come to man who lives life according to earthly actions tied to virtuous living: "Your fields and grain shall be bountiful, your sheep and cattle shall multiply, the fruits of your orchard and the grapes of your vines shall yield abundantly" (Deuteronomy 28:1-6). Such blessing requires our on-the-ground efforts: plowing, seeding, tending, and harvesting. God blesses us with the fruit of our hard work.

Indeed, it is our divine calling to cultivate the physical around us. The first announcement God makes to man is in the realm of the physical, and it requires our action. "And God said, let man have dominion over all of the earth, replenish the earth and subdue and harness it" (Genesis 1:28). This is from the first book in the Bible, and only those who see the Old Testament's vision of man as philosophically central will take this to heart. Other faiths heavily demarcate between the physical and the spiritual, the earthly and heavenly. (In a later chapter, we will explore this further.)

We are to harness nature and have dominion over it, for in nature lies all the physical elements necessary for man's physical well-being. God created nature, not only as something to be admired but as the ongoing treasure chest for human survival. If we harness and replenish it properly, then man need not worry about overpopulation, for in the same verse where God announces our need to have mastery over nature, He announces "Thou shalt be fruitful and multiply and fill up the earth" (Genesis 1:28). So long as humanity learns how to harness nature and replenish it, the filling up of earth by humans is not a threat, rather something good and the expressed intention of Creation itself. Overpopulation can pose problems, however, in societies that lack the vision found in the Judeo-Christian outlook.

★★★

In order to have dominion over nature, man needs to first understand it. If he is to harness and replenish it, the human being must first learn the rules by which nature is governed. The rules of nature were made by the Creator Himself, so that the study of the physical laws under which our universe operates is a virtuous undertaking. "How great and many are Your works O Lord, You made it all through wisdom" (Psalms 104:24). The study of God's world, known as science, is a mandate from Genesis, and unlike what the detractors of religion assert, complementary to religion and part of man's divine calling. We are students in God's classroom.

Antagonists to religion continue with the deliberately false accusation that religion is the enemy of science, that we religionists are at war with it. No doubt, the persecution of Galileo and Copernicus had a hand in shaping this belief. Certainly, our emphasis on matters beyond science, things such as faith and theology which go beyond the laboratory and test tube, make it easy for antagonists and atheists to assert their erroneous claim. By doing so, they reveal their absolute ignorance of the Judeo-Christian philosophy of man.

There were no greater scientists and men of rational thought than Isaac Newton and Albert Einstein, both of whom spoke of their work confirming the hand of God within creation and of uncovering the mysteries in the Almighty's scientific rules. Both, especially Newton, had enormous regard for the Old Testament's vision of man. George Washington expressed that same conviction: "It is impossible to reason without arriving at a Supreme Being."

Islam, in contrast, calls for human beings to be submissive absolutely to the Koran. Today's imams preach the doctrine that man cannot understand nature and that Allah's operation of the physical world does not conform to principles understandable to man, so that most of science constitutes heresy. To the imams in today's driver's seat, the rational is an affront to the Koran.

It is high time that the Judeo-Christian outlook not be tarred with the same "religion-is-against-the-scientific-and-rational" brush that is applicable to other ideologies. Religions are not the same, except to the secularist who, because he is on the outside of religion, assumes all religions spread the same message and are variations of the same theme. They are not. Judaism and Christianity are partners with Western thought. The Judeo-Christian outlook has as one of its primary goals our personal growth and understanding of the things around us, which comes about through deliberation. We believe God gave us a mind to *think*.

★★★

The secularists will not do our job for us; it is up to us to assert the singularity of the Judeo-Christian outlook. It is not politically correct among liberals to distinguish between the outlooks of people, claiming, as they do, that we are all the same and each culture is but a complementary piece in the grand jigsaw puzzle and mosaic of multiculturalism.

For an ethos to survive, subscribers to that ethos must have the confidence and courage to assert the efficacious singularity of their ethos. If not, it will wither and be smothered by those asserting contrary ideologies. This is the crucial test right now in our civilization and for our people: Do we have the guts to assert who we are, what we believe, and insist that the Judeo-Christian ethos constitutes our civilization and heritage, and we will not allow antagonists to rob us and our children of it?

The blessedness within our outlook comes not only because God shines His grace on those following His law, but also because inherent in the Judeo-Christian ethos is *success itself*, due to it being action oriented, rational, individual-centered, thereby creating independent and responsible human beings living by kindness, cooperation, and transcendent purpose.

What we have written demonstrates that in the Judeo-Christian ethos man is not merely a passive entity within the great masses, but an individual with the assignment to be action oriented. Being human is not being a mere cog within ideologies and movements, but a strong being, capable of harnessing and holding dominion over his circumstances. It is the polar opposite of those religious ideologies and social-political movements that see man as an almost pitiful subject to be taken care of by the State or relegated to submissive status in his spiritual and moral life.

Man is directly capable and responsible to take care of his position within the universe. Rousseau with his underestimation of man's innate greatness and potential, and Voltaire with his vile antagonism toward the Bible, along with the socialism, communism, and political leftism that grew out of these French philosophies, is at odds with the American Judeo-Christian attitude regarding man's unique role and his independence here on earth.

★★★

The Judeo-Christian outlook is comfortable with the notion of prosperity, and furthermore believes wealth is not something to be rejected by those seeking a religious and spiritual life. Wealth is a blessing. That being the case, it is not a coincidence that Christians and Jews came together in seventeenth century Holland and created the most effective means of generating wealth for all, namely, a market for stocks, wherein individuals could buy shares in companies that were launching new businesses. These purchases were called investments and allowed people who bought such limited ownerships a chance to prosper as the company prospered. The formation of companies and corporations and the ability for outsiders to become partial owners, shareholders, in these growing enterprises is called capitalism, where one risks his money (capital) on the reasoned speculation that his investment will grow.

Neither is it a coincidence that Jews and the Dutch made up the management of the Dutch West Indies Company that, as a business, brought people to America to settle its land and provided them with an opportunity for a fresh start in a new world. One of the first things that began unfolding in Judeo-Christian America was the gathering of men under a tree at the corner of Wall and Broad streets, where they, in what was called a stock exchange, could buy, sell, and trade shares in burgeoning companies. Ownership and wealth creation were part of Judeo-Christian America from the very beginning.

In the Judeo-Christian outlook, wealth, through capitalism and business, is spread across the widest possible range. It is not redistributed or given away for free. It does require that those desiring wealth work for it or actively contribute from earnings into those risk-taking ventures, such as stocks, that may bring future returns. There is wealth in the Muslim world, but it remains in the hands of a select ruling few—the sheiks and clerics. Such is the case in communist countries where wealth is limited to those in the apparatchik party leadership. As with Islam, communism and the welfare state distribute the income of others, but that does not make prosperous individuals nor independent ones, but an indistinguishable mass dependent on the top religious or political bureaucracy. It works against the whole notion of equality of opportunity, individuality, and upward mobility. Equality does not mean being inferior as everyone else, but being what *you* can be.

Our Founding Fathers were religious men dedicated to the Judeo-Christian outlook on life, be it regarding direct political choice or in economics. The work ethic was part of their religious upbringing and civic outlook. Benjamin Franklin wrote of it in his pithy sayings in *Poor Richard's Almanac*. He spoke of thrift, industriousness, prudence, and discernment. "Early to bed, early to rise, makes men healthy, wealthy and wise" was his formula for a life revolving around work, study, and general separateness from constant leisure and entertainment. Success does not come to those who are lazy and preoccupied with fun.

During the last fifty years, with the ascendancy of liberalism, scoffers have repeatedly made the claim that our Founding Fathers were not religious men. The ACLU and other left-wing groups make this false assertion when trying to stifle religious expression and public references to those things biblical, including the placement even of the Ten Commandments on the frescoes of public buildings, despite the fact that such carvings were commissioned by our very early statesmen.

Any objective perusal of the statements of our Founding Fathers demonstrates clearly that they were not only advocates of the Judeo-Christian ethos and culture but proponents of the religion itself. We will cite a few examples. But before doing so, it is important that we differentiate between religious vs. religiosity. Many people are religious, though not engaged in religiosity, certainly not to the extent to how religiosity is today displayed.

What is it that renders one religious and not secular? It is a belief in God the Almighty; God the Creator; God who has an ongoing hand in human history, i.e., Providence; the sublime efficacy of Scripture; recognition of a biblical outline for living; prayer; and an identification with a religious institution such as a church or synagogue, where formal communal worship takes place. Communal worship raises individual belief into public expression and association. Each one of these seven beliefs and characteristics was unequivocally found in each of our Founding Fathers. Perhaps not even one of these is found in the secular person.

Benjamin Franklin was the least outwardly religious of the Founders, yet the church he attended remains in lower Philadelphia, two hundred feet from the Delaware River. George Washington worshiped at St. Paul's Chapel in lower Manhattan on Church Street, where atop the altar sits the name of God, Yahweh, shining forth in golden Hebrew lettering. In his first inaugural address, Washington spoke of "the Almighty Being who rules over the universe; who presides in the councils of the nations; and whose Providential aid…"

Later Washington said: "Do not let anyone claim to be a true American if they ever attempt to remove religion from politics." In his first Thanksgiving proclamation he said: "It is the duty of all nations to acknowledge the providence of Almighty God, to obey His Will…and humbly to implore His protection and favor." He likewise said: "It is impossible to account for the Creation of the universe without the agency of a Supreme Being."

John Adams said: "The general principles on which the Fathers achieved Independence were…the general principles of Christianity." Throughout this book, I have made the point that it is not the details of

Judeo-Christianism that guide us as a nation, but, like Adams said, *the general principles*. When speaking of Christianity, Adams included both Testaments, Christian in the sense that it relies on a Christian understanding of both Testaments. (Adams was known to be the most religious among the Founders.)

Thomas Jefferson declared: "The God who gave us life gave us liberty." He continued, "The Christian Religion...is a religion friendly to liberty, science and freest expansion of the human mind." And to future would-be members of the ACLU, Jefferson responded: "My views are very different from the anti-Christian system imputed to me by those who know nothing of my opinions."

In the foundational year of 1782, a congressional resolution was passed: "The Congress of the United States recommends and approves the Holy Bible for use in all schools." James Madison said: "Religion is the basis and foundation of government." He, of course, meant the Bible, not the Koran. Benjamin Franklin announced: "I believe in one God, the creator of the universe. That he governs it by his providence." Later in a letter to the President, Franklin said: "I therefore beg leave to move that henceforth prayers imploring the assistance of heaven..."

Only a deliberately blind person would not acknowledge the absolute tie and identification these men had to biblical religion. What else could they be called if not religious? All this talk of them not being religious is wrong, except to the extent that they may not have been involved in daily religiosities and rituals. I dare say, if any candidate running today for President expressed his or her loyalty and pride in religion as did the Founding Fathers, the media and liberals would disqualify them as candidates. "They are too religious and unfit," the media would blast. The only candidate who could be as avowedly religious and get away with it would be someone espousing a non-Christian religion, a religion approved by the multiculturalists, a religion that would be an in-your-face challenge to the over two hundred million serious Christians the media despise.

No, our Founders were not involved with religiosities, nor did they wear their religion on their sleeves. Would liberals, who question whether our Founders were religious, be more convinced if Washington had, at every decision-making moment, brought his staff around in a circle, holding hands to pray for guidance? Do liberals expect, so as to verify their religious bona fides, these men should have been writing religious books?

Were they supposed to drop everything and go to church every week to prove they were religious? They read the Bible every week, and more—that says a lot.

Those who call the Founders non-religious are measuring them against a type of religiosity found today, a religiosity not essential to people who are religious. Both my grandfathers and father were religious men, as were my grandmothers religious women. They lived by the seven religious principles mentioned above, except they went to synagogue, not church. But I never saw in them outward, overt religiosity. They were deeply religious, but no one on the street would have known; except, of course, by the morality by which they lived and the carriage and bearing that often distinguishes the religious person from those secular.

Yes, George Washington liked to dance. Why not, he was a Christian, not a Puritan. Jefferson loved fine things and delved into science. But science, as mentioned, is keenly compatible with biblical religion; nor do we take vows of poverty and minimalism. They were not clergy, but philosopher statesmen grounded in action, courage, determination, and reason. But what they represented was Christianity and the Judeo-Christian moral outlook.

★★★

Throughout American history, when leaders and citizens have called this a Christian country it is to this moral and values-laden outlook they refer. No one has ever evoked the phrase so as to erect a theocracy or require the country be run according to the details or rituals of Christianity. Most reasonable people understand what is meant in America when the colloquial term "Christian country" is employed. Liberal Jews, for example, need not fear a theocracy is in the offing when all that is meant are the morals, values, and respect for the individual and free markets characteristic of Judeo-Christian Americanism.

My fellow Jews should accept this, especially since they employ the very term "Jewish values" to mean not theocracy but a set of social values. Even Franklin Delano Roosevelt used the term "Christian nation," as did the Supreme Court in 1844. Proof that such terminology is not some disguised agenda to enact a Christian theocracy or exclude Jews is nowhere better evidenced than how its pronouncement has never resulted in a theocracy and that Jews have flourished freely in America as never before.

While hosting radio shows in New York and New Jersey, I had the opportunity to interview Reverend Pat Robertson and the late Reverend Jerry Falwell. Each interview was thirty-five minutes long. In the world of radio, that is mammoth air time. Never once during the interviews did either man make any attempt at proselytization, fixed only on the special moral tenets involved in the Judeo-Christian ethos and how important it was for my listeners to continue strong support for Israel.

Being that calling us a Christian nation or a Judeo-Christian society has nothing to do with religious practice but social values, those who deliberately wish to change our identification are doing so precisely because they disagree with those historic American values. They wish to upend these values and seek, therefore, to replace the phrase Judeo-Christian. They wish to change our identity. There can be no question that when President Obama declared, "We are no longer a Christian nation...We are one of Muslims, Christians, Hindus...," he had this as his intention and goal.

The fact that even the liberal New Deal President, Franklin D. Roosevelt, referred to us as a "Christian nation," and Obama wants to change that, demonstrates that Obama does so not out of liberalism but, it seems, a dangerous and radical multiculturalism, secularism, and affinity for Islam. It goes beyond liberalism to an assault on the historic values and morals that have guided us and capitalism itself. Does he wish to change our identity? He has no right to do so. He was elected to be a caretaker, not an outside revolutionary conquering us from within. Humbleness and gratitude toward the American people who elected him should result in upholding what *we* hold dear. Instead, he has used his office to rob us of what we have been as a nation hundreds of years before he was born and overturn the system we had before he came here from Indonesia.

Others arrayed against our Judeo-Christian heritage and values are those who call themselves "progressives," a nice sounding euphemism for socialists, hedonists, rich communists, and revolutionaries. But such progressivism is actually regressive for most of us who will not be a member of the ruling apparatchiks and who want a wholesome American life. We will be the first to lose our freedom of speech and assembly, our right to any form of self-defense, and will slide from comfortable middle class status to dependency or a much lower standard of living and diminished opportunity, once the effects of socialistic "progressivism" take hold, as is already the case in England, Portugal, Greece, and communist countries.

Mr. Obama and other progressives seem to like and have endorsed the

Muslim Brotherhood and curry favor with Hugo Chavez. Progressivism is for those who seem to see progress in everything un-American; and who find everything outside our culture interesting and illuminating, while what is American is, for them, boring and rooted in racism. Justice Ruth Bader Ginsburg tells us our Constitution is outdated and not appropriate for 2012 (yet, ironically, she decides our constitutional law). President Obama prefers U.N. laws to ours, and Harold Koh, Obama and Clinton's legal advisor at the State Department, wants us to live according to progressive international law, forfeiting our own sovereignty. *Progressive* is the enemy of the Judeo-Christian ethos. It is at war with historic America and our identity.

EIGHT

Compassion

[Compassion is given to those with unusually distressing circumstances.]

Before we begin clarifying some of the basic moral terms and values that define our lives and have significant influence on our politics and policies, let me state that the forthcoming clarifications are based within the philosophical moral context of the Judeo-Christian outlook, not on any particular religious creed or theology born out of it. People of differing religious views and subsequent ecclesiastical interpretations of Scripture arrive at different religious conclusions. Throughout the book, I will stress that it is not the particulars of religion or the man-made conclusions of a brand of religion that are essential to our nation living by the Judeo-Christian outlook. We are not a theocracy, rather a nation that has been informed by the broad moral principles of the Judeo-Christian ethic, as opposed to secularism, socialism, collectivism, or particular religious brands.

Our civic attachment to the Judeo-Christian ethos lies strictly in its broad biblical moral principles; otherwise it begins moving beyond the realm of the civic. Once it moves beyond that broad understanding into post-biblical emanations of councils and synods, we have gone beyond the civic mandate of biblical Judeo-Christian principles.

There are four hundred different Protestant sects, many orders within Catholicism, and different groups among Orthodox Jews who have their own particular evolved religious formulas. We are not always united by these nor do they constitute our common culture. We are united by basic Scripture, the Word of God.

The broad moral principles of the Judeo-Christian ethos come out of a combination of the Old and New Testaments, rooted in a uniquely American respect for the Old Testament. This bears repeating. As proud as I am about my forefather Abraham, it is not the Abrahamic Code we follow in America, but the Judeo-Christian one, for Abraham lived before either Testament was written. The Bible called Abraham "the father of nations," and he was the first one to formally concretize and promulgate the idea of one God, but he left no specific writings as did the Bible. Many imams now arriving in America are pushing to replace our national Judeo-Christian ethos with one that will include the Islamic vision of life and government, doing so under what they wish to call the Abrahamic Code. At the White House on November 5, 2011, President Obama referred to our shared Abrahamic faith at an Islamic *Eid* celebration he hosted. In June 2007 and in March 2008, Mr. Obama used this phrase, instead of what has always been referred to by us as our Judeo-Christian heritage. On these occasions he also said, "America is no longer a Christian nation, and the 'religious right' is trying to hijack our nation by declaring so." None of this is accidental but part of the Left's age-old, bit-by-bit push toward our society's reeducation. (One need also note the difference between a *lineage* to Abraham through Ishmael vs. the *faith* of Abraham carried forth through the seed of Isaac and Jacob.)

In a French television interview on June 1, 2009, Mr. Obama said that "population-wise America is one of the most Muslim countries in the world." This is a fabrication of the first order given the much larger numbers of Muslims in thirty other countries and that America's Muslim population is only one percent. This was probably intended to weaken the French into accepting the inevitability of Muslim influence in its country and conditioning Americans to believe we in America have no choice but to accommodate a large American Muslim population.

The Koran is quite different than the Old and New Testaments in its value system and in its application of who is entitled to equality. It claims ownership of Abraham, Moses, and Jesus as Islamic forerunners and figures so as to advance Islam. But it does not defer to them so as to give equality to Judaism and Christianity, or Christians and Jews. The Koran referenced the Torah and Gospels but often changed biblical stories when it did not suit the specific Islamic agenda, something Christianity and the New Testament never did regarding the Old. The New may differ theologically and attitudinally from segments found in the Old, but it never rewrote it.

The early settlers who came to these shores had great regard and fidelity to the Old Testament's actual words. The reader had a direct relationship to Scripture and God Himself.

Furthermore, I emphasize moral terms and values, as opposed to religious, because we in America understand that while we differ religiously, we should be able to agree morally. Therefore welfare state liberals routinely advance their agenda under the moral phrase "social justice," though we know it is really a heart tugging plug for socialism and doesn't have anything to do with morality. To them social justice means socialism. Though one may feel a particular sentiment, and admirably so, from that does not derive a moral responsibility to act accordingly.

★★★

Now let's examine compassion, our topic for this chapter. Though we may feel compassion for someone, from that sentiment does not necessarily derive a moral obligation to perform an act of compassion. The subject of our compassion should fall into the category of those deserving compassion: the truly needy, as in the economically bereft widow and orphan so often mentioned in the Bible, the sick, the elderly, or those who have been dealt a terrible blow of unfortunate circumstance. There are others. Webster says, compassion is "granted because of *unusual* distressing circumstances affecting the *individual*" (emphasis added). One does not automatically become an object for compassion simply because society or groups have willy nilly made them objects of compassion. We may certainly sympathize with those in conditions we would not wish on ourselves, but our moral obligation for direct acts of compassion depend on certain conditions. As with everything else moral, we extend compassion when it *ought* be extended.

For example, has a person brought his circumstances upon himself? Has he tried those things that inevitably lift people out of these circumstances, as is the case with others who have done so? Is the person fashioning himself into an object of compassion so as to take from others? Is the person taking advantage of our good will?

Does the person refuse to live by the moral conduct that is the axis upon which acts of compassion are reciprocated? Is the person shirking his own human need for personal responsibility? Does the person feel a sense of entitlement that precludes him from assuming his obligations toward himself? Is ingratitude his response to our acts of compassion?

Are we simply enabling bad behavior by our continued acts of compassion? Are these people, of themselves, deserving of compassion or simply straw men used by those who have an agenda to take our earnings and redistribute them to potential voters? Are our acts of compassion temporary or will we be forced to continue them indefinitely to those refusing to change course and make necessary changes? Is our compassion to be given to individuals or groups (and thereby political)? And, finally, do our acts of compassion make it harder for us to fulfill our obligations to those in relationships we have freely chosen, which, after all, are where our primary obligations lie and where we must first direct our acts of compassion?

No category, not even that which is demanded in the name of compassion, is so absolute as to be beyond assessment. Every act in life must be weighed and pass the test of whether it is a moral obligation or not. Feelings of sympathy are good, though they do not necessarily require acts of compassion. In some cases, as we will discuss, even sympathy is uncalled for and misdirected—even dangerous—when extended to those who wish to destroy us, our family life, and even our society. Often, for the sake of society's survival, it is crucial not to be snookered by appeals to compassion.

After Adam and Eve's failure to act with personal responsibility and their indifference to accountability, God chose tough love and stopped their cycle of dependency. He is a God of Love, but He taught us that compassion, when uncalled for, prevents His children from living by the operational law upon which the foundations of His earth were laid—personal responsibility.

When Abraham beseeched God to spare the city of Sodom from total destruction, his appeal was not that the evil, out of compassion, be spared punishment. No, he knew that the repeat offenders in Sodom did not deserve compassion. Rather, he asked that the innocent not die because of the deeds of the evil few. It was a reasonable request. We all grapple with the ongoing condition of the innocent sharing the same fate as the evil: "Far be it for you to slay the innocent with the wicked, so that the innocent should be as the wicked" (Genesis 18:25). Request was denied because, as God answered, there were no innocent ones in Sodom; it was a place of principled and recidivist evil. Never once did Abraham ask that, out of compassion, Sodom and its ways be allowed to continue.

★★★

Naturally, we wish to extend compassion to those suffering and hurting. And this country does—just look at its response during Hurricane Katrina. Americans poured in by the thousands, donated millions, as they do during other catastrophes around the world, and took in the Katrina homeless by the tens of thousands. But not everyone making a claim to our acts of compassion are worthy candidates for it. Even with our own children and friends, we know to withhold when we are simply enabling dreadful conduct, be it drunkenness, laziness, or the addiction to other people sending you checks and taking care of your needs. If such is the understanding when it comes to our own family, then certainly it should apply on a national scale. Most people know that our social entitlement programs are breeding millions of dependency junkies, but they fear being called uncompassionate or bigoted.

Some people can never say yes. But equally worrisome are those who can never say no. It is hard to say no to those making demands of you in the name of compassion. But when one knows in his heart that he would say no to his own children if they were not living up to their responsibilities, he should be equally able to say no to others acting with gross misconduct. Yes, it is hard to say no to those accusing you, but being able to assert a set of values brings strength and maturity.

It is not easy to overcome the butterflies in one's stomach when standing against that which is not politically correct. But unless the American middle class is willing to begin acting with some moxie and courage—confident in its across-the-board set of standards—they will slowly be written off the page of the American scene by those who demand and demand and see the weakness and fear in our eyes. More than anything else, middle class America must begin believing in itself, stand tall, and push back.

★★★

No one should go hungry. No one should go without basic clothes. Everyone should have some type of roof over their head, heat in the cold months, and some access to basic health care. These duties come from being a member of a community. They are not bankrupting us. What is bankrupting us is the overly generous, unnecessary quantities, and way-beyond-subsistence provisions that we give people on welfare who end up living far better than they would from the pay of an average job. Such a system is rooted in political calculation and not morality. There is nothing moral about a system that declares there is no personal responsibility, no accountability, no need to choose correctly, no need to be independent, no need to work, no need to take care of yourself and your obligations—all the qualities that constitute being a free moral agent. Everyone must live with some range of obligations. Without it, we compromise our humanness.

Citing the specific ways our government should react to real poverty and need vs. professed poverty and need is not the purpose of this book, but the morality of conservatism seems beyond question. We conservatives would love people to have jobs and fend for themselves. Jobs provide dignity, inculcate good habits and values, and all the other emotional dispositions that help shape a moral being. Who would mind if the once previously poor or unemployed man used his wits and strength to become wealthier than most? On the contrary, that affirms the greatness of America. But jobs come from free enterprise, and liberal policies are punishing free enterprise and small business, jeopardizing the millions of jobs associated with it. Many on the Left prefer such a scenario and work against private job creation so that more will become dependent on government—all in the name of compassion!

The American people have been a compassionate people for three hundred years and need not prove their bona fides by succumbing to those on the Left preaching and gaining from the politics of compassion. We should ignore those who tell us it is we "who must do some soul searching." On the contrary, perhaps Mr. Obama needs to search his own soul as to why he continually casts Americans in such a negative light, especially after being elected President by them.

There are far too many who think our moral obligation to those in need is to make them economically equal to the middle class footing the bill: "to each according to his needs from each according to his ability." But this scenario results in taxing earners heavily and asking them to do without so that non-earners can equalize their living standard with those who earn. We pay for other's amenities such as the internet, telephone, cell phones, and air conditioning. The compassion that liberals feel for those receiving never seems to extend to those actually doing the work, making the sacrifices, deferring gratification, saving, and who continually give to others. Selective compassion for receivers but never for the providers is a sign of politics, not compassion. It is not a reaction to need and poverty but the use and facilitation of it in order to create the welfare state.

Isn't it about time we heard some compassion for the hard working, no-nonsense individual—the fellow who can't sleep in because, unlike the receiver, he has to be at work every morning? Why is compassion never evoked for the millions who do the right thing, demand nothing, and pose no harm to anyone: the forgotten man, the purposely forgotten man?

★★★

Let me provide an example of why it is unwise to guide our civic laws and ethos by that which is strictly religious. A friend of mine mentioned how one ancient rabbi opined that the demands of charity go so far as to require society to restore a man fallen down on his luck to the status he was before. If he was a baron or wealthy man, he opined, we must restore him to that previous wealth. Evidently, his opinion did not take into account how burdensome that would be on others and their families, and how society would go bankrupt if such was duplicated thousands of times. That was simply his religious belief, and it made him appear and feel generous. It is far more reasonable not to decide these issues according to religious peculiarities or social-workism, but on rudimentary Judeo-Christian philosophy and morality. It is the most practical, non pie-in-the-sky morality the world has ever known. The crucial part religion does play in all this is in its unwavering support for our Judeo-Christian biblical values and moral outlook.

Nor should we be guided by the *laissez faire* purists who disapprove of any financial arrangement between the government and the citizen. They are, for example, against Social Security and Medicare. But these are not outgrowths of an entitlement state. We receive Social Security not because of entitlement but because we earned it and payed for it. The same is true with Medicare—we paid for it along the way, as we did for unemployment (though unemployment weeks should not be extended so far that people do not seek work or see it as vacation time). Veteran's benefits were earned. All of these represent moral, reciprocal arrangements different than the entitlement welfare state.

Obamacare, on the other hand, is completely different. Unlike Social Security that does not reduce one's choices in life or standard of living, Obamacare will diminish our standard of medicine and deny us medical choices. Social Security and Medicare are not anti-liberty. The people wanted them, unlike Obamacare where between two-thirds to three-quarters of Americans do not want it. Social Security met its goal as a stipend for the elderly, whereas our health care needs will not be met by Obama Health Control. Health care needs could have been met without taking over our lives. No one's life has been taken over by Social Security, but all our lives will be taken over through the institution of Obamacare.

And herein lies the crucial difference. Obama's healthcare was specifically designed to transform America so that government and those who run it will have direct control over us. Though not wanted by the people, liberal politicians, in the name of compassion, ignored and overruled the people. For—and this is important—more than wishing to meet the desires of the people, there are those who wish to *control* the people. There are people like that even here in America. We now see that America is not immune from the ills of human nature. The immorality of the welfare state bred another, more colossal, immorality—Obamacare.

The word *compassion* has always been a part of our lexicon of virtues, our sacred literature, and our philosophic and moral history. It is shameful how liberals have hijacked it as a political tool for a political purpose. Like so much else in liberalism, they have corrupted it and robbed it of its sacredness.

It is up to us to retake our language and refill our moral vocabulary with the accurate and uplifting content that characterized it for centuries, from the time of biblical antiquity. Let us no longer allow liberals to politicize a language that belongs to the respectful and predates the communist definitions found in Saul Alinsky's *Rules for Radicals*. What a noble undertaking that would be and what a wonderful gift to our children, and all future Americans—the gift of language!

NINE

Love

[*Whom we love reflects our values and who we are.*]

Love is the most precious of all human emotions, the greatest gift we can give. It should not be taken for granted nor seen as another entitlement. What import and quality does "I love you" from a mother to son or husband to wife have if we love everybody in the world equally, even those we do not even know? Just as there are gradations to love, there are instances where love cannot be extended at all.

The one we love, according to Webster, is the object of our attachment, devotion, or admiration. Sometimes we can hardly help loving another, as in a romance or with our children. Other loves reflect what and whom we admire, and to what and to whom we feel attached or devoted. Our loves, our attachments, and our devotion tell us a lot about ourselves: our values and priorities, and what speaks to our soul.

Loving everyone equally is but an abstraction; it is not real love. Such across-the-board love diminishes the proprietary specialness that should be directed toward those who deserve our attachment, devotion, and admiration. If indiscriminately scattered, love is cheapened and commodified. Extending love to all of humanity no matter their conduct depreciates the love for those whose conduct and morals make them worthy of love. Extending love, therefore, requires discernment and forces us to choose. We should love those we morally *ought* to love.

Christians tell us that God so loved mankind that He gave to them His only begotten Son. I have spent fifty years thinking about what my Christian friends mean by this and have heard opinions, over my lifetime, from not less than a thousand people. The only conclusion I can reach is that such love is exclusive to God, and that no man can love all of humanity in a fashion similar to God. It is not duplicable among us mortals, nor even desirable given that we must make moral judgments. We all possess values that directly determine what we admire and who, therefore, should be receiving our devotion and attachment. Love for mankind is best defined as seeing the humanity in individuals.

Those who claim they harbor no gradations in their love and do not take into account the actions of men live in a different mental world than I—far too theoretical for this man occupied by what is needed to preserve this world. Loving all men equally, no matter what, because of their possibility of being *saved* is similarly found among the Jewish mystics (they simply differ as to what brings salvation). However, that speaks to a unique spiritual and religious realm, quite separate from the plain, moral categories I have been emphasizing. The moral and the spiritual are not always synonymous. Religion includes morality but goes on to include more. But *that* more which it includes is not always appropriate for statecraft or in behalf of what is necessary for preserving society. The two realms may, at times, collide.

I have a particular religious view where the two can operate in tandem; others do not and, on behalf of statecraft, need to draw a line between the mystical and the operational. In a later chapter we will review the famous verse, "Loving thy neighbor as thyself." At this point it is best to characterize that love, not as equal to what one has for one's spouse and children, but in apprehending the humanity and dignity of one's neighbor.

★★★

Love is a gift and not an entitlement. Hence, love—to those outside our family and friends—is not a moral absolute. At first, we greet all in the spirit of love and hope to continue giving love to all people. But the use of the word *love* is exaggerated and out of proportion if we feel compelled to give strangers the same degree of love we offer our family and those who we already know deserve our love. Regarding mankind in general, instead of love, I would use the word *embrace*: at first we embrace all people. But even embrace is not absolute and requires discernment and ongoing assessment. We embrace all we first meet because we see the humanity in them.

A man recently came by to do some work in our house. He told us of how his elder son and wife had adopted seven children who had no family. He was a believing Christian who saw the humanity in people and felt impelled to embrace them and bring them into his home and take care of them. I remember, as a boy back in Cleveland, knowing such a man. He was our gardener and over decades had brought dozens into his home. He believed strongly in the Bible. Some remained with him and his wife, others left. Over the years, that which started out as embrace became actual love for those specific children who remained and became his own children.

What are we to do when the person we first wish to embrace turns out to be someone acting in an evil manner and repeatedly so? What are we to do when the repeated evil begins harming us and those around us, including those to whom we are responsible? What is our moral obligation? Do we allow abstract and lofty religious ideals to stand in our way of doing what is in the best interests of society and our families, which is our primary moral obligation? When does the ersatz give way to the real and crucial? Are we to continue to embrace him who represents that which is not admirable or live with continued attachment and devotion to such a person or association of persons?

What does it say about us that despite the repeated and ideological evil in front of our eyes, we continue extending love—which here we mean to be attachment, devotion, and admiration—to him and that which should repel us? Are we not, then, loving the wrong person and accepting his ways? Is such love or a perversion of it?

I am positing all this not because of some academic or intellectual joy in extrapolating on moral and philosophic theory. No, I do so because I firmly believe our survival as a free society, including our freedom of religion, depends on religious and moral people freeing themselves from purist notions that stand in the way of us defending ourselves from a leftist and Islamic crusade out to harmfully change our lives. Seeing people as human beings does not mean we must always love and embrace them. At times, we must separate the two.

All of this came to the forefront recently. A statesman in Austria, a loyal Christian man, expressed concern in an article published in *The Wall Street Journal* that theological purists are at a distinct disadvantage today in Europe when living by a code of always loving one's enemies. What the statesman was warning about was the inertia and passivity, the unwillingness to stand at the plate and fight those who have declared their intention to subdue us, our children, and the entire civilization. "How," he asks, "can Christian Europe withstand and survive if it lives by an ethos of always loving your enemy while your enemy lives by a creed of destroying you, the infidel"?

This very question led a famous seventeenth century Italian philosopher to the conclusion that what may be valuable in the realm of pure religious theory can be harmful in the area of statecraft and national survival, and for general moral well-being. For morality is centered on doing what we ought for men as mortal beings, not necessarily for that involving his immortal soul. (Personally, I see the immortal soul expanded by courageous acts directed on behalf of man's mortal status. I do not see a dichotomy between the godly and the temporal. To use a colloquialism, I do not set up a wall between church and state.)

This "loving all" theory is fine when "enemy" refers simply to your hostile next-door neighbor or a time when Europe was not beset by an outside religion setting its sights on overpowering and destroying Europe of its innate Christianity. But today there exists a real enemy who has made his intentions known. This enemy is no longer far away and theoretical but lives within our borders.

As an Austrian, this statesman who wrote the article is living among fellow Christians challenged by a European outlook that sequesters virtues into absolutist categories. He knows the difficulty posed by an absolutist-type of love that never demarcates. (In a later chapter we will address this whole Platonic notion that sees the world in a duality, that is to say, absolutist categories where distinctions are not possible. Plato's belief in *dualism*, categorical opposites, had deep and lasting effect on early Church teaching.)

America's Founding Fathers were not dualists and knew when to embrace and when to reject. Nor were they bogged down by Emanuel Kant's *categorical imperative* that saw no way out from the iron confines of something being either always good or always bad.

I personally go beyond *division* and maintain that certain traits normally considered bad are acceptable not simply for practical reasons but are, at certain times, as Ecclesiastes implies, the *right* thing when done at the right time. In other words, when appropriate, they become actual moral *virtues*. As virtues acted upon, they develop strength, maturity, and nobility—the keys necessary for choosing morality and living by it.

One has to be careful, though, about not going over the line into what is called situational ethics, where people begin to choose values or divide moral categories according to how it suits their emotional desires in a given situation. It was out of that fear, perhaps, that many theologians retained indivisible, absolutist categories as opposed to allowing for the demarcations often necessary in life. They felt better safe than sorry. However, there is a bona fide litmus test for all this—Is the application based on true wisdom, or is it based on desire, convenience, or appeasement? Wisdom is rooted in the fear of God: "The beginning of wisdom is fear of God" (Psalms 111:10; Proverbs 9:10). First a person must be honest and probe his intentions: Are they motivated by lust, convenience, human frailty, or appeasement? When (1) satisfied his intentions are pure, and (2) after concurrence from other good men and women, he then should (3) look to the Bible where wisdom based on fear of God is found.

The Bible is not a thirty page document of do this and don't do that. It is voluminous in offering accounts, stories, and history of virtually every possible situation where man will have to make choices and use biblical *precedent* and wisdom in deciding when a characteristic remains bad, when it is practical and OK, or when it becomes even virtuous. The life of King David, among others, is a learning model, illustrating wrongly chosen love and war versus rightly chosen love and war. We need to proceed carefully, but the clarifications can be exhilarating.

In fact, assessing and deciphering God's will is part of the *struggle* inherent in a religious life. Religion is, in my view, not simply about panacea and inner peace but includes ongoing philosophic and religious struggles. Certain foundational principles remain fixed and to which we aspire and yield. But we are not indistinguishable, passive objects driven to crystal-clear ends. Part of the *personal* aspect of religion is struggling to ascertain those ends, and with that struggle comes personal growth.

Extending love and understanding to those engaged in barbarism and cruelty not only diminishes the glory of love but cheapens it as well, inasmuch as we extend to them that which they hold in disdain. This whole notion of loving the murderer or terrorist is, to me, not an exhibition of love but an indifference to their victims. It is callous to those relatives who have been eternally wounded. It reflects a "love of love" more than a "love of life."

I often wonder about survivors who continue to love those who have murdered their loved ones and family members. Are they victims of a type of Stockholm Syndrome, or are they dealing with grief through a type of escapism, or are they providing sacrificial purpose to the death of their loved one through the rescue of the soul of the very one who killed him—he died so that others may be reborn?

We need not hate but we can continue to value them as human beings created by a loving God. However, we *ought not* extend love—meaning our earlier definition of attachment, devotion, and admiration—by embracing such individuals or people. Continuing to love under such circumstances is asking that we dampen that part of us which is flesh and blood. But flesh and blood emotions should not be squelched. The soul is to live in this world, side by side with flesh and blood, not replace it. As noted in a previous chapter, I consider the inability or refusal to make demarcations an outlook philosophically lazy and morally hazy. It is an abandonment of moral clarity. Absent moral clarity, no society can survive, nor is a theology being honest.

★★★

"Loving the sinner but not the sin" is acceptable in normal everyday circumstances. However, when the sin is done as matter of *ideological principle* and indeed *harms* others, the sin and the sinner become one. The sinner cannot be separated from the sin. He becomes united with sin. When repeated, we must *remove the sinner himself* so as to protect the innocent from the harm that will continue from his plans and hands, since he does so ideologically and with intent to continue harming. Although we are called to forgive seventy times seven, we are also not commanded to embrace and admire the one who harms us and those we love.

Yes, we can open ourselves to forgive recidivists who may one day repent, but meanwhile we cannot continue to live with them, even out of a hope of repentance down-the-line. To do so would be rejecting our responsibility to protect the innocent and our obligation to those in relationships we freely chose. To allow his continued living among us is to care more for a possible, renewed soul than the actual life and body of our loved ones and society. Once again, this points to our need to decide based on Judeo-Christian moral principles and not mystical religious yearnings. "Before worrying about a man's soul, first worry over another's physical survival."

That we must remove and excise from our midst those engaged in repeated brutality, based on their ideology or a sense of their entitlement, is a biblical motif. As mentioned before and as will be mentioned throughout this book, eradicating the evil around us and in our midst is the single greatest moral obligation the Old Testament assigns us. There is much that God can and will do for us. But He leaves to us the task of removing evil. That is our Job One. He affirms this mandate to us six times in Leviticus alone and again in Deuteronomy. By insisting we personally eradicate evil, God is telling us that we must first learn to discern evil and call it what it is and by its name. But will one really stomp out those who, despite their horrid evil, remain objects of your love for whom you make excuses?

God tells us in Deuteronomy 22:4: "Do not hide." Removing evil is a duty from which we are not allowed to hide. He warns us in Deuteronomy 29:18 not to think that by ignoring and wishing away evil it will just disappear. No, I leave it to you, God says, to do away with the evil in your midst. That constitutes our moral obligation and makes us a defender of the Lord, a man of spirit. One of these instances is the *Meisit U'meidi'ach*, the one who wishes repeatedly to harm society as a service to a terrible ideology. The war on terror is our moment in history in the never-ending moral undertaking of excising evil.

The enemy the Bible speaks of as the one we are to forgive is not someone who has set his life goal on killing you and your children and forcing you to live life his way and under his control. The Bible is speaking of a wholly different person who is our neighbor. In Leviticus, when it speaks of not hating your neighbor in your heart, it refers to someone with whom you've had altercations of the civil type, not one who is out to destroy you and your family.

We know we need not love those intent on killing us, for the Bible in Exodus 22:1 and other places (Deuteronomy 22:26, for example) tells us that we may kill in self-defense. It did not say: "But first try to understand your killer. Tell him how much you love him. Speak to him of your tolerance." No. Love and defend your children, wife, household, friends, community, and country. That is your obligation of obligations. Failure to do so is not an indication of your love of another's soul but a shortfall in loving your own family.

Pacifism in the face of an evil out to destroy your family indicates a lack of regard for family and the society around you. I do not see it as a strength or virtue but as moral weakness. If our souls were to be untouched by the grime of life, God would have kept them up in heaven and not have placed them in real bodies in this earthly world of action. The soul is elevated when it fulfills its earthly obligations of fighting evil and defending family. It misses the opportunity for elevation when it stands aside from the duties of life. Our souls would certainly have remained pure if they had remained in ethereal heaven. But they were brought down to this earth of action to attain what they could not have if remaining above—the nobility in acting on behalf of family and societal obligations.

No greater human love is there than to defend your own. No greater embrace is there than to embrace your country over its enemies. No greater morality is there than that of moral clarity. No greater human sacrifice is there than sacrificing on behalf of your family and those who truly deserve love.

Frankly, instead of hearing how much we are to love malcontents, criminals, jihadists, and angry rabble rousers wanting to bring us down, I'd like to hear people begin talking about loving the conservative Christian, loving the upright, middle-class guy, the caring family man and loving wife and mother, and the patriot—all our unspoken heroes. I would love to hear of loving those who deserve love not simply because they were born, but because of the good they actually do.

I am one of those from the school of King David, the inspired author of Psalms. He spoke of loving the righteous, loving the man of clean hands and upright heart. Perhaps it is easier to love the scoundrel than the straight-laced. No one gets brownie points for loving those who deserve love. Special credit is given in our society to those who seem able to love those whom most of us, often correctly, choose not to love. King David, progenitor of the Messiah, thought otherwise. He understood that society is moved in the direction of that which is acclaimed. If you continually announce your love for the bad guys, society will beget more bad guys. For society's sake, and for the sake of wholesomeness and proper role-modeling, it is best to celebrate and announce your love for the good guys. Love the believers, love the righteous, love those who work hard and love the Lord.

TEN

Tolerance

[*Tolerance cannot result in abandoning standards.*]

Tolerance is allowing others to believe and act as they wish so long as it does not harm anyone else or violate fundamental standards and tenets under which our society operates. But it does not require that we respect or endorse those beliefs and actions, nor is there a need for us to understand them.

We conservatives have displayed bountiful tolerance toward things others believe and do. It is we who have, during the last decades, been called upon to make all the adjustments. But the liberal Left will never be satisfied until we actually respect and accept their ideology and endorse it as mainstream, wholesome, and equally valid to what we believe or the lifestyle we live. We cannot and should not do that. Tolerance does not mean that one throws out one's entire value system and casts one's brain, heart, and soul into an intellectual garbage bin.

The liberal Left wants our endorsement of its values and lifestyle so that it no longer is faced with a competing set of values, and we, especially our children, will live by its values. They wish to have the ease of not ever being challenged, of not having to defend that which they wish to impose on us. They do that by calling us names: racist or misogynist, homophobic or Islamophobic, Israel-firsters or jingoists, mean-spirited or polluters, sexist or speciesists (believers in the primacy of human over animal). They cannot tolerate those who think differently, which has given rise to the apt description of them as the thought police. Each one of us has been or soon will be labeled some type of extremist by the thought police, not for what we do but simply for the beliefs we hold. A thoroughly un-American wind is sweeping across the land.

The Left knows that if you control thought, you control action; and eventually you own the people and the country. If you own the brain, you own the body. If this country ever goes down, it will happen because of the success of the thought police and the pressure they have exerted. Weapons will have not been necessary.

What is ironic is that the Judeo-Christian system the Left wishes to overturn is the only religious and civic system that has within it, and actually abides by, the principle of tolerance and living *according to conscience.*

Our response must be to continue thinking and expressing what we think and live by it outwardly. Our dear friends, Granma Miller and Marguerite used to say: "Know what you believe. Do not let them take from you what you believe. And believe what you know." Once you believe something—really believe it—you will act upon it. Confidence is born in conviction!

In the name of liberal tolerance—as opposed to real tolerance—the Left is enforcing a monolithic national view. Its tolerance is intolerance, just as its liberalism is non-liberalism. Words and phrases mean only what the Left says it means, even if their definitions are the exact opposite of what is the truth.

Genuine and reasonable tolerance is done when showing tolerance for that which *morally* ought be tolerated. Four conditions are necessary for what is called tolerance to actually be tolerance: (1) those claiming it must reciprocate it; (2) it cannot simply constitute a lowering of standards; (3) it cannot be self-contradictory and something wholly different than what it purports to be; and (4) it should be a virtue and not a political tool.

First, over the years we have seen that while the Left calls for tolerance for those things it prefers, they have not extended that same tolerance for what we believe and prefer. They never give in! As mentioned, they have called us names and have tried to shut us down. There is no reciprocity, and a relationship absent reciprocity cannot be characterized as a moral endeavor. What they mean by tolerance is the institutionalization of what they prefer—the pushing of their preferences. Instead of using fists, they corrupt and exploit the honorable term of tolerance. What they do should not be called tolerance but rather liberal preference pushing.

Second, most of what has happened over the last forty years in the name of tolerance has concluded in a drastic lowering of personal and national standards. Some was unintentional, but a lot was intentional. Either way, standards have been severely lowered, as well as the norms under which our society has operated. Fundamental tenets have been discarded, be they social, educational, cultural, habits, or entertainment, the arts, and what used to be called good taste. (Just recently, my wife came back from a visit to the Museum of Modern Art in NYC and was appalled by the inferior and depressing exhibits throughout much of the museum's "progressive" gallery.)

What is passing today for tolerance is simply a suspension of good, historic judgment; a capitulation to bullies and the uncouth; and a rejection of the standards born of our accumulated wisdom over centuries of Western civilization. By lowering standards, we are forfeiting our power for good judgment and discernment so vital in making us mature human beings, as opposed to infants and copycats.

Society places itself at risk when it lowers its standards. Often creating lesser standards is a sign of a weakness to stand up to those, who in the name of inclusion, demand that we lower our standards to match theirs. We excuse our lowering of standards under the banner of tolerance but eventually embrace what have become the new standards, bringing society down by steep notches. Let us call today's tolerance what it is: a lowering of standards arising from our weakness to demand our previous high standards because of our fear of being called intolerant.

Third, in the name of tolerance, the multiculturalists are demanding that we tolerate (a) that which is intolerable; (b) those who will not tolerate us; (c) those who do not live by tolerance. All of this is self-contradictory and shows that what is at play here is a demand not for tolerance but for control and out of fear, a lack of national self-respect, and a rejection of our own cultural identity. Tolerance is not what it purports to be.

In fact, tolerance has led to a voluntary suspension of our rights to free speech, publication of our views, and true liberty—all of which are God-given rights. But God-given rights should not be forfeited, even for such things as tolerance. When viewpoints are forced upon us, the results are a suspension of our rights, which is an act of immorality since as moral agents we have a right to these freedoms.

For example, editors all over America not only refuse to print certain cartoons Muslims considered offensive but also just about anything the local or national Islamic organization considers offensive or unflattering. These editors represent newspapers and magazines that pride themselves in routinely publishing and exposing information offensive to Americans and Christians. Regarding Islam, however, they refuse to print anything offensive out of what they call tolerance.

We cannot say many things, no matter how factual and necessary, if the multiculturalists consider them intolerant. They label as intolerant anyone who tells the truth about matters that shed a negative but realistic light, though these same people relish doing so regarding Christians, Orthodox Jews, dwellers in the cities of Judea and Samaria, and Republicans.

We are similarly told, in the name of tolerance, not to do anything that could enflame Muslims overseas. When reminded that all this infringes on our fundamental right to free speech, we are told that we must "learn to understand different cultures and be tolerant of their ways, even though they are not our ways." In other words, we must forfeit our ways of open debate and free speech so as to accommodate their ways where free speech does not exist. Implicit in all this, is that their ways and standards must take precedence over ours—truly a multiculturalist's ultimate dream.

The upshot is that we are being told to be tolerant to those who are not tolerant to us; to accept conduct from others that is intrinsically intolerable; and to provide our Judeo-Christian ethic of tolerance to those who spurn, as a religious principle, the very concept of tolerance. It is the epitome of self-contradiction. It demonstrates that none of this is rooted in genuine moral tolerance but in capitulation to the Left's ethics and as a means to make us inferior to the culture of others. Out of tolerance, we are told that Islam should be allowed to plant mosques all over the West, while at the same time we are told to tolerantly accept the prohibition of churches and synagogues, Torahs and Gospels, in Muslim countries. We are told not to get upset over the reality that Jews and Christians can no longer live as equals to Muslims, and without oppression, in Muslim countries.

Even worse in Scandinavia, Swedish and Norwegian girls are being raped and even gang raped by packs of Middle Eastern men who are living there and being given monthly government welfare checks. In the minds of these rapists, Swedish women are fair game, precisely because these men do not live by a code of tolerance that demands people provide respect for those outside their own group. In other words, their code is: You shouldn't rape your own, but you can rape the outsider. Those who have tried to alert the public about this intolerant belief system and attitude have been scolded as being intolerant for even raising the point.

The definition of liberal tolerance is that if, in the name of tolerance, you remark about Muslim's endemic intolerance toward the infidel, you are called intolerant. In other words, in the name of tolerance, you cannot demand tolerance from others, and you are intolerant for expecting it!

Obviously tolerance is being used by Sweden's multiculturalists as a political tool, to wit, the slow de-humanizing of and attrition against its own historic population, so as to create the identity-less, post-native-culture, multiculturalist state. It will not stop in Sweden or Norway. The Left has found the ultimate workable tool. It is but a word, but the most dangerous weapon in an arsenal that will not need real weapons. That word is *tolerance* as defined by the Left. It is not moral and ought not to be construed as such.

How pitiful it is that the elites of a nation would rather have their young women raped than be called intolerant. They are fearful of being called intolerant by the very people who loathe the whole concept of tolerance! This is national suicide. I do not call it murder, precisely because so much of the West is voluntarily digging its own grave, at a time when its demographic majority does not require that it do so. The question is: Have Europeans been emotionally eviscerated by years of being criticized by Third Worlders or by their own never-ending criticism of themselves? Islam benefits by not living with the ethos of self-criticism, guilt, and self-loathing endemic in today's Western societies. What we are witnessing is not murder as much as it is purposeful, self-inflicted suicide. Much of the West seems willing to kill itself to show how tolerant they are of those who, in their intolerance, wish to kill them.

★★★

All of us who practice genuine, moral tolerance feel right in doing so. Each of us knows it is the right thing, the American thing, to provide opportunity and friendship to all worthy individuals. We want everyone to get a fair shake, and we pride ourselves in being able to see beyond the limited confines and scope of our own personal upbringing. We are better for it and more enriched. Nowhere in the world has tolerance breathed as a living reality—not simply as theory—as it has in America: "Give us your tired, your poor, those wishing to breathe free." People in America mingle, socialize, work together, and appreciate different backgrounds to a degree not quite found elsewhere. For the last half century, there has been no greater and time-sustained project than that of middle-class America accepting others and living with tolerance.

But the key in all this is *discernment*. Eventually, an open-ended, non-discerning, and self-loathing form of tolerance can lead to an acceptance of low standards born of an across-the-board, dangerous tolerance for everything. Some of these standards will be those of barbarism, cruelty, and inequality. In the name of inclusion, a dark civilization could replace the previously enlightened one we and our parents enjoyed.

History has shown how unchecked openness leads to a flirtation with iconoclastic, self-destructive forces and isms. A nation and civilization can go quickly from enlightenment to darkness. Rome experienced self-destruction when it went down the path of boredom, internal cynicism, and self-loathing by elites. The only antidote to this oft-repeated historic tragedy is a system that refreshes itself through its own living waters and utilizes the power of God-given discernment and morality. The ethos that has that capacity is God's Judeo-Christian blueprint. "It shall be a blessing to those who follow its statutes and to those who guard its inheritance" (Deuteronomy 5:40). It is up to us to fight for it. Nothing could be more worthwhile. Yet, nothing seems to require so much courage.

★★★ ELEVEN ★★★

Peace

[*Vanquishing evil and ensuring tranquility within the borders*]

Peace between nations is either a formal acceptance of each other so as to live in coexistence or simply a lack of hostility born of a belief that it is wiser to refrain from hostility than to engage in it. Peace among individuals is either a live-and-let-live relationship or an actual comity between the two. In all situations, peace can go beyond the simple cessation of hostility and rise to an actual appreciation and friendship between the two parties.

The ultimate circumstance of peace, wherein nations shall live in actual agreement, harmony, and even fraternity, is the one God Himself will bring: "He shall make peace" (Psalms 29:11); in other words, it is not something that represents a mere absence of hostilities but something tangibly affirmative, requiring "a making of it." Though during Creation God made light and darkness and all the tangible things we see and feel, He is withholding the creation of peace as a tangible phenomenon until the Latter Days. This condition is in the hand of God and represents what the Bible calls the final period of worldwide redemption, the messianic period. I shall call it the state of *ultimate* peace. Until such a period arrives, men and nations will attempt to facilitate peace within the parameters possible and the unique relationship under which the two parties operate. But peace as a guaranteed and forever condition cannot be permanently cemented in this earthly circumstance.

A peace process can lead to hoped-for conditions, but the process is not an ultimate or final goal within itself. It is not an absolute category but a conduit to some form of possible end to hostilities. It all depends on who is involved in the process.

The ultimate goal of nations is for its leaders to provide its citizens with a state of tranquility. At times, it can be achieved through peace processes and treaties but very often not. A peace treaty in itself is meaningless if one

100

party knows it will be breached the moment it is convenient for the other party to resume hostilities. Such a treaty, while a feather in the cap of those diplomats who do whatever they can to bring parties to sign it, is but a temporary charade. Furthermore, it is dangerous if it lulls a population into harmful concessions or a feeling of complacency that causes them to disarm themselves or forget the need to remain vigilant and prepared for the hostilities that will surely come.

Most of the world does not operate under the type of comity and shared values as seen between, for example, the United States and Canada. Most peace has been secured only after one side has vanquished the other, while the other side realizes that it can no longer successfully engage in further hostilities without doing more harm to itself than its former adversary.

Domestic tranquility, where citizens can go about their daily business not worrying about being attacked, is the ultimate goal for leaders of a nation. When it is understood that such tranquility cannot be achieved through bogus gestures of peace or insincere documents, it is the best and only alternative to vanquish the enemy so as to ensure domestic tranquility for the citizens.

Leaders are obligated first to the domestic tranquility of their citizens, since leadership constitutes a relationship freely chosen. No leader is required to run for office but freely chooses to and does so with the understanding that it obligates him to provide that tranquility. As mentioned, relationships freely chosen bring obligations and are moral paradigms. Many times, domestic tranquility is achieved only by vanquishing an implacable enemy. That is why military power remains the ultimate weapon and guarantee for domestic tranquility and peace.

Countries run by dictators, as are found in the communist and Middle Eastern worlds, suffer under leaders whose relationship to the people is not freely chosen. They are not moral relationships. Such leaders are not concerned with the domestic tranquility of their people, except to the extent that unrest may lead to their ouster from power. In negotiations, therefore, they have a lethal advantage over freely chosen leaders who have a reciprocal relationship with their people.

There is a great temptation and pressure brought upon leaders to engage in peace processes so as to appear peace loving. The result is that communist and Islamic dictators have greater negotiating powers during these processes than do democracies. Many come from ideologies where peace, unlike in the West, is not something to be extended to the infidel or reactionary. The peace process will be used by them as a tool to exploit our concept of peace as a virtue and wring from us dangerous concessions. They use the process as an interim, stalling apparatus until they feel military victory is on their side. Western leaders, on the other hand, allow themselves to operate within peace process rules they know are one-sided and false but seem to lack the political stomach to resist or overcome them. Our enemies know how to play the peace card.

As mentioned, a lasting peace treaty works only if each party lives by shared values and holds peace to be a virtue. Unfortunately, so as to get these treaties signed—and the accolades and relief of the populace that follows—Western leaders are fabricating a notion that everyone shares our values. They don't. The greatest psychological weakness in today's world is the naïve and ignorant assumption—an assumption being forced upon Western populations—that we all share the same values. Such is not the case; for if so, there would have been no need for a contrasting Koran or Communist Manifesto, nor a continued following of these ideologies by tens of millions. These ideologies were not made to affirm that which came before but to chart and lay out a different set of values and agenda, and a route toward it.

★★★

It is often asked: "But don't all enemies harbor different values yet we sign treaties with them? Who else are you to sign a peace treaty with if not your former enemy?" The answer is that the best and most enduring peace treaties were those signed by enemies we had vanquished. In our vanquishing of them, they became *former*. For example, we vanquished the Germans and the Japanese.

Our peace treaties with those two countries came about and were built upon the removal from power of those leaders who represented the belligerent ideology that precipitated the launching of war to begin with. Nazism and Japanese militarism were ideologies that had overtaken the people. They were temporary, and the people were happy with their removal. These treaties insisted on an uprooting of the pernicious ideology over the Japanese people and of Nazism over the German people. These ideologies had to go if a peace treaty were to be signed. With the removal of these aberrant ideologies, Japan and Germany could once again become who they always were. Such is not the case when dealing with communism or Islamism. These ideologies remain even after the treaties are signed. Such treaties are, thus, meaningless.

The belligerent ideology of violent jihad remains because it is not limited to a single leader or a temporary ruling clique that has taken over, but because it constitutes a national and religious ideology. It is not something that is temporary but a national and shared ethos. Treaties will not be able to remove that which the national ethos does not want removed. Nazism and Japanese militarism were not longstanding national identities rooted in the people as a people, but *Ummah*, peoplehood, *is* tied to Islamism.

Through Ronald Reagan, we halted Russian communism by vanquishing it. We did so by (1) crushing it economically; (2) implementing a missile defense system and installing Pershing missiles the Russians could not overcome; (3) identifying it as an evil empire; and, here is the kicker, (4) stripping it of any pretense as a moral ideology. In the end it crumbled when its leader, Michael Gorbachev, said that hardcore communism must go—a crack that led to its quick demise. The people were happy to see communism go. They felt liberated without communism. In contrast, many Muslims feel liberated *with* Islam. We vanquished communism because Reagan had as his goal the *vanquishing* of it. He was "a leader willing to fight our battles" (1 Samuel 8:30). The vanquishing of evil is the ultimate moral activity.

★★★

The plight and situation in which Israel finds itself will illustrate many of the points mentioned above. It finds itself in a nonreciprocal relationship with its neighbors. Not only is she willing to live in an absence of war, but she is willing to recognize and coexist with her Arab neighbors. She wants a real peace. Her Arab neighbors, on the other hand, do not want coexistence, will not extend recognition, and continue to bombard Israel with rockets and suicide bombers. Israel provides the best medical services to even its enemies, who, in return, offer not life but death. The Arab states surrounding Israel, and those in the West Bank, want Israel destroyed, lusting to be the ones who will execute the destruction.

Too many liberal American Jews seem willing to relinquish that which God has promised the children of Israel, a promise that spawned the great Zionist inspiration to rebuild the land. No other people did for the land of Israel, *Eretz Yisroel*, what the Jewish people have done, because no other people have had a biblical mandate and compulsion to do so. Too many liberal Jews are willing to forfeit their genuine historic identity while granting a falsely manufactured identity to West Bank enemies.

No matter how generous and risky are Israel's peace gestures to her enemies, she is continually rebuffed. Many liberals seem unwilling to accept that Israel's enemies will never accept her. They remain under the illusion that the problem lies with Israel, and she must make more concessions and do more; when the fact is, her enemies will never accept the infidel. There is no reciprocity in this relationship. It is not even a relationship.

Using the peace process, Arabs have shrewdly tried to weaken Israel bit by bit, piece of land by piece of land. The Oslo Accords, a peace process document involving the late Prime Minister Yitzchak Rabin, an acquaintance of mine and a good man, turned out to be an interim ploy by the Arabs to extract from Israel whatever they could until they felt strong enough to destroy her. Indeed, that is what Islamic leaders told their people when Western cameras were not around and while speaking in Arabic. We in the West need to be wary of those who use peace not to achieve peace but as *war by other means.*

Morality demands that leaders protect the people and not be seduced into schemes resulting in dangerous concessions, even if, by so doing, the elites accuse a leader of not being a peace-loving man. Leaders need discernment, the ability to distinguish between that which is real and that which is a dangerous charade. Church and synagogue leaders need discernment as well. Our physical and spiritual enemies are adept at beguiling and confusing us. They know how difficult it is for people to resist the glory, the prizes, and the awards that accrue if you simply play ball. If you do, you will be labeled a lover of peace and dialogue. But being a man of peace means knowing what ought to be done for real peace and with whom you ought to do it. Peace that is not true peace is not a virtue; it is worship of a theory. As Jeremiah said to leaders scrambling about in peace processes: "Peace, peace, but there is no peace" (Jeremiah 6:14).

★★★

The war over Israel is not a battle over a plot of land or a parcel but only part of the Muslim's global jihad. Back in 2003, I mentioned this to a member of the Council on Foreign Relations, but he did not agree. Today, however, he concedes that what we are seeing regarding Israel is only part of the jihad—the springboard and testing ground of it—and Israel's enemies will not stop until they have taken over every Jewish holy site and rename them as their own. It is a battle to defeat *Adonai*, the God of Israel, and declare *Eretz Yisroel*, God forbid, to be *dar al-islam* (territory of Islam). Though we never hear presidents announcing from their podiums "Christianity is a religion of peace" or "Judaism is a religion of peace"—as they love to do about other religions—we need not risk our futures in phony peace processes just to prove it. We know who we are! It is better that we have as a leader "a mighty man of valor" upon whom "rests the spirit of the Lord" (1 Samuel 9:1, 16:13).

America could use a man of valor right now as President. Mr. Obama seems to be doing his utmost to slowly disarm America. In a promise to the Russians, he spoke off-camera of reducing our nuclear capacity down to that of France, while not demanding equal concessions from the Russians. He is leaving the men, women, and children of this country terribly vulnerable. It is a major dereliction of duty, especially as the Commander-in-Chief's first obligation is to protect American citizens. Perhaps, like many on the Left, he believes America is not worthy of military superiority. After all, being the lone superpower allows America to do what is in the best interests of America and not bow to the socialist demands of the U.N. and others in the international arena. But Mr. Obama freely chose a relationship where, in return for the American people electing him their President, he vowed to protect them. This relationship, in which one party no longer wishes to uphold his primary obligation, is stripped of its reciprocal, moral axis. I can see no upside to American security through Mr. Obama's draconian disarmament schemes. If he follows through on his plans, what is his moral claim to the office of the presidency?

★★★

Peace is used by some as a bludgeoning tool. In March and April 2012 in Sanford, Florida, we heard the thuggish chant: "No justice, no peace." It was being used to railroad George Zimmerman to prison for an act Sanford police reasoned was done in self-defense and not as a hate crime. When Jesse Jackson and Al Sharpton rode in to town from their northern headquarters in Chicago and New York to stir things up, the crowd screamed "no justice, no peace," and it means *do it our way or else*. In other words, if you want peace in the streets, give us the justice we want, not what the law demands. Mr. Sharpton used this slogan many times during his protests in New York City to bully police and politicians, and we learned that when it caves in, society gets neither justice nor peace.

It is a sad commentary how so many in the liberal community assume that, until proven otherwise, a white individual is a racist and what he does must have a racist motivation. The decades of friendship of whites to blacks and the years of instituting policies to redress wrongs from decades ago matters not to those who self-satisfyingly retain their own bigotry against southern whites and gain celebrity by so doing.

The best peace in the world and the one most worthy of pursuit is peace with your family and especially your spouse. I would venture to say that maintaining a loving and peaceful relationship with your spouse is on a day-to-day scale harder than the flash-in-the-pan diplomatic attempts at peace making. Those that do it are the real peace lovers: Blessed are the family peacemakers for they bring God into the world. I admire those men and women all across our land that coalesce their family in warmth, love, and peace, creating something spectacular.

We speak of God lowering His countenance upon us and planting His grace among us. It does not happen because of diplomats around the negotiating table but because of spouses relating peacefully over the kitchen table. The Talmud tells us that Aaron, Moses' brother, was a pursuer of peace. His peacemaking had nothing to do with international relations but domestic relations and family life. Aaron let Moses do that which was necessary to vanquish enemies and secure tranquility. Aaron concentrated on bringing peace within families and among neighbors. He pursued it. And so should we.

★★★ TWELVE ★★★

Equality and Fairness

[Equal justice under the law that is objective and impartial]

Equality means *equal justice under the law*. There has never been a better definition and realization for equality than this. People in America often do not realize how unique this biblical and American founding principle is. Throughout history, most people have lived under systems where certain groups or privileged classes lived by a set of laws above the rest, or within caste systems, or as exploited infidels. The Magna Carta was a seminal document erasing legal distinctions based on hierarchy.

"All men are *created* equal." We take this phrase for granted today, but until the Declaration of Independence, no document or group of men had distilled this soaring concept into such a tight and impactful phrase. It hits you square in the face: "Hear ye, Hear ye." No other sentence has changed mankind as did that one except the passage in Genesis from where the Founders drew their inspiration: "And God *created* man, in the image of God did He *create* him." Man is equal because he was created at one time and by one Source. There are not different men from different sources and from different times.

Not *some* men are created equal, but *all* men. Why all men and not a few? It is because God created *all* men. By what are they made equal? They are made equal by having been created by God. Where do they get those equal rights? From God who created them and made them equal. Because God created us, we are equal under the law. Our American heritage and our understanding of who we are stem from Genesis and the Judeo-Christian ethos. Our civic culture is tied to it. Without it, the basis of everything we have and hold dear is gone, including our liberty. Furthermore, because our equality under the law is tied to Him; absent His law, we will become unequal.

No other philosophy or ism in history has as its core this announcement and outlook on the individual as does Genesis and the Declaration our Founders built upon it. Communism does not believe in God nor Creation. Islam separates out as unequal those who are infidels. It is not found to any matchable degree in Zoroastrianism, Hinduism, or Buddhism.

The Founders were wise, sharp men. They knew all men were created equal but understood that once created, each man chose differently. As individuals with free will, men's lives would certainly differ as each life progressed according to the individual's choices. All they had to do was look at the world around them. How, they wondered, is equality among men maintained when everyone chooses separate and different paths and do not end up the same? In moral terms, what *ought* that equality be? There could be only one answer, equality under the law. Equal justice for all. Men maintained their equality not by staying the same and having the same possessions—free will made that impossible and undesirable—but in their treatment by the law. They were helped by the Old Testament's declaration: "One law for all the citizens" (Exodus 12:49).

★★★

The French Revolution too spoke of equality for the common man. But like the socialism that grew from it, it defined equal as an equal sharing of material goods, an equality of *result*. In contrast, the Founding Fathers saw equality as equal *opportunity*. It foresaw the negative social engineering that comes about when governments decide to *force* people to be equal in ownership. Such a goal ends up punishing and keeping down people with greater talent, ingenuity, courage, energy, or stick-to-itiveness. It dampens the human spirit. Ultimately, it leads to the *soft tyranny of good intentions*.

The Founders, as the Old Testament, aspired to a civic ethos where the law would be equally applied so that each individual had the opportunity to live, and become, according to his own efforts and abilities. The Declaration spoke of our right as individuals "to pursue happiness," not of a government obligation to guarantee individual happiness.

Government, the Founders believed, could be used in a limited way to make sure legal or man-made roadblocks were removed so that an individual's ability to pursue his happiness was not artificially blocked. They also understood that economic prosperity, so necessary to the well-being and dignity of all men, was made exceedingly more possible when individuals were allowed to script their own destiny and ambition, and not precluded from doing so by those in government regulating civic life to ensure sameness.

Men as moral agents of free will must be able to freely choose and not be stymied by a government wishing to keep them down in the hope that citizens become materially the same as others. Equality lies in sameness in law and opportunity, not sameness in property. How and to what degree one pursues his happiness depends upon the degree of personal responsibility he brings to his life and projects. Our Founding moral principle lies in the individual's right to pursue, not in any one group's right to claim or possess.

There will never be sameness, since each individual is endowed with different talents, lives by his own sacrifice and drive, and subscribes to different philosophies of life, each yielding uniquely different results. Those wishing to impose a philosophy of sameness are motivated by a desire to control and stand above those whom they consign to inferior sameness, a sameness they do not impose or choose for themselves.

Sameness is also championed by those who wish to keep down those who excel and attain material levels above them. This constitutes the worst characteristics in the panoply of human emotions: envy and jealousy, and the desire to rob people of what they can be and their God-given right to individuality. It smacks of mobbism. Under any other perspective, it would be labeled what it is—sinful. Such inhumane and ungodly emotions, however, are given license and extolled when done by those running nanny-state governments under the misnomer of equality.

★★★

Individuals or groups do not achieve material sameness when living by different philosophies. Concerning individuals, the Talmud says: "Just as our faces are different so, too, are our ideas and conclusions." We often become the realization of the very ideas that shape us. It is ironic that those advocating multiculturalism—the belief that different groups must be schooled in their own cultures, philosophies, and goals—later complain when there is not sameness among all groups. But since people live and achieve according to the differing expectations of their ideologies, aren't such complaints irrational? Except, of course, when one recognizes that the multiculturalists have as their goal the obliteration of our prevailing American Judeo-Christian culture and cite this lack of material sameness as justification for ending it.

Nowhere in our admiration of the Judeo-Christian ethos do we claim that every pleasing outcome resides in it only. Each culture matriculates something pleasant not found as pronounced in another. There is, for example, a certain quality of life and exquisite rhythm in everyday eating and socializing found in Italy or parts of France not found here in America. In other cultures, extended family life is easier. America excels in the idea of freedom and liberty, industriousness and hard work, experimentation and risk taking, ownership, fairness and openness, thinking big, and being able to be the author of one's own life and, over a lifetime, writing one's own personal story in a way never possible before in history. It also provides the greatest opportunity for economic achievement.

Those who insist on rejecting the American way and display their cultural pride by living under counter-philosophies should not complain when they have not attained the same American dream as have those who live by the rules that make that dream possible. Nor should those who desire and opt for the stress-free, predictable, easygoing life decry our system when they do not own as much as others who work long hours and take risks. They should be happy that America allows them the freedom to choose their preferred lifestyle.

There is no American birthright for owning equally what your neighbor owns or has. The birthright lies not in an equal material result but in equal opportunity. The socialist-communist notion of man is rooted in materialism, not things spiritual. It ignores the grand achievements of life that come from things beyond the material, which center on the satisfying outcomes of the religious, spiritual, and family aspects of life. Beyond that is the nobility and personal fulfillment that comes through study, friendship, duty, service, the aesthetic, and the dignity of being a person of character and living with a purpose beyond the material. We all know people materially rich but not wealthy, and people with less material possessions but with lives filled with abundance.

Equality comes in being able to choose your life and goals, and work toward them. It is made possible in a Land of Liberty, not in a paradigm social-engineering sameness. What is important is not sameness but being *special*; and for that to happen, a person needs freedom.

***

As mentioned earlier, every relationship requires reciprocity. Those within society living by equality under the law must extend to others their right to live equally under the law. That is the reciprocity upon which every relationship stands. It is a two-way street. In March 2012, a young black man was killed in Florida, the circumstances of which were not clear during the first few days after the shooting. Was it self-defense or did the shooter have malicious intent? Initially, the shooter was not charged, out of the belief it was self-defense. In response, the Black Panthers issued a Dead or Alive Reward against him and offered a $10,000 bounty for his head. The Justice Department, under Eric Holder, did nothing to stop the Black Panthers from doing so, just as Holder had dismissed a charge—video-taped and eye-witnessed—of the Panthers' intimidation with bully clubs, at Philadelphia voting precincts during the 2008 election for their candidate, Barack Obama. Worse, Attorney General Holder did nothing to help an elderly couple forced out of their own home when their address was twittered, in error, by Spike Lee, as that of Mr. Zimmerman, the shooter and defendant.

Aside from the un-American spectacle of a lynch mob roaming the streets is the necessity to repeat that trial by jury—habeas corpus, innocent until proven guilty—rule of law by courts and police, not mobs, is a condition to which all are entitled. It is not enough to expect it for yourself, but something that the Black Panthers, Louis Farrakhan, and others of the Left must be willing to extend others. Equal justice is for all, even for members of people outside your group. Reciprocity. Without such voluntary reciprocity and absent law-enforcement agencies willing to take action against those with whom it politically sympathizes, the mob rules and the innocent of society are suddenly left without protection.

★★★

Fairness is the condition of being treated equally under the law by rules that are objective and impartial. Such is a condition that *ought* to be. There are, of course, many factors in life beyond the purview of government requiring us to rise above our personal situation so that we get a shot at life. It is good and proper to help those who need that push or extra help in their own ongoing, personal efforts at a shot at life. Families do that for each other, and our government offers free schooling, libraries, and museums so we all have that same footing.

There is no country in the world like America where so many successful people have parted with their wealth to provide scholarships for others in need of a leg up. Mr. Julius Rosenwald, founder of Sears Roebuck and Company, is but one example. He paid for the building of good schools throughout many of the black neighborhoods of the South during the beginning of the twentieth century. Andrew Carnegie established free libraries, and Walter Annenberg gave hundreds of millions in scholarships for poor youngsters. Regular Americans, in their penchant for fairness, give energy, time, and money for projects not for their children's benefit but for those less fortunate. We can never equalize the material condition and opportunity of all when we take into account the dozens of circumstances that shape and surround our lives. When government tries to do the same thing, sooner or later, tyranny sets in, for it gets stuck on the road of incrementally readjusting a reality of life impossible to overcome. The utopia becomes a nightmare and, finally, hell for all. It is fair only in the sense that all become equally miserable.

Fairness is also receiving that which one has earned. The worker receives the wage that is fairly his, based on the agreement he has with those that employ him. It does not mean, however, we all get what we want or what we feel entitled to, simply because we were born or live in a country where others have more.

Parents are familiar with the constant refrain by children: *But it's not fair*, meaning it's not fair that I don't receive what I want and what I am asking for. It's not fair that I have to do my chores. But all of us adults know that fair is living by personal responsibility and not making claims to something you did not earn. In fact, that would be unfair to those who did work on behalf of getting the object they worked for, and unfair to those who live by personal responsibility and accountability.

A society is immoral that lives by a two-tiered system where we demand personal responsibility from some but not others, and where those who have not worked for something can have it for free from a government that takes from those that did work (and worse, may not be able to get what they worked for because it was taxed away). It ought not be. It undermines the whole concept of fairness, which is to deal by rules that are objective and impartial.

THIRTEEN

Marriage and Life

[*Beyond the civil and onto the sanctified*]

Marriage is that which takes place between a man and a woman. Relationships that are not between a man and woman are arrangements or partnerships. Business relationships are not marriages nor are sexual relationships in and of themselves marriage.

The phenomenon of marriage is as old as Adam and Eve, which makes it older than any other relationship except the one between man and God. That being the case, its definition is exceedingly important and the most classic. For conservatives, words and definitions are not things to be manipulated nor hijacked to fit a cause or preference, because civilization depends on how we define the concepts by which it operates. Conservatives like our civilization—we wish to *conserve* it. Redefining a concept is redefining civilization, thereby jeopardizing the continuation of that civilization along the lines of what it was, is, and will become.

Marriage is a definition tied to history and cannot be recalibrated so as to conform to preferences. It is not a civil rights issue but fidelity to a definition, and words do matter. Words are not to be played with as was done in *Alice in Wonderland* when Humpty Dumpty said, "Words mean whatever I want them to mean." Words and concepts, properly defined, endure.

If those engaged in protecting the definition of marriage were motivated by prejudice, they would be calling for laws outlawing the practice of homosexuality between consenting adults or asking they not be allowed to vote, hold jobs, or rent houses. No one is. No one denies homosexuals any rights because of who they are or what they do; even marriage is open to them if done, as marriage is defined, with a member of the opposite sex.

The Bible, in Deuteronomy 22:13 when speaking of marriage says: "And when a man shall take a woman for a wife…" Marriage in the Judeo-Christian tradition is between a man and a woman. This is separate from its negative opinion of sexual homosexuality mentioned in Leviticus. Even absent sex, marriage between members of the same gender is not marriage, while marriage between a man and woman is marriage (even without sexual relations).

The Bible confers on marriage a special designation it gives no other relationship. In Hebrew, it is called *k'du'shin*, which means *sanctification*. No other relationship, partnership, or arrangement is entitled by that term. Man and woman bound in the contractual relationship of marriage is separate and above any other relationship. It is sanctified. That is what makes it *marriage* and not simply a partnership. The sanctity of marriage is rooted not in how much one loves the other but in its unity of man and woman.

K'du'shin also means separate and unto itself in its holiness. Marriage remains separate and above any freely chosen relationship, the most inviolate of any we have. Those who breach it are not guilty simply of fornication but adultery itself. Fornication is doing that which is outside proper and conventional confines, whereas adultery is a piercing of that which is holy, the sanctified relationship.

★★★

As mentioned many times before, there must be reciprocity to relationships. Many relationships involve reciprocity, but no relationship carries reciprocity to the degree of marriage between man and woman. It is the moral relationship par excellence. In Genesis, God declares marriage between male and female and lays its foundation in their being to each other *helpmates*, which is the essence of marriage. No other relationship is defined as people being helpmates. God *announced* His taking of male (*za'char*) and female (*n'kei'va*) and uniting them as one. The concept and institution of marriage was a creation of God, and it was done with a male and a female.

There is an ultimate reciprocity between male and female that exists in no other combination. Beyond sex, there is *completion*. A male lacks a multitude of things found only in a female, and a female lacks many things found only in male. Together there is completion not possible when uniting two of the same sex. Together the husband and wife have within themselves the potential to do what God did—bring forth human life. It is *marriage* because it brings about fullness, a singularity that makes it separate and above every other relationship.

To those of us who cherish the concept of marriage and wish to pass it on to our children, it is vital that it not be made into something that it is not. It is a matter of moral clarity.

★★★

Life lies at the center of the whole moral enterprise. We who are alive owe to others the right to live. The right to live is a God-given right and as the Founders stated in the sentence that shook the world: "are endowed by their Creator with certain unalienable Rights, that among these are Life..."

All relationships involve obligation and reciprocity. We who have life have a reciprocal obligation to protect and preserve life. The only exception is regarding actual self-defense, wars of self-defense, or operations to stave off imminent threats. Such killing is not called murder. Though some may disagree, justice requires that we put to death those who have murdered the innocent human being already born. It is the reciprocity of taking from him that which he took from others. It is not a form of revenge, but a way to protect society from another life being taken and demonstrates to society the value we place on innocent life.

Life begins in the womb. Be it at the moment of fertilization or heartbeat is a religious question. So is the question of when exactly the soul enters our lives. Therefore, there is a grave moral imperative in protecting the fetus. As science and technology have advanced, so have we begun witnessing an even earlier beginning to life than we had previously thought.

There is, however, one morally acceptable situation where we supersede the life of the fetus and that is when the mother will die if the pregnancy continues. It becomes a matter of heartbreaking self-defense. Furthermore, there exists only one degree of life greater than the fetus', and that is the already-born, living human being who, as God said in Genesis, has "breathed into it the breath of life." The self-defense of the mother already born, breathing the breath of life, takes precedence.

Killing a fetus for convenience sake, however, is an abomination. Never in the history of civilized sociology has there been a phrase so utterly detached from reality and selfish as "a woman's right to control her body" to justify killing the fetus. Her body is not the baby's body. They are attached by an umbilical cord, and she provides nutrition, but they remain two separate entities. When a woman dies, so does her hand, her leg, and all parts of her body. But, at the proper moment, a baby can live outside the womb even if the mother host is gone and her body departed.

I do not see this as a woman's issue but a life issue. Women, like men, must preserve life. An umbilical cord does not make the mother the baby or the baby the mother; each has a separate heart and a separate brain and arms—separate bodies, one big and the other tiny. It is not a civil rights issue. It is another case of those who have a preference for what they want to do, calling what they want to do a civil right. In moral terms, the life of the child takes precedence over the inconvenience of the lady who is carrying him.

Liberals claim that taking the side of the fetus is getting into one's bedroom. But abortions take place not in the bedroom but the hospital room. No one is intruding on someone's private sex in the bedroom. This has nothing to do with contraception. Nor is there any credence to the claim that it interferes with someone's reproductive rights. Wrong again; no one in our society demands that someone else reproduce and have children or not have children. They can use condoms, diaphragms, or whatever to prevent a pregnancy. If they choose, they can remain childless or barren. What is at issue is whether there is a right to destroy life and not give birth to that which you have *already* reproduced and is biding its time in the womb.

★ ★ ★

We often hear people say: "But you can't legislate morality." The answer is: you cannot legislate religious beliefs or practices, whereas we enact laws based on society's moral perspective all the time. Laws against theft, murder, rape, you name it, are based on society's moral belief system. That is why I have gone to great lengths to address all issues from a broad moral perspective and not as religious undertakings.

We all agree society has a responsibility to protect life. Only a few people would argue that life starts only after birth. The fetus may not yet be a human being that has already breathed the breath of humanhood, but it is life. What else could it be but life? It isn't just amorphous tissue.

To those who say that our moral laws are limited only to areas where someone's action harms another, well, that is what abortion does—it harms the living fetus.

Laws do more than limit people or provide rights. We make laws regarding action to reflect our deepest moral beliefs. The issue here is not sin, but proper conduct; it is not centered on theology but morality.

True, we cannot legislate moral sentiments. But laws are not passed for the express purpose of changing or deciding how one feels inside. Altered sentiments can be by-products of law but are not the purpose of law. As mentioned in an earlier chapter, sentiments and morality are separate categories. Sentiments deal with feelings while morality deals with action.

When people say we cannot legislate morality, they are confusing sentiments, which cannot be legislated, with actions, which can be legislated—provided they are rooted not in religion but morality itself.

Redefining marriage and continuing to allow abortions are moral issues and harmful to the vast majority who need the definition of marriage and of beginning of life to endure. It is not simply a desire but a need, a societal need.

FOURTEEN

Social Justice

[Has it become social engineering that is penalizing the middle class?]

Social justice is the application across society of equal justice for all, that all citizens within society are subject to the same laws. When liberals speak of social justice, what they really mean and want is socialism—the welfare state. If left unchecked, they would go beyond even the welfare state. Everyone agrees we must help those truly in need, but what social justice advocates really want is redistribution of wealth. Remember candidate Obama in 2008 telling Joe the Plumber about "spreading the wealth around." In fact, seven years earlier in a 2001 interview on Chicago's WBEZ he said, "It was a shame the Warren Supreme Court had not gone even further and taken up redistribution of wealth since everyone has a right to housing." Like everything else in the liberal playbook, today's liberals exploit and hijack endearing terms such as compassion, tolerance, fairness, and social justice on behalf of instituting the welfare state or a cultural Marxism that reflects their lifestyle preferences. Redistribution of wealth works solely on behalf of the groups they prefer, which is not the hardworking, straight-laced, conservative middle class.

There is a very popular maxim among social workers, liberal clergy, staffers, and others who have made themselves the arbiters of social justice that I have been accosted by my entire life. They say it is society's obligation to "afflict and make uncomfortable those who are comfortable, and give comfort to the uncomfortable." To me, that does not sound like a pursuit of justice as much as pursuit of vengeance. There is no doubt that many in the self-proclaimed social justice community dislike mainstream America—you and I. But they have no moral right to arrogate to themselves the authority to afflict and make anyone uncomfortable. Who do they think they are?

Moreover, they reserve this discomfort for others beyond their circle while they themselves generally live very comfortable lives. Indeed, when we challenge some of their notions and demonstrate how what they propose is hurting many fine upstanding Americans, they flee from the debate for they do not wish to be made uncomfortable.

Their whole maxim is fallacious given that the middle class they call comfortable is working hard to attain its level of comfort by sacrificing and taking the time to strengthen family life and teach their children the proper virtues. Their comfort was not given to them, and most are just getting by. They are not so comfortable as to be free of daily stress and worry. Anyone reading this book knows how much effort is put in to just keep daily life flowing and operating. Hardly anyone's life is a picnic. Nor is there any sin in being comfortable, the proof being that these arbiters live quite comfortably and beyond the economic means of the very people whom they wish to discomfort.

Nor are those whom they call uncomfortable entitled to attain their comfort on the backs of other people's hard work—that is simply legal thievery. Nor should they be morally free from the personal responsibility that facilitates comfort and is the key to the modicum of comfort achieved by others.

★ ★ ★

Another aphorism of the professional social justice crowd is that "a society is judged on how it treats the poor." It actually is a variation on what Gandhi said specifically regarding India during the British Empire years, referring not to the poor but the "weakest"—the *untouchables* of the caste system. Gandhi was right regarding giving rights to the untouchables. Liberals today, however, are using it as a moral charge to immediately enact the welfare state. Nice sounding as the phrase may be, regarding establishing a welfare state, it is wrong on three counts:

First, a society is judged on applying equality under the law to all. That is a just society. No society can distribute equally all its goods and money unless it wants to be a communist society. What it can do is make sure that equality under the law and equality of opportunity is available to all of its citizens. A society is judged on being just, not on its being redistributionist.

Second, it is exceedingly important how we treat the poor. But the need to treat people well is separate from a political desire to underwrite their life or their lifestyles. We treat people well by extending them courtesy, not talking down to them, being mindful of their human dignity irrespective of their economic station, inviting them into our churches and synagogues, availing them of all the public institutions such as libraries, museums, and parks, and by letting them vote. There is no greater sign of equal treatment than giving everyone, no matter their station in life, the right to vote. It means they have as equal a say in how this country is run as do wealthier Americans. That is *very* good treatment.

Our treatment of people is personal, one-on-one, and has nothing to do with either redistribution of wealth or a preference for a person simply because he is poor. This is opposed to the system where some are preferred simply because they are rich—both are equally wrong. What is very important is to make sure that we, as individuals, relate to other people in a respectful manner. When done by millions and millions, a society can be labeled as one that treats its people well.

Indeed, Americans treat people of other ranks far better than those societies where there is a type of aristocracy, where the upper classes do not mingle with those economically below them. Many of those societies ironically are in Europe itself, the cradle of the welfare state. Except for going to a soup kitchen once in a while, many high-brows advocating social justice do not mingle in the everyday forums where regular Americans go and miss the opportunity to directly treat others with dignity. In lieu of mingling with the lower economic strata and directly interacting with them, they instead advocate high-brow social justice.

I personally have always felt comfortable living a life without social demarcation, talking to and working with anybody and treating them as an equal. Therefore I have felt no need to look to social justice schemes to replace what I routinely do in a matter-of-fact way in everyday life. You and I do not treat people nicely out of some affectation and display of social justice but simply because we look at people as people.

You and I may not have met, but all of us read in magazines about the good works Americans do. All of us hear stories about how generously average Americans treat people poorer than themselves. Pick up any magazine and you'll read about the ladies throughout America involved in church projects that bring clothes to those who need them and stand behind the serving lines feeding turkey and sweet potatoes to those down on their luck. You and I know many dads who volunteer once or twice a week with the Boy Scouts and give all sorts of kids a helping hand, teaching them how to do practical things and providing them with a sense of belonging.

Back in Cleveland, I knew all types of Main Street businessmen, just like many of you reading this book, who gave poor kids their first opportunity at a job, taking a chance on them. These men, Jewish and Christian, made it possible for poor kids to leap beyond their environment and enter the wider world of customers, commerce, and managing their own work sphere. The America you and I know is filled with stories of people treating those poorer with respect and giving them opportunity and hope, a leg up, and the satisfaction of responsibility. For example, there's my friend Mike down in Alabama—we call him Coach—who sets up sports camps so that the underprivileged youngsters can enjoy athletics and learn about healthy competition.

Our names aren't publicized because we do not choose to run for public office on the plank of social justice nor earn our living by being staff members of social justice organizations. No, tens of millions of Americans do not preach social justice policy from above but actually live it down here on our streets.

And third, there is this assumption that America is made up of the permanently comfortable and the permanently uncomfortable, and those that are uncomfortable are so because of what the comfortable did to them. These notions are based on what happened in Europe or Russia decades or centuries earlier. But this was never our American model. It is an erroneous importation to America of theories based on realities in European life that did not, for the most part, exist here.

Many of us come from itinerant immigrants, legal immigrants. We need not make amends. We just need to make sure the laws are equally applied to all and, when we can, give a boost to those who show a willingness to rise above their station and teach them the tools, good habits, and sacrifices necessary to get to where we now are.

Although there were many initial bigotries against one or another people group who came here—witness the Irish or the Italian experience, for example—many of those who were from families once poor are no longer poor. Of course there was the whole slavery debacle. This tragedy took laws being passed to rectify the situation. But pass them we did, and now there is a fair opportunity for all. We all got to where we are now not by oppressing or cheating anybody, but by hard work, perseverance, and by delaying material gratification.

The paradigm of leftist social justice is based on age-old conditions in

Europe where, to begin with, there was no application of equal justice, society was specifically structured to a socially and economically tiered system, and unlike America, there was not the social integration and access to all public institutions. Too many in the liberal social justice community wish to remake America into a European-type model for the sins and mindset that were of Europe but are not committed here in this day and age nor have they constituted our mindset and atmosphere.

★★★

In 1971, John Rawls wrote an influential liberal book, *A Theory of Justice*, in which he asserted that social justice is best achieved when society's public institutions are arranged to the benefit and condition of the least advantaged and those who have not achieved. This became the mantra and calling card of those in the social justice movement. As we mentioned in our chapter on tolerance, a society is at risk when it lowers its standards. Have we not seen since 1971 how, in the name of inclusion and understanding, our institutional standards have been lowered in every segment of society? It is not a good idea. Have we not seen, during these last forty years, how bringing everything down to lower levels has created an underclass and many inner city schools that do not function? On the other hand, we have all seen examples of other inner city schools whose students were challenged to achieve beyond their perceived abilities and who met and surpassed those challenges with flying colors.

Rawls was wrong and showed a rather condescending view of those he consigned as being below him. Societies prosper, create, achieve, and inspire by raising standards, not lowering them. Our institutions should be geared to raising people's standards upward, not lowering them downward. His formula disenfranchises the vast majority of Americans who crave the highest standards. In the name of social justice, he is punishing the bulk of Americans. Why, for liberals, are "the people" only those who underachieve? Why should the majority of Americans paying for these institutions not have institutions with high standards, and why should these institutions not be shaped for their *benefit*?

A true egalitarian would believe that all people can rise up. Society's institutions should work to spawn future achievers. Equality does not happen by bringing achievers down to lower levels but by inducing and inspiring underachievers to rise to higher degrees of accomplishment. Societies are best served by those who wish to excel. However, many elitists have a very dour, pessimistic, foreboding view of ordinary people. As materialists, they do not account for the human spirit, but that is un-American.

America became America by strivers, dreamers, and doers. America is a land that admires achievement and is filled with people who achieve. It is our ethos. It is not something to be undermined and shattered in the name of social justice. Left-wing social justice will ruin the spirit and ingenuity that made America grow into America. Our people of excellence have served as an inspiration to others, and our achievers have produced a wealth that has made everybody's material life better. Here there is no limited pie where achievement comes at the price of the poor.

America is more prosperous today because of the outstanding achievements that suddenly burst forth with the rise of inventions in technology and medicine, and improvements in business and finance. Material life is better than in 1971 because, while the Rawl-ites in charge of our institutions decided to lower cultural standards, business did not listen and decided to raise output standards. People, even poorer people, are far better off today than before. It matters not that some are vastly wealthier than others. What matters is that so many today have air conditioners, cars, phones, and lifesaving blood pressure and cholesterol pills whose market price is but four dollars for a month's supply. Because of business, a poor person today can save his life with mere quarters whereas the greatest millionaires of yesteryear could not do so even with their millions. To me, that is social justice—the raising of everybody's standard of living. Social justice schemes will destroy America and bring down the standard of living for everybody. Just look at England.

Social justice is not achieved by bemoaning that others are more successful or by disregarding great successes just to keep in place an ever-indicting and ever-complaining social justice hierarchy *kvetching* about the lack of social justice. The gloom-and-doom Rawls never anticipated the rise of the black middle class, the technology boom, and the growth in housing. He wrote his book before the economically invigorating policies of Ronald Reagan.

Fortunately Rawls' influence was limited to the institutions under the control of the social justice elites. The decay they ushered in is not found in American business. Decay is not a moral aspiration. When social justice becomes a formula for decay and lowering of standards, it is not justice but surrender as a result of misguided guilt. It is national suicide, and we should have no part of it. It is a moral wrong committed against those who wish to live by personal responsibility, accountability, and discernment; to those who wish to choose the highest in life, not the lowest. It is a road-block to a sunny tomorrow and all those children whose future depends on striving to be the best because their institutions have shown them the best.

I have visited some of the children's museums geared to the lowest among us. They are boring, uninspiring, plain, and do not engender the stardust needed for future leaders. I remember the late Senator Patrick Moynihan writing an article about the dumbing down of America and the lasting negative impact it was having on our culture. He wrote how, post-1960s, it was instrumental in paving the way for an underclass. I had invited him to speak in front of a group of rabbis in one of the Senate's hearing rooms. He must have been 6'4", a very affable and urbane Irishman, quite older than me. I introduced him as the Senator-philosopher who had coined the phrase "the dumbing down of America." I thought, perhaps, he might have reconsidered his early article, having been pilloried over it by social justice left-wingers. Towering above me, he put his hand on my shoulder and, in front of everybody, said, "Yes, my dear, young Rabbi Spero is correct in quoting me that the dumbing down of America is one of our greatest tragedies," the cackles of the professional social justice crowd notwithstanding.

Many in the social justice movement believe we middle class, conservative Americans deserve some sort of cultural and economic punishment. For them, our punishment is justice. They call it social justice, but it is social *injustice* to most of us. Americans need not be patronized but set free to rise above their patrons. If we bring our standards down, prosperity, strength, and intellectual vigor will shift to those countries opting for higher standards. What many call "progressive politics" is, as has been eye-witnessed countless times across the world, a regressive, downward slide to soft tyranny and loss of essential freedoms. How can that be called justice?

***

The push for social justice has broadened its mandate to now include providing illegals with free schooling, free medical, welfare, housing, and food allowances—the full basket of freebies paid for by hard-working, play-by-the-rules taxpayers. The professional social justicers cite the Scripture that says: "Do not afflict the stranger" (Leviticus 19:23). How ironic that those so concerned about not afflicting the stranger have had as their mantra the need to afflict the comfortable—the regular citizen.

It seems they have, indeed, been successful in afflicting the comfortable taxpayer. Some schools, emergency rooms, hospitals, and basic services in rural and smaller communities are teetering on bankruptcy or have been shut down in those areas where the overflow of illegals using these services has overwhelmed them. So now, taxpayers can no longer be serviced by institutions they paid for because of their use by those who do not pay for them. But those in the social justice circle need not worry since they do not live in the rural and small town areas affected by these shut downs.

When the Bible in Leviticus spoke of not afflicting the stranger, it meant not to harm or cheat the stranger as was the practice at that time among most foreign societies. It did not mean to fully support the stranger and provide him with more than what you yourself have. Do we call the American middle-class taxpayer afflicted simply because he is not fully supported by government programs? No. Then neither can we be accused of afflicting the stranger simply because we do not wish to fully support him with government programs. If the Bible's definition of "not afflicting" is translated to mean that we must pay for another's entire life, including all members of one's family, then it would have likewise demanded that every citizen in society be fully supported so as not to be a victim of affliction. It didn't.

Clearly, what the Bible meant was that we not afflict the stranger by viewing him as a type of infidel on whom we can inflict the types of cruelties not allowed against a member of the sect. Later, the Bible says, the stranger should not be forced to live by a law inferior to the rest. Here in America, no one would countenance an illegal being beaten up just because he was a stranger. Nor would we say he was not entitled to stand before a judge in a courtroom. We would not have him charged a second time for a crime for which he was already acquitted. But requiring basic protection is a separate category from granting him the benefits of every government program. Only proponents of welfare states equate government handouts as the equivalent of natural law and legal protections.

In ancient Israel, the stranger could, like everyone else, take strands of wheat from the corners of the field the Bible no longer considered the owner's. But the farmer did not have to take from his own money, or earn two salaries, so as to fully support the entire economic, medical, and family needs of the stranger. That was not an entitlement, as the social justice class wishes to claim. If the farmer wanted, he could perform a voluntary act of *charity.* But imagine someone from Outer Mongolia coming to your door and demanding that you fully support him and all his family members. Never would the Bible have opened up society to the suicidal paradigm of having millions of outsiders be allowed simply to storm the country and demand the Israelites fully support them and precipitate their own economic and national demise. In the name of helping A, the Bible never demands that B perish.

When one sees the extent to which the social justice pushers wish to take this country and the harm they are willing to impose, one has to wonder if it is really justice they want. Feed the hungry and clothe the naked, in a moral sense, means providing two or three basic meals and a change or two of clothing. It means soup kitchens, missions, public shelter, foster homes, orphanages, modest clinics, vaccination centers, and limited stipends for families. It does not mean extending benefits equivalent to $50,000 and, in some cases, $85,000. Nor does it mean a basket of benefits surpassing the take-home pay of those being taxed, who now live beneath the scale of those receiving their taxes. There is nothing moral about this.

Neither is it moral for a social justice system to be enforced where hard-working families must limit the amount of children they can have because of their huge tax obligation to support those who trump the system by having as many children as they want, and who view childbirth as a direct avenue for collecting further welfare checks.

There is no justice nor morality in vast amounts of Americans working two or three jobs to pay the taxes required so that entrenched segments of society can live off the sweat of their brow and stay home, receive an additional check for each new child, get babysitting, electric, phones, and cable, an overflow of food, housing, and who knows what more, because they have been told they are entitled. This is middle-class servitude, a type of serfdom. This is a penalization of those who live by the ethos of taking care of one's self and family. None of the above is justice, nor is it even charity. God never saw charity as a *punitive* vehicle for establishing income equality or parity in life. Nor does it seem like equal justice under the law. I think we can agree that this is not what Jesus had in mind when speaking of feeding the hungry and clothing the naked. A note to liberals: regular Americans are people too.

★★★

Too many in the social justice crowd enjoy feeling they are better and more compassionate than the rest of us. Self-righteousness and moral superiority make many feel good, special, and *better* than the rest of us.

Sometimes people ask me: "When will the social justice crowd be satisfied?" I answer, "Probably *never*." Many in the social justice class clamor loudly not only because they make a living from it, but because their personal identity, as someone *more* concerned and *more* compassionate, is wrapped up in it. If they are not out daily advocating, they feel a loss of *important* identity. Much of the noise made by social justice advocates is rooted not in real societal need but in their own personal need for daily self-identification and importance.

I have been around for a while and have seen that though we have enacted almost all of their demands from thirty or forty years ago, every year brings a new set of demands. Having been told that if we did A and B, social justice would be achieved; we are told years later that unless we do C and D too, we will be living in a society with no social justice. The Left needs to continually expand the parameters of social justice to keep it alive, especially after previous demands have been fulfilled. Whereas just a few years ago we were, for example, warned that we needed X amount of billions to achieve social justice; we are now told, since we already gave it, that social justice requires much more. In fact, the social justice Left today is even more critical of America than it was years ago. They are in a self-generated group frenzy that continually criticizes America despite our decades of accommodations to them.

Many people in the social justice class speak endlessly about police brutality. There is something disingenuous and cynical about those who, in moral superiority, are always eager to condemn the police but with the knowledge that the police will always be there to protect them when the time comes. Deep inside, they are confident the police will function not by left-wing rules but commonsense ones. They are quick on the trigger to condemn the military and our soldiers but know their criticism will never affect them personally since the honorable men and women of our military will always be there to defend even their critics. Deep down, they know the military will keep its high standards for combat effectiveness, despite their criticism. Criticism that never puts the critic at any disadvantage or risk and carries no personal downside is *cheap* criticism and mere grandstanding.

I often wonder what would happen if we divided the country in two.

Liberals would live in one half according to the rules they demand of police, taxpayers, the military, and regarding the environment. They would live by socialism and secularism only. Their society would have to live strictly according to each of their man-made rules designed to display their moral superiority. We conservatives would live in the other half. My bet is that after five years, with none of us to pick up the slack for liberalism's mistakes and errant notions, they might live in a social jungle, amid rampant disease and poverty.

★★★

I know many in the left-wing clergy who also feel a need to continually rebuke mainstream America. Acting like prophets of old who chastised their society, they stand on their podiums looking down on us callous-hearted Americans who do not seem to see those receiving, for example, $40,000 worth of government handouts as equivalent to the truly destitute widows and orphans of 2,500 years ago during Jeremiah's time. The truth is that Jeremiah never saw a society as good as ours. America does not need constant rebuke and chastisement.

I call what many of my clergy colleagues do *religious correctness*. They have taken the politically correct and culturally liberal positions and provide them with a religious holiness. They do so because most were liberals before they entered the ministry or rabbinate, or because it is the easy way out. No one gets a bad rap for being *too* compassionate, whereas we conservative clergy are maligned for being mean, coldhearted conservatives, indifferent to the poor and disenfranchised. Religious correctness has gone so far in bowing to politically correct left-wing causes of so-called "justice and compassion" that many are crusading on behalf of terrorist rights and genuflect every time a Muslim organization concocts some bias charge. Like peacocks, they preen how they understand different cultures, something that makes them more compassionate and worldly than the rest of us.

Many religiously correct clergy are promoting the idea that all religions are the same. That is liberalism and pantheism. Pantheism is the belief that although your god is not my god, all gods are acceptable. Religion is about *the* God and His values. The values of Islam are very different than the values of Judaism and Christianity. The values of Allah as depicted in the Koran are different than the values that God bequeathed to us in His sacred Bible. People may have in common the worship of a single deity, but the one they worship can be as different as white is from black.

To see the difference between the One we worship and the values He imparts from theirs, one need only look at the communities made in His behalf. How are Mecca and its people in any way similar to Jerusalem and its people? How are Rome, Lynchburg, Virginia Beach, San Antonio, or even Salt Lake City, and the beliefs and values of its people, similar to Kabul? What liberal religious correctness preaches is spineless and confused political correctness. It is an affront. It is cowardice. It is *religious appeasement*.

Just as the political left-wing is partnering with political Islam, so will the religious Left begin discarding the Judeo-Christian for the Islamo-Christian and, heaven help us, partnering Jesus with their prophet. Already left/liberal rabbis are twinning synagogues and mosques. But why should we be surprised? Just as in biblical times when there were false prophets, in modern times there are false rabbis and false ministers and priests. Indeed the Bible warned about this repeatedly.

As mentioned, no one in our liberal-oriented society gets brownie points for defending the needs of his own group. No one will be lauded for sticking up for the white middle class, and certainly not for defending Christians because the liberal white community relishes charging other whites with racism. By constantly criticizing your own group, you parade your concern and compassion as being so broad that it cannot be contained to your own tribe—it extends beyond and embraces every group or cause outside your tribe. *I am above my own*, *therefore I am better*. But soon, one becomes absolutely indifferent to his own kind. Perhaps this explains the silence of so many liberal ministers and priests over the genocide being perpetrated on African Christians by Muslims.

This selfish need to feel morally superior to the rest of your group is leading to a tragic condition among many left-wing clergy and political activists within the Jewish community—their vociferous campaign to delegitimize Israel. It is a mind-boggling phenomenon that only a few could have imagined. Many liberal clergy and Jewish academicians side with those who wish to dismantle Israel and kill her children. Nothing Israel does is ever good, according to them, and whatever atrocities its enemies do are understandable. (One left-wing Jewish academic claimed the fact that since Israeli soldiers never rape Arab women, contrary to Muslims who capture Jewish girls, it is a sign of how racist the Israelis must be!) The feeling that you are better and more moral is based in bloated egoism and results in an inversion of morality.

There is no question that something else is at play among Jewish left-

129

wingers. They simply can't take the heat. Their liberal world has made Israel a target. Instead of being courageous and standing up for her, they have abandoned her. They are embarrassed in front of their colleagues to defend Israel in the liberal world that has made the Muslim cause, in just about everything, the liberal cause. Islam is the cause célèbre of the Left, the new civil rights cause, precisely because it represents that which is not Western, that which is not American. Leftism today is rooted in anti-Americanism and anti-Israelism.

Instead of acknowledging their own inner weakness and need for introspection, the Left has decided to label Israel's enemies as moral and Israel as not moral. Israel is held accountable for everything while its enemies are held accountable for nothing. They have created this *inverse morality* by demanding from Israel an unattainable perfection, and from Israel's enemies they demand nothing. It is certainly wrong to be a traitor, but it is worse even to sanctify one's treachery into some new moral paradigm. But the Lord works in mysterious ways. For every Jewish leftist who seeks to destroy Israel, God has given Israel three-fold in Christians who befriend her: "And five of you shall chase a hundred" (Leviticus 26:8).

I knew this day was coming since I had witnessed how for decades the Left had always found fault with America but never communist Russia. We think the Left are creatures of wrong politics when actually, they are creatures of their own distorted thinking.

FIFTEEN

War

[*Defending citizens takes moral precedence.*]

War is the necessary action a government undertakes when a country and its citizens have been attacked. Defending its citizens is the first and primary responsibility and obligation of government. It is based on the moral reciprocity in a relationship where the people grant office to officials in return for those officials protecting them.

The protection of citizens is certainly not achieved through disarmament, though progressive politicians like to claim so, inasmuch as disarmament treaties fit their notion that peace is achieved "if we just get along," in other words, appeasement. Progressives also believe it is annoying when one nation, especially America, is a superpower because they have long felt that America is not morally better than other nations (after all, we are not socialist) and does not deserve to be in a position above other nations. Thus, back in the 1980s, many progressives were denouncing the assertion put forth by Ronald Reagan that it was good for America to pass the Soviet Union in superpower status. Just as progressives believe in economic sameness, they similarly believe in parity of military power between antagonists.

During the Grenada invasion of the 1980s, when Ronald Reagan successfully sent in our military to rescue American students held by Grenada's communist regime, Jesse Jackson and like-minded others wailed at the unfairness of America using its overpowering military strength to rescue the students. Instead, Jackson wanted negotiations, for negotiations imply sameness and equal footing, something ideologically and emotionally comforting to progressives. It is as if life is but a game, and it is unfair when one side has an advantage over the other, especially if that advantage is held by capitalist America. Military superiority by capitalist America is a verification of how capitalism (as a result of the Judeo-Christian ethos) is the single best mechanism not only for producing wealth but for protection as well. This knowledge sticks in the craw of those, like Jackson, who like neither capitalism nor our unique and historic American approach to life with the values of a society built by those Dead White Males, known to us as the Founders.

Some liberal politicians and opinion shapers are embarrassed by superior American military power because it demarcates us from others. They believe power in itself is something nefariously gained, except of course, if that power is used on behalf of socialist and liberation causes they endorse. Rarely, since 1965, have they supported military action for purposes beneficial to America only but have done so only when our men and women in uniform were deployed to liberate other peoples living under dictatorial oppression. In such instances, the use of American power was, for them, not embarrassing. In other words, the use of the American military for non-American needs or non-American human rights situations is, for them, the proper use of the American military. It is our service to others. For a while, our war on terror was acceptable to them because the terrorists affected other countries and peoples too.

Many in the diplomatic corps, the striped pants fraternity, would negotiate endlessly before conceding it was time to hand the situation over to the military. After all, their stature and career longevity depends entirely on the jawboning process, even if it results in ridiculous concessions on our part in order to keep them center stage.

As we have seen, any freely chosen relationship brings with it obligations, and the President is to protect and defend the people from outside enemies. Presidents freely choose to run for office and are thus morally obligated to fulfill their part in their reciprocal arrangement with the people. As Commander-in-Chief, a President's first moral obligation is to his soldiers, making sure that when they go into battle, everything is done to protect and spare their lives over the lives of the enemy. While we need not indiscriminately kill, a President is morally obligated to put America's sons and daughters above those of the enemy. These soldiers are our brothers, cousins, fathers, and sons. Any President uncomfortable with putting our combat soldiers first should apply, instead, for the job of Secretary General of the United Nations, where he will not have to make the partisan decision of putting American soldiers above general humanitarian interests.

Many of us are aware how our American soldiers on the battlefields of Iraq and Afghanistan have had their hands tied from doing what is needed to protect themselves as opposed to worrying about what are called innocent populations. These rules of engagement have come from the very top. I have personally heard the stories and frustration of returning soldiers who spoke of unnecessary combat injuries and deaths to our soldiers due to these rules of engagement. Millions of Americans are sickened by the suffocating rules imposed on our soldiers and the consequences to families who must live with the devastating by-product of these politically correct concerns. Our soldiers are not serial numbers, there to die in service to the locals but whose own health and lives are but secondary. How many orphans, widows, and forever bereaved families stateside must be made in sacrifice to the twisted liberal morality that cares more about the enemy than our own? In Orwellian fashion, some liberal elitists have redefined military courage as restraint on the battlefield.

In the moral context, I simply cannot laud a policy that places concern for others over the primary moral obligation to protect the lives and fate of soldiers under the auspices of a leader freely choosing to be Commander-in-Chief. His moral obligation is to them first. Soldiers should not be placed in combat situations where decisions on behalf of their lives are decided by lawyers who lean toward what the international community might favor. If general humanitarianism is their prime motivation, they should work for the U.N. Our obligation is first and foremost to the American soldier fighting in the American army.

In war, we try not to be cruel. But in battle, it is not cruel to think of your life and the lives of your men first. Saving yourself is not done out of a desire to be cruel but to remain alive. The rules of war are different from the rules of civic life and even the rules that are operational in police work and in the apprehension of criminals. In civic life, killing is a rarity, and we try to avoid it, but in war the overriding and natural condition is killing. If not focused directly and exclusively on saving yourself and your men, you will be killed by the natural condition surrounding soldiers in war, which is killing. It is not cruel to be thinking of yourself or your men instead of sparing a mosque or Islamic holy place, as some have been ordered—their bricks trumping our flesh and blood. Going house to house, instead of bombing from above, so as to spare those deemed innocent (who may well be in league with the enemy) is a reckless endangerment of American life. Too many soldiers have been maimed or killed that way.

Many in the liberal world see war as an action against criminals and

133

impose impossible police guidelines on our soldiers that are more apt for civic life. Some see them as a meals-on-wheels enterprise, as was the case when President Clinton sent them to Somalia, a naiveté resulting in the tragedy of Blackhawk Down. Today, some see them as a type of social worker. But soldiers are not social workers. If liberals want social workers, then strap helmets on the heads of those from New York's New School of Social Work and send them over to do the social work of the killing fields. So much of the problem besetting our war policy is that those in leadership come from backgrounds that give them no idea of what the military and war is all about.

★★★

A pivotal device for saving American lives comes from the intelligence we gather. Some who wish to remain innocent delude themselves into thinking that our intelligence needs can be met through spy satellites alone. We know, however, that our best intelligence and discovery of terrorist plots and plans have come through our interrogation of captured terrorists. Terrorists do not fork over such information voluntarily—they need to be induced. It is the President's duty to make sure we have that intelligence because it saves American lives. Under President Obama, however, there has been but scant interrogation of captured terrorists.

Those opposed to waterboarding call it torture. I do not agree. There is no lasting negative affect from waterboarding; in fact, some of our soldiers undergo it during their own training. There is no burning, hitting, nothing brutally physical in its pain. It is mostly psychological. It is not pleasant, but it is not torture. We do not administer it to be cruel but to gain information that will save the lives of our people and citizens. Unlike the enemy we are fighting who actually tortures for the grotesque pleasure they get from watching people cry out in pain, we do not. Their torture consists in the actual infliction of pain through burning, maiming, and other atrocities with lasting bodily effects. Waterboarding does not. Yet some still like to call it torture. But just because someone calls it torture, does not make it so.

And who was it that we waterboarded? A terrorist behind 9/11 that killed three thousand innocent Americans, sliced the throat of Daniel Pearl, and decapitated many others. Besides getting information from him, it seems a small, momentary discomfort and punishment for the crime of slaughtering innocent Americans.

Those who claim that if we waterboard, we are "no better than the enemy" are purposely trying to undermine us. Any American, no matter his political office or social standing, unable to distinguish between who we are and who our enemies are lacks moral clarity. Anybody who centers the difference between three hundred years of American history and that of Arabia on one issue called waterboarding lacks basic discernment.

But the crucial point is the moral one: It certainly is morally acceptable to place someone in a few minutes of discomfort if by so doing you save the lives of thousands of innocent people. The lives of tens of thousands are a more important consideration than the discomfort of a terrorist murderer. Those who disagree are morally challenged and victims of liberal *moral inversion*. Some care more about their image with Paris or Oslo than what is needed to save American lives. Many want to be in a position beyond any international reproach, even beyond reproach from Muslim countries. There is no question in my mind that left-wing radicals would be OK with waterboarding a white supremacist in order to discover a plot to incinerate a million from whatever they envision.

To many of our elites, the sensitivities of captured Muslim terrorists loom larger than the lives of Americans. Too many regard the honor of Islam more than the survival of Americans. When does it come time to accord honor to Americans? They speak of compassion, but when it really counts, they show more compassion for the terrorist than for Aunt Betty on Walnut Street. They may answer that it is not so, but the proof is in the pudding. We are not even to eavesdrop on the cellular calls between terrorists because of their so-called civil rights.

If someone from Mars was looking down and saw a civilization where thousands of a nation's sweet children could be saved from death, and all that was required was a terrorist (who wishes to kill them) be put under water for a few moments, they would wonder as to the sanity and morality of a people who would not do such a thing. Such a society should not be lauded for its humanitarian concern but rebuked for not loving its children enough.

Leftism is the polar opposite of Judeo-Christian morality. When one begins moving away from biblical morality, the other road traveled leads often to the gates of *Gehenom* (hell). I knew the grandfather of a man who devotes himself now to protecting the rights of terrorists, disregarding the safety of the American people. The grandfather was a religious Jew from Poland, near the Russian border who died more than thirty-five years ago.

He gave millions to charity. He would be turning over in his grave if he knew that his grandson had been so captured by leftist ideology that he devotes himself to representing the very murderers who want to kill Americans and destroy Israel and every Jew on the planet. He has gone over to the other side. I am forever astonished and perplexed by what self-hate does to a person.

Mr. Obama, according to reports, is against almost any form of interrogation. A March 2012 column in *The Wall Street Journal* indicated that Mr. Obama prefers drone strikes that kill terrorists as opposed to taking them alive and bringing them back for interrogation. He dislikes GITMO and other detention centers overseas because of what the world will say about the heavy hand of interrogation. As a result, according to this column, just about all the information we have regarding terrorist plots is from the Bush years. The U.S. is not able to obtain much current information. Michael Mukasey, U.S. attorney general from 2007-2009, reiterated this in a May 1, 2012, Op-ed in the *Journal*, saying "refilling our available intelligence apparatus is of no importance to a President who on his second day in office signed an order that results in no classified interrogation program. We are dipping into our past [Bush] reservoir." If this peculiar value system results in the death of Americans who could have been otherwise saved, I think it constitutes actual immorality.

Jose Rodriguez led the team of those interrogating Khalid Sheikh Mohammed, the mastermind behind 9/11. He states unequivocally that our enhanced interrogation methods yielded information that led to the capture of Bin Laden and revealed future plots we were able to foil, thereby saving countless American lives. Yet in 2009 and again in 2011, Mr. Obama spoke of outlawing enhanced interrogations saying it is "not who we are." And he did outlaw it. We do know that our enemy cares little about their women and children, placing them in front of themselves during battle as shields. We, on the other hand, protect first our women and children. If some ten to thirty second waterboarding or sleep deprivation is all it takes to save our women and children, then we need to do it. You see, Mr. President, protecting our women and children is *who we are*.

★★★

During the last ten years of our war on terror, we Americans have seen the astonishing campaign of many within politically liberal circles standing against any of our government's efforts to secure our protection. No sooner does the government do something than outfits calling themselves civil rights organizations go to court to stop us from protecting ourselves. They have become the enemy of our soldiers on the battlefields and enemies of Americans wishing to protect themselves from jihadists hellbent on killing us.

As I have mentioned before, no one in today's Western world gets brownie points for sticking up for his own group. Loyalty is labeled tribalism; it doesn't count. The exception, of course, is if it's done by groups outside the conservative mainstream. In such cases it is called pride. Many liberal activists live by an all-consuming self-righteous vanity in need of showing they are more moral than the rest of us. They show their moral superiority by taking up the causes of those outside the tribe, and these days nothing seems to represent that more than taking up the cause of Muslims. Those on the Left showcase themselves as being morally and intellectually better than us by taking the side of our enemies. That it results in risk to fellow American means nothing to those so intoxicated by their own so-called superiority. They can do this to fellow Americans because they consider themselves apart and above the American population, crusaders in causes that are, in their mind, more worthy than mere Americanism.

We in the Jewish community, as is becoming more apparent each day, have also suffered from the hands of those wishing to boast of their moral superiority. It is now the fashion in left-wing Jewish circles and among left-wing rabbis to be anti-Israel. This makes them stand above us tribalists who live by a respect and love for Israel. Every time an Arab sneezes, they condemn Israel but remain silent when Israelis are rocketed by Hamas and Jewish children and families are blown to smithereens in their homes and cafes. To show how they have risen above mere tribalism, they have initiated boycotts against Israel, lobbied Congress against Israel, and remained utterly silent and complacent to the calls of Islamists to destroy Israel and Jewish people around the world. Perversely they are not condemned by many in the establishment Jewish organizations who live in the world of absolute, liberal political correctness.

These liberal Jews call what they do courageous when, in fact, it is nothing of the kind. In the insular left-wing world they inhabit, such as academia, liberal political activism, the international and Islamic set—the only circle they care about—they are celebrated and given honor they could not achieve among commonsense, patriotic groups. What would be courageous is if they stood up against their left-wing clique so fashionably anti-Israel and worked hard to support Israel instead of doing the morally weak and easy thing of becoming part of the mob against it. This is the perfidy that arises from those whose self-centeredness and false sense of moral superiority guides whatever they do.

These moral superiorists boast of their unparalleled understanding that we plebeians do not possess. They even understand the jihadists' desire to destroy Israel as well as those Jews around the world supportive of Israel. Vain fools that they are, they think they will be spared and enjoy an ever-lasting friendship in the transnational caliphate of tolerant multicultural brotherhood.

Even in the Christian community, it would be heartening to see a greater outcry against the wholesale slaughter by Islam against Christians in Africa and other parts of the world. Entire Christian communities, each hundreds or almost two thousand years old, from Iraq to Tunisia, from Turkey to Sudan, are being wiped away. The few Christian leaders who have spoken out on behalf of brutalized Christian brothers are labeled Islamophobes. If you demand Islam stop the killing, you are, in the eyes of elitist liberals, guilty of something much greater than the killing itself, namely, criticizing Islam.

★★★

It seems no one gets moral credit when defending their own, not in today's liberal politically correct West. Political correctness is ignoring the rights and needs of your own on the altar of what is best for those outside your group. Human rights, civil rights, and all the platitudes emanating from the Left, are selective and not objective. The Left, so eager in its demands for equality, has an unequal concern when it comes to the application of these rights. Their compassion is limited, it seems, to those arrayed against us, not those who stand with us.

The Talmud offers a very pithy and profound insight to this sad situation. It says: "Those who display compassion to those who are cruel end up showing no compassion, indeed cruelty, to those who actually deserve compassion." There is great depth to what the Talmud says. When we begin investing our emotions and compassion in those who do not deserve it, we eventually identify with them and their cause because so much of it is now in us. We begin seeing what they wish us to see. We understand them. Soon we see only their side and become indifferent to those whom they have declared their enemy. Finally, in our new tunnel vision, we start hating those they hate. We become cruel to those who deserve compassion, for we no longer see them as worthwhile. Many on the Left did not begin being indifferent to regular Americans. They began with a personal need to show compassion to the cruel or belligerent out of a sense of being morally superior to the rest of us. But once on the road, they could not turn back. It is important, therefore, that we stand back, wait, and really assess to whom we are offering our compassion, and what they are *really* all about.

There is something even deeper than this. The Talmud is telling us that those who extend compassion to the cruel are actually, to begin with, soulmates of the cruel. It is not something that comes step-by-step, but a simpatico already there, endemic from the start. They are cruel to those who deserve compassion because they always despised them and their cause. They have warped, twisted values.

None on the Left ever seem to have any compassion for regular, hard-working, honest, religious Americans. They dislike us because they hate our values. They are on the side of our tormentors—those who love to afflict the middle class and call us racists because they are of that ideology, their fancy degrees, fancy language, and fancy clothes notwithstanding. They are on the side of darkness; they have chosen not to fight evil but to be of it. Either it happened step-by-step over their years of understanding, later in their identifying with it, or because that is who they were to begin with.

They claim to be more moral, but they are not; smarter, but are not; more concerned, but it is not so; more compassionate, but select their compassion. We conservatives should stop caring what those on the Left think, especially since they have exposed themselves to be morally bankrupt. If America unravels, it will not come from tanks in the streets but from naively and foolishly listening to those bedeviled by the sins of unadulterated vanity who want to control and lord over us.

SIXTEEN

The Founders

[Inspired men who affirmed Scripture's broad themes]

The Founding Fathers were influenced not only by the great philosophical debates and discussions of their day but by classic schools of thought, including the Bible. Though they did not look to the Bible as a guide for daily ritual practice, they saw in this classic work profound moral themes centered on justice, equality, liberty, and pursuit of happiness, as well as an outline emphasizing local control as opposed to centralized power.

The Old Testament, for example, underscores the paramountcy of the individual and its corollary of personal responsibility, both crucial elements in shaping what was to become a unique civilization: America.

In Deuteronomy 24:16 it is written: "Each human by his own sin is to be judged." In other words, people are judged as individuals, not as members of groups. We further read in Deuteronomy, 24:16: "Do not punish children for the sins of their fathers." These two verses underscore how, when it comes to the law, we are free of group identity and even family identity. This emphasis on the individual is in sharp contrast to how for most of the history of mankind, the fate of the individual was tied to things beyond him, such as group and family identity.

The overriding importance of liberty to those within a nation is highlighted in Leviticus 25:10, which states: "Proclaim liberty throughout the land and to all the inhabitants thereof." Liberty is not reserved for a particular class nor based on one's being politically correct but is a God-given right to all within our society.

It is similarly so regarding man's ownership of his own life. The Old Testament often remarks: "Therefore choose life" as well as "The law is given so as to live" (Deuteronomy 30:19). Man's right to life and liberty are salient biblical aspirations.

Throughout the Old Testament, an acknowledgment and respect for private property is promoted: "And each man shall sit under *his* vine and under *his* fig tree"; and "He shall till *his* field," or *his* property, *his* estate, *their* inheritance. All this rounds out to: *Life, Liberty*, and the *Pursuit of Happiness* (private property). As we will examine later, Deuteronomy clearly emphasized man's attachment to his house and field—his property—and honored that part of human nature.

Wealth is seen as a blessing, not something shameful nor a cause for guilt. Charity given from one to another is an essential and abiding feature of the Bible, but collectivism and the nationalizing of production were never biblical paradigms.

A majority of the Old Testament's directives are addressed to the individual, "And you…" you in the singular, not the collective. And that's because the Bible is not determinist in outlook but believes in free will. People are not viewed as entities within a great mass, rather as individuals. As individuals, they must choose freely and be responsible for the choices they make. This sets the Old Testament apart from those religions that endorse either submission, collectivism, or determinism where man is but a victim of his circumstances.

This motif originates in Genesis: "And man was created in the image of God," in other words, with individuality, creative intelligence, and moral responsibility. His destiny is very much tied to his making proper choices. This is a very American theme and something outside the general pale of European thinking and the socialism that grew from it.

Much of the above constitutes Americanism and distinguishes our American Revolution from the emotions and principles that fired up the French Revolution. Besides, the French Revolution was driven by a rejection of religion that had sponsored the old-line monarchies, while the American Revolution, in contra-distinction, embraced the broad themes of the Old and New Testaments that supplied promise to our Founders.

Because the Founders envisioned a nation where the individual was to live in liberty and freely choose his way of life, they were adamantly opposed to a government that ruled top-down, preferring instead a structure built on local control, one more amenable to the role and rights of the individual. In the Old Testament they saw a model for a loose confederation. In ancient Israel, there were thirteen tribes (including Levi), each living by their distinct habits, loosely confederated, similar to the notion of state's rights found among the original thirteen colonies tethered to a central government only in areas of war and treaties for the purpose of common defense.

The Old Testament had much to say regarding the architecture of government. In Deuteronomy 16:18 we are told: "Judges and officers shall be set in each of thy city gates." This was a model for local control, where laws of daily life and routine are set by local people, while only questions of war or other national and capital issues were decided by the Great Court in Jerusalem. As James Madison and others saw it, local control provides *domestic tranquility*, for it doesn't force communities to subdue or shed their heartfelt convictions and mores on very personal issues to a centralized power. These great men, who had no desire to control others, understood the danger to human autonomy and self-respect that comes from monolithic uniformity, especially a uniformity created in the image of faraway elites or a governing clique deciding how we the people should conduct each aspect of our life.

Our whole form of government rests on state's rights and on localities deciding the personal issues of life, such as marriage, divorce, gun laws, driving, and punishment for crimes, schools, or abortion. These matters should be left to state legislatures. The Founders recognized, as Madison told us, that for domestic tranquility to prevail, it is essential that the personal issues of life not be decided under a monolithic, national one-size-fits-all edict, but be left, instead, to localities and states that better reflect the wishes of the people within these freely chosen districts. It should be a government where the people have a voice, a situation where the personal aspects of life are decided by the local people themselves. The people should not be stifled. Paradigms that give people greater decision over how they choose to live are moral paradigms.

The serious problem we have in America today is that of one or two state judges disenfranchising the people from exercising their voice and will. It is now commonplace for one judge within a state to overturn the will of millions of people, doing so after the issue has been publicly debated and its constitutional questions discussed as part of that robust public debate. These individual judges are ruling by fiat. They are hijacking the votes of the people.

They decide according to their own personal belief, and how they think society should live, and espouse their antagonism to what the people have decided by charging the voters with having "acted unconstitutionally."

These judges do not offer any new, previously unheard of constitutional rationales. The people and legal scholars have already weighed in on every aspect of the constitutionality of these issues before these measures are even put on the ballot. We have seen how judges can be arbitrary and contradictory in their decisions, picking and choosing legal principles, inventing anything out of thin air to justify their decisions.

Be it regarding marriage, parental notification, or mandating a full array of benefits to illegals at the expense of the taxpayers (services not offered for free to the taxpayer himself), individual judges are daily thwarting the will of the people. Illegals seem to have more rights than parents who are citizens. These judges have arrogated to themselves veto power. They have assigned themselves the status of State Executives, not satisfied with their limited authority as but local judges. They are not, however, the Supreme Court.

I am sure the Founding Fathers would agree with me. When the Republic began, there were probably three million people in the country. The Founders would not have allowed one man to decide by himself the rules of the nation's daily life. They made a revolution precisely to overcome one-man rule. They did not even give the President unlimited power. He was not to be another King George. Today we have more people voting on behalf of these issues than lived during the time of the founding of our nation. It seems impossible that the Founders would have granted to one man, a judge, the power to overrule the expressed and voted-upon wishes of the people. Would they have given one man power over the will of the tens of millions voting in our present day referendums when they were unwilling to do so over a mere million? Absolutely not.

★★★

Even the contours of the Executive, so ably determined and demonstrated by George Washington, were reminiscent of the Hebrew kings whose powers, as recounted in Deuteronomy, were limited and who had to live by the same laws as every citizen. Though the Hebrew kings, like our President, had certain prerogatives and privileges, they were to eschew, while in office, an extravagance and ostentation that set them too far above the people: "His heart shall not be lifted above his brethren" (Deuteronomy 17:20).

In addition, so as to identify personally with the ethos and people of the country, the President had to be American born and raised, as is found in the Old Testament command that "Ye shall take a king from among your brothers" (Deuteronomy 17:15). This in contrast to the monarchial situation in Europe where countries were often, through marriage, ruled by foreign families. The Founders were aware that the philosophy they envisioned regarding society and the place of the individual within it was unique and not always fully understood and shared by those coming from outside American territory.

The original Pilgrims of 1620 and 1630 heard sermons from William Bradford and John Winthrop declaring the establishment of this colony as a new Promised Land and identified with the ancient Israelites who knew the time had come to declare their deliverance from "Egypt and Pharaoh." They had "crossed a modern day Red Sea to a New Zion." The Founders saw their independence from King George as that of the Israelites and Moses and proposed a seal with the biblical Pillar of Fire, encaptioned: "Rebellion to Tyrants Is Obedience to God." No man was to have such arbitrary power over the citizens. So attached were they to this piece of biblical history that the Ten Commandments and *In God We Trust* were enshrined as national touchstones and sentiments.

The majestic themes that guide our country are found in the Declaration of Independence, while the structure and organization of a government most suitable to enable those themes are outlined in our Constitution. Later a Bill of Rights was added. What did the Declaration mean when it proclaimed *All men are created equal?* Did it mean, as the French *philosophes* and later Marxists claimed, that all men were to possess material things equally? Our Founders said no. All men achieve equality when no law is devised and enforced that would preclude a particular individual from *pursuing* his happiness. In other words, equality means equal justice and equal opportunity under the law. This is a direct gleaning from the Old Testament.

I have no doubt that the following three verses from the Bible clarified for our Founders the meaning of equality. In Exodus 12:50, it states: "One law for all the citizens that reside therein." Later in Deuteronomy 16:19 it says: "And ye shall judge them all the same—do not favor one over the other, do not alter your judgment." Indeed, in another section of Exodus 23:16 it states: "Do not favor the rich, nor the poor." Nothing is a more compelling illumination of what constitutes equality than these three verses: justice under the law. All men are created equal is made real by living under one set of laws for all.

★★★

Much of what separates our Founding from how other countries operate is rooted in how the Founders understood the nature of man. John Knox and John Calvin, John Locke and Thomas Reid, indeed Isaac Newton himself, were great admirers of the Old Testament and, therefore, reached conclusions vastly different from Rousseau and Voltaire as to the nature of man and, thus, what type of society and form of government would facilitate the best in man.

Beyond doubt, the Founders were influenced by Montesquieu's notion of a separation of powers between three branches of government: a system of checks and balances. Equally were they influenced by Locke's propositions of free will and life, liberty, and a right to personal property, as well as his call for government deriving its power only from the consent of the governed. But they were *moved* by the Bible, especially those elements that matched their philosophic predispositions.

They saw the nuclear family unit as central to the maintenance and survival of society, something more important than the hierarchal institutions of state or church. An abundance of Old Testament citations and commands are directed not to the state, not to the religious institutions, nor to a special ruling class—but to the family: "A Passover to the Household," and "Each *family* according to its history" (Exodus 12:3). Family as a unit is central to the Judeo-Christian ethos more than in other ideologies.

In classic philosophy, the family unit takes on more importance than is found in the romantic (social) philosophies of France and Germany. As mentioned, the Founders deliberately rejected the French philosophers and chose instead the classic philosophy of Aristotle, a philosophy grounded in human nature and not utopian social theories. The great professor of philosophy and psychology, Daniel Robinson, once quipped that one sees the difference between classic philosophy (human nature) and those of France and later Germany (social utopias) through the following: "In his will, Aristotle asked to be buried next to his wife, while Hegel [a German social philosopher] wished to be buried next to Fichte, an 18th Century philosopher he admired."

Though many wish to claim that the Founders were not influenced by religion, history refutes this. Indeed, the foundational American principles of work and productivity as virtues and pillars are rooted in the Protestant work ethic, found in Exodus, which sees in work a religious mandate, something noble and virtuous: "Six days shall ye work" (Deuteronomy 5:13). Many other cultures see in work something demeaning and certainly not a religious goal.

Similarly, believing in individual responsibility, our Founders—be it Adams, Washington, Madison, and even Jefferson—insisted that for liberty to survive a society must live by a moral code. Our founders and pioneers referenced the Bible and God as the fountainhead for living by the essential traits of prudence and morality. Furthermore, our rights come from God, not men: "See, I have set before you this day, life and good" (Deuteronomy 30:19).

The miracle of the Philadelphia story is how such a large group of men, scattered from different parts of the country, were able to come together during a singular, propitious moment in history and create what was never created before. It was an idea monumental in its fusion of philosophy, religion, law, sociology, and morals. They brought forth a Republic, not born in anarchy, meanness, and violence to its people, as was the case with the French Revolution. The Constitution was something workable for the ages—a once-in-history gift to citizens, as long as the people continued embracing it and did not set themselves above it.

Walking through the streets of Philadelphia, as our family did two summers ago, and seeing the streets where these great men had come to discuss, debate, and conclude, one is struck by the sheer Providence that graced this moment and place—and these men. Aside from Mount Sinai itself, I know of nowhere and nothing else where divine inspiration was so revealed. Like Sinai, it was complete and for the ages.

Years later, as these men separated, each continued with their special talents, but never again did any reach the summit they had together climbed in Philadelphia. For several years, between 1774-1789, these men as a group touched the sublime and drank from a spirit rivaling the prophets of old. As an ordained assembly, each achieved a majesty that none could have possessed by themselves alone. We are the fortunate heirs to this providential moment where intellect, spirit, emotion, and reason combined as no mortal moment before. From it was born a nation and a godly ethos.

★★★

Aside from a refreshing moral clarity, America believes in ethics, the principle of telling the truth and dealing honestly. Commerce and business flourish, and so do we all, when there is a national ethos of openness and telling the truth. Such an ethos makes for trust among neighbors and those interacting. Trust and honesty, as national characteristics, make life easier, sweeter, and more productive.

We assume all societies operate similarly by such an ethic. Not so. In Islam, for example, there is a rule called *taquiah*, which means one can lie on behalf of advancing the Islamic religion. When one takes into account that just about everything in Islamic society is tied to religion, the use of *taquiah* becomes widespread and permeates much of daily life. Furthermore, cultural guidelines, everywhere, are influenced by religious guidelines and attitudes. That being the case, a religion urging *taquiah* results in a rather sly culture, a day-to-day life lacking forthrightness and plain honesty.

The American penchant for candid straight talk grew out of a religious culture rooted in: "Be forthright in your talk" (Deuteronomy 23:24) and "Remove yourself from speaking falsehood" (Exodus 23:7). Movie roles by Gary Cooper and John Wayne are terrific indicators of how religious ideals end up becoming cultural norms and touchstones. Religious ideals shape the personality and character of a nation and its individuals.

We are fortunate and blessed to be heirs of this noble heritage we call Americanism. We took it for granted and sometimes assumed that most Western countries lived by the same ethos. Accordingly, too few stopped to take the time and contemplate what precisely has made America wonderfully exceptional—awesome in its power while sweet in its idealism and good will. Indeed what we most often hear from liberals is how unfair we are, how blameworthy we are for almost everything. That is hogwash.

Now that our country is under nonstop assault from within, and there is, for the first time in our history, talk of transforming the country, it's best that we first know what has been the specific philosophic engine that has brought us such across-the-board prosperity, freedom, and physical security, lest those with malevolent designs rob us of those things we hold dear, including our historic morality. For up until recently, we Americans, our leaders, and Presidents possessed this moral clarity.

★★★ SEVENTEEN ★★★

God-Given Liberty

[*The God who gave us life gave us liberty.*]

Because of our Judeo-Christian outlook, the United States has stood separately, and in distinction, from much of the rest of the world in determining what is right and what is wrong. Looking at the U.N., we see the U.S. position rarely supported by other nations, with the exception of Israel and some European governments when under a conservative leader. It is no surprise that communist, Islamic, hard-core socialist, and authoritarian governments have not voted with us. They operate by a value system completely different and at odds with ours. Our Judeo-Christian culture looks at morality and what *ought* to be—at what is right and what is wrong—through a different lens than other religions and ideologies do. As mentioned previously, cultural attitudes derive from religious attitudes. The unique aspects of the Judeo-Christian religious view demarcates it from the cultural perspectives and attitudes found in other parts of the political world.

It has become clear to most that the Obama administration has veered dramatically from historic American foreign policy: it supports the dangerous Muslim Brotherhood; it feels cozier with Russia and Hugo Chavez than it does with England and Germany; it has been belligerent to Israel; it has failed to support democracy movements in Iran and has not shown seriousness nor a heartfelt desire to stop Iran's nuclear bomb development; and it has coddled authoritarian leaders while standing against leaders, though imperfect, who have tried to be friendly to the United States. Does all this indicate that Mr. Obama and his appointees subscribe to a morality far removed from the Judeo-Christian value system that has guided this country's foreign policy until now? Does Mr. Obama construe right and wrong and what ought to be by a very un-American, non Judeo-Christian outlook?

I would have to say Mr. Obama's outlook does differ from the historic American ethos and that his view of what is moral differs from what is found in the Judeo-Christian vision of morality. Judeo-Christian morality is centered on *liberty* and the right of the *individual*. Mr. Obama, in contrast, like all hard core socialists, is focused on *top-down control* and favors the rights of *groups* and the causes of those groups. He has more emotional simpatico for leaders, who in the name of "the people," exercise their authority with a command and control attitude. Top-down control and authority provides him the means to empower groups and causes he deems worthy and whose *political time has come*. This is the *revolutionary* part that defines the inner political man of Barack Obama (separate from who he may be as a regular family man).

For Mr. Obama, the *time had come for Islamism*, a "worthy" cause in his mind, to take control of the lives of Muslims in Egypt. He quickly called for the removal of Hosni Mubarak, the leader flawed but friendly to America. He knew, as we all did, the Muslim Brotherhood would soon begin to gain power and command and control, on behalf of the Islamist cause. Indeed it has already happened. It was obvious from the start, and I said so at the time during a radio interview on a D.C. station. Putin in Russia controls from the top as does Chavez in Venezuela. As with all hard-core socialists, such control is deemed worthy since it is done in the name of the people. The image problem other dictators have is in their failure to announce that what they are doing is on behalf of "the people." They forget to tie their authoritarianism to some lofty sounding cause, movement, or ism.

Those who see people not as individuals but as members of preferred groups engage in what is called "identity politics." The Judeo-Christian ethos and Western enlightenment, on the other hand, see people as individuals and do not remove from them their God-given right to live and choose based on their own decisions. The Judeo-Christian ethos demands neither conformity nor erasure of one's innate personality to group identifications made by political leaders. Each man is given his own soul by which to intuit and his own brain by which to think.

Socialist leaders engage in identity politics and group rights, for it brings to them large blocks of immediate power—a power much more difficult to obtain than when appealing to individual people alone. With that power, they push for special group rights and then demand that individuals outside the preferred groups forfeit their rights on behalf of the aspirations of these groups. In the end, identity politics and the cause of the group chip away at the freedoms individual citizens had enjoyed and had taken for granted. The slow removal of individual rights is the end goal of the top-down leader, since the only thing standing in the way of a top-down leader's overwhelming control is the rights that citizens still possess. None of this is moral according to the Judeo-Christian outlook. Leftism is philosophically incompatible with the American Judeo-Christian outlook and a betrayal and frontal assault against that for which our Founders pledged their "lives, fortunes, and sacred honor."

★ ★ ★

Leftists have a different view of morality and what ought to be. In their mind, societies should be controlled by a select, anointed few who rule over the rest of us. Naturally, Mr. Obama and those who put his policies into effect (the clique) convince themselves that what they are doing is in the best interests of the people. But, in truth, it is not in the best interests of *We the People*, and it is high time the vast majority of individual Americans stood up and said we are the people as well.

We are slowly seeing the erosion of our individual rights in deference to group rights. The Black Panthers were given the right by Mr. Obama and his Attorney General to set a Bounty and Dead or Alive warrant against George Zimmerman in Florida, and were allowed to intimidate voters with billy clubs in Philadelphia. Such rights do not exist for other Americans. Mr. Zimmerman's father, a non-minority, was not extended the right to protection from hoodlums outside his door.

In foreign policy, American socialists align with those leaders who preside over their countries in similar controlling fashion. None of this is moral. But for all this to be possible, top-down leaders must first convince the public, and convince us into believing that they are working on behalf of noble and moral "for the people" causes, be it minorities, feminists, Islam, the downtrodden, or the sexually disenfranchised—all *groups*.

Denial of individual rights for group rights directly conflicts with the Declaration of Independence and undermines the Old Testament. Jefferson encapsulated the Declaration and the Bible when he declared: "*The God who gave us life gave us liberty.*" Our rights come from God and not from the state or some supreme leader who decides and assigns rights based on what group we come from or whether a citizen's rights fit into the nationally social-engineered scheme he and the clique envision.

Rights deferred are rights denied and rights selectively provided foretell suspension of most basic rights. This is not some arcane policy issue, but the soul of the Republic itself and heart of a civic heritage bequeathed to us by men far greater in every measure than Mr. Obama. We need not be impressed by Mr. Obama having attended Harvard inasmuch as our Founding Fathers themselves attended Harvard, Princeton, and Yale. God, the Grantor of our liberty, holds greater academic degrees than Mr. Obama, the remover of our liberties. What God has given, may no man take away.

★★★

One incident remains etched in my mind. It was back in 1991 and I was living in lower Manhattan. It was the case of the Central Park Jogger. A young woman had been running on the park's jogger path and was assaulted by a gang of young black men. They gang raped her repeatedly, beat her to a pulp, crushed her bones, and left her for dead. They left the scene joking about what they had done. But somehow she did not die and was spotted and taken to the hospital. After weeks of miraculous surgery, she made a type of comeback.

After a couple of weeks, the parents of the rapists, as well as those in the black political leadership and white liberals, who shape their moral thinking by whatever black political leaders demand on any given day, declared: "It is time to let the 'boys' move on from this incident and go back to the community college so they can continue on with their young lives." Hear this: they should carry on with their lives, while the young woman's future remained in jeopardy, and she forever would feel the horror of being repeatedly raped and mercilessly beaten!

How, I wondered, *do "boys" joke about raping and beating a young woman? How*, I wondered, *do parents and "community leaders" evince such selfishness and callousness to the life of a human being their children nearly destroyed?* It comes out of a sense of entitlement and an ongoing provision of special group rights at the expense of the rights of others. For almost twenty years, mainstream individual Americans—not members of a "group"—were told that they had to forfeit their blue-collar jobs or college slots in the name of affirmative action; then, their children had to endure bussing and leaving neighborhood schools for the sake of others. In Cleveland, for example, business owners were forced out of hamburger franchises they owned so as to sell them (at reduced rates) to minorities in the neighborhood. All of this was demanded of and given by the government. The young men, their parents, and the community leaders got the message: if you were not from a preferred group, a minority, your rights to liberty and property were limited and conditional. Well, it is only a short leap from "I have a right to your job," "I have right to your children's schooling," "I have a right to your business" to, "I have a right to your body and even your life."

Those taught to believe that rights come from government end up believing that, if from the "right" group, they are entitled to whatever they demand. They have no respect for the rights of others. Rights, in their view, are not innate, but conditioned on whoever screams, bullies, and intimidates the loudest. *We have* a *right to her*, so now let the boys move on with their lives, schooling, and jobs. We need to assert and be ever vigilant regarding our God-given rights as individuals. Forfeiting any individual right in the name of the "more important" cause of preferred groups can never be countenanced—not even one right.

As we have seen one sure-fire way of convincing people to forfeit their individual rights on behalf of the group is to attack them with guilt and responsibility for the group's plight. Another way is to assert that the cause of the group is the more moral one. How is that achieved? Liberal politicians, social workers, and many clergymen know the formula. It is by placing that group into an already predetermined moral category, assigning them victim status and automatic nobility because of the group they come from. It goes like this: if you are from those perceived as less powerful, automatically you carry the moral high ground. You have been oppressed and are a victim. Your group constitutes "the people," those set upon by the harsh and selfish ruling establishment, those of special privilege.

Yet it does not seem to me that victimhood is God's preferred ideal for mankind. The Almighty hopes we make our way in life not by exploiting victimhood but by becoming strong, independent people.

★★★

When men arose in the eighteenth and nineteenth centuries, as now, to construct political systems by which other men could be controlled and their lives socially engineered, they were able to exploit the timeworn antipathies to wealth, power, and war. These hatreds were passed on to them by centuries of attitudes that arose from the absolutist categories of *dualism*, a society-shaping philosophy we will examine in the next chapter.

Karl Marx could speak against wealth, the bourgeoisie (middle class), power, and "wars born of capitalism." He called for class warfare against all these. He could bring society down and restructure it by invoking the old reliable standby: it was "for the people" and "for the poor" just as, a century earlier, Rousseau successfully romanticized and immortalized "the noble savage." Rights would be granted not to the individual but the group he called the working class. Liberty, property, and the pursuit of happiness beyond what the state considered worthy of pursuit were all targets and had to be removed. It was all done, of course, in the name of justice.

Marx spoke of "religion being the opiate of the people," but, as we have seen, *Marxism is the real opiate of the people*. It is the false dream that utopia will arrive by dismantling what others have and redistributing it to the poor and the preferred classes. They no longer would be poor except in liberty. The "taking from others" would not be characterized as greed, but the right to keep your own earnings and that which you owned would be called greed. The state would redefine rights as being only that which advanced the state. It would corrupt language and decide what the "proper" emotions are. This system has failed every time it has been tried, and yet, like a drug, people always fall for it. I pray that America will be the exception.

The public falls for it because those selling it are shrewd and come across as doing it because they love the people. But the people they love do not include those whom they wish to bring down—the successful. The salesmen are looking for a route to power and the people are but their cannon fodder. The salesmen, like Marx himself, are always from an intellectual and upper class that live separate from the people they adore and will remain separate from them throughout the utopian years. They wish to become the new aristocracy. Like all those craving power, they know to say that the powers they want are only those that can help them in their altruistic mission of helping the people.

Who was Karl Marx? He was first and foremost an outsider—a nasty, self-centered, arrogant elitist, and a bad father and husband. He was no lover of people as individuals, but he "loved the masses." He was not the first to propose communism, but he was the first to transform the sociology and philosophy of communism into a scientific formula.

Mr. Marx's inner feeling of being an outsider was central to his formulation of communism. So as to have opportunity in a society that disqualified Jews, Marx's father converted to Christianity. Marx was raised with no

Judaism at all and was not part of the Jewish community. Like many Jews on the Left, Marx rejected anything Jewish and his former people as well. He was a virulent anti-Semite and hated all religion. Yet he was never accepted as an equal in general society. The Europe of 1860 is not the America of 2012. He was a member of no people and was angry at those in the general bourgeoisie society that did not consider him as one of their own. His family had come from Germany, and as an adult he lived in England.

I have long felt that it was this sense of alienation that impelled him to upend the society and the bourgeoisie who eschewed him, and create a new segment called "the people" with whom he could identify, though he never socially aligned himself with them, feeling superior to them as do all elitists. My intuition was confirmed years later when reading *Against the Current*, a series of essays by the noted English philosopher, Isaiah Berlin, himself Jewish. Marx is not the first intellectual, community organizer, or protestor who threw his personal psychological problems onto society through the instrument of revolution.

In light of the deplorable economic and social conditions in Russia and the harsh edicts imposed by the Czar, communism seemed like a new path to utopia. Europe during that period was on the cusp of upheaval, transitioning from a monarchial system to something new. Communism and other leftist political paradigms provided those seeking power the facile ability to do so under the banner of "for the people." But none of these ivory tower thinkers had ever dreamed of how American freedom and free enterprise would reshape the world. They never envisaged an America where workers could become owners and entrepreneurs; where people were no longer cogs in the mills but well-paid individuals exercising their talents; where economic and social opportunity propel upwards the vast majority into a self-sustaining bourgeois, middle class. Americans do not need class warfare in a society where class is not an impediment to success. Class warfare does not seem to me to be God's prescription of justice.

★★★

Even 150 years after Marx and decades of proven American upward mobility, the concept of "for the people" remains, along with the patronizing notion by elites that the people are inadequate and incapable of deciding like adults and shaping their own destiny. Back in 2009 when the Obama administration had taken over General Motors and basically gave it to the unions, the talk show host, Larry King, held a discussion. King remarked how glad he was that Obama would decide for the auto companies what type of cars were best for them to manufacture. King said: "Someone has to make these decisions for the American masses." What a pitiful remark, how condescending, and how utterly ignorant regarding who the American individual is. Larry, we are not "the masses," nor are we incapable of decisions. In fact, during the last three hundred years, it has been the individual American who has made these decisions and created our products. In contrast, top-down, command-and-control societies, run by the all-knowing leader on behalf of the masses, continually languish and fail.

Having spoken twice to Larry King, I can attest that he is not an arrogant man. But Larry lives in the Los Angeles/New York City cocoon and does not know the heartland or the American people. He is part of the liberal milieu that sees the job of those smarter to take care of those below—we of the masses.

I still remember how back in Cleveland, Dennis Kucinich ran for mayor on the platform of "For the people." He did so by vowing to shut down the independent Municipal Lighting Company of Cleveland. In class warfare, "the people" win when they can shut down a business. The wealthy are evil, and the people's power comes from destroying the wealthy. Suddenly, *power*, when used by "the people," is no longer a vice. Thirty years later, the demagoguery we witnessed in Cleveland has moved to D.C. via a detour in Chicago. No matter the evidence of how American Judeo-Christian free enterprise and freedoms benefit people better than anything else ever conceived, elitists, snobs, socialists, and dangerous control mongers will zealously continue their pursuit against us and our heritage—in the name of "the people." Even if the people don't want it.

EIGHTEEN

Victimhood

[*Laying claim to victimhood—the ultimate political prize*]

Why is it that only the poor and less powerful are considered "the people"? Many middle-class, wealthy people are wonderful, kind, and generous human beings, and not all poor people are angels and would not be angels if wealthier. Why is strength or power bad if such strength and power is arrived at legitimately—as is found in the U.S. military—and has come about precisely because great sacrifices were made and discipline enforced, a condition absent those with less power? Why is American power bad in light of how it has come through adhering to the success innate in following the Judeo-Christian paradigm? Others have the option to do so but refuse. Perhaps those weaker are so because they have not been willing to endure the hardships necessary to make one stronger.

In today's liberal politically correct environment, if a group can grab for itself the appellation "minority," it has won the game, for society places that group into a type of automatically moral category. But why? Are people from minorities inherently better than those from the majority? While a group may be a minority here, Muslims for example, worldwide they may constitute a majority. Do the traits or beliefs of an individual suddenly change the moment they transfer from majority group status to minority group status? And why are persecuted Christians in Africa not considered a minority?

The answer to all this lies in what is called *dualism*, which is the simple classification of things into either bad or good, placing just about everything into predetermined, easy moral categories. Plato (Greece) and Zoroastrianism (Persia) were guided by dualism. They believed there were predetermined categories of light and darkness, good and evil. What dualism lacks, though, is discernment. For the convenience of categorization, it relinquishes discernability.

Persia and Greece, both powerhouses during their times, had profound influence on Western civilization and thought through this ideology. Dualism divides the body and soul into two polar opposites: the material and spiritual into competitive entities; the good and bad into irreducible elements; and the moral and immoral as irreconcilable. Different civilizations may have filled these categories with different content, but the system of duality, either all good or all bad, remained. Judaism, which preceded both philosophies, resisted the onslaught of dualism, as we will later explain.

Dualism had its merits in answering the age-old question of how a good God could allow evil. Their answer being that there is a force of evil separate from the good, that works independently and contrary to God. Men, even non-biblical men, were always confronted by how we rise above the material to reach that which is spiritual, and how we ascend beyond the physical to touch that which is the soul. The answer lies in separating the two, the body from the soul, and keeping the earthly and material apart from the heavenly and spiritual. To attain spirit and nourish the soul, it was felt that man had to *renounce* the earthly and physical cravings.

The apostle Paul was heavily influenced by Plato, the philosopher having preceded him by almost four hundred years and prevalent among the thinking of the Greek colonies, Antioch and Asia Minor, that Paul traversed during his work on behalf of the Church. The early Church fathers also relied heavily on the philosophy of Plato, since it was centuries until Church philosophy adopted, along the lines of Thomas Aquinas, the views of Aristotle with his emphasis on the individual and personal virtue through action. The late Pope John Paul II and the current Pope Benedict have displayed a great respect for Aristotle. In fact, with the full embrace of Thomas in the mid 1500s, Platonism was in many ways rejected and Aristotelianism was elevated, and the groundwork was laid for a refreshed and vibrant Judeo-Christian ethos.

Renunciation was never part of biblical Judaism. Mainstream Judaism believed in taking that which was mundane and sanctifying it; not separating the soul from the body but attempting to reconcile them by utilizing the earthly things of flesh and blood and elevating them by infusing them with sanctity. There was a fringe sect called the Essenes who did believe in renunciation, but they died out because they would not engage in that which was carnal, without which there is no reproduction. Carnality as a means for reproduction is part of a divinely blueprinted life inasmuch as the Bible itself in Genesis instructs man "to be fruitful and multiply." As to how God allows evil, Judaism looked to the Book of Job, which revolves around the very issue of a righteous man afflicted by what appears to be unwarranted pain and tragedy.

Once in the mode of dualism, however, one can easily fall into the convenient trap of dividing life into good and bad, with those things of an earthly nature being bad and those of a spiritual nature needing separateness from and a renunciation of anything considered earthly. Under such thinking, the proper religious life becomes only that which is ethereal, almost otherworldly. I am inclined to an old *Midrashic* saying: "The world was not created for angels" but for earthly humans whose duty it is to decide "when to" and "when not to." I have always cherished this task as a religious undertaking to find the road to human nobility and majesty in choosing correctly.

Judeo-Christian life is fulfilled not in total renunciation or absolutism but in an engagement that requires ongoing clarifications and choices. One does not dismiss entire categories of life but makes distinctions within categories. Making distinctions requires discernment, and religious discernment comes from wisdom, biblical wisdom. We garner biblical wisdom by poring over biblical stories. The Old Testament is filled with stories that are real, and flesh and blood, for it is in the arena and context of real life that we humans make decisions based on discernment and assessments based on distinctions.

Renunciation is for the select few—for a religious elite. It is an unlikely biblical ideal for man created by God as flesh and blood, who lives in a world where God purposely made our food pleasurable, our bodies sensual, and our conflicts and wars inevitable. By dismissing those things as not spiritual and too earthly, we place things that are vital for life into the non-moral category. Treating war as something immoral leads to pacifism, something quite easy to advocate when knowing others will fight the wars on this earthly plain that protect the pacifist. Placing it in an immoral category narrowly confines the moral options for war. But often war ends up saving tens of thousands who otherwise will be killed during the years of attrition where war, in the name of morality, is forestalled.

It is hard to celebrate the heroism and sacrifice of soldiers when what they are involved in is labeled a necessary evil. For that reason, the Old Testament called soldiers "men of valor," since they are engaged in the ultimate moral mandate of eradicating the evil against us. In fact, uprooting evil when necessary is as much a fulfillment of the divine will as is the moment we extend comfort to a bedridden neighbor who is in the hospital. In one we show mercy to the individual and in the other mercy to society now freed from the horrors of evil.

The Old Testament devoted a chapter in Deuteronomy to speak of the necessity for war against our enemies, so we would not hide behind morality in order to escape our responsibility. It did not dismiss war, but instead, clarified and gave us discernment into how to conduct it morally. So as to give credence to the soldiers and virtuous nation undertaking it, God even declared Himself "a man of war" (Ex. 15:3).

Even absolutists who refuse to make distinctions should admit to a hierarchy among categories. Not all categories in life are equal; in fact, there is a hierarchy among categories. We must weigh and assess among categories. The highest category is life—protecting and preserving innocent life. Let us take, for example, lying. The category of preserving life outweighs the category of not lying. Thus while not lying remains constant within its category of routine civic life, when needed to actually save life itself, not lying should be superseded by the highest category of all—the preservation of life. It simply cancels out those things below it. The philosopher Kant, and theologians of absolutism, should have recognized that hypocrisy does not exist when one takes into account the importance of one category over the other as opposed to wondering if we can make "an exception to the rule." Failure to recognize an escalating scale of importance among different categories led certain absolutists to the conclusion that during time of war one should still not lie to save one's life.

★ ★ ★

What could be more earthly than wealth? Dualism renounced it and characterized it as something non-virtuous. Furthermore, during the years of the Gospels, the wealthy were the nefarious Romans and those from the Sadducees who bought the priesthood and aligned with the Romans against the common folk. If having wealth is a vice, then those who do not have it are its opposite—virtuous. Wealth was in the hands of a few not the people. "The people" became virtuous precisely because they did not have wealth. Thus began the symmetry between being poor and the virtue of being "the people."

What could be more earthly than power? Being earthly, it is something to be renounced. Furthermore, power showed its cruel side when in the hands of the Romans lording over the Second Temple Jews—the few killing the many. If power and those who used it were bad, then those who did not have it were good. Who did not have it? The people! Thus was tied the knot of powerlessness and the virtue of being the people.

These two elements of life—power and wealth—were consigned to the *vice* side in the *either-or* ledger of dualism. If the point was to now live a life of the spirit over the life of the flesh, and the spiritual and the physical were irreconcilable, then dualism demanded that power and wealth be stigmatized as things unbecoming men of the spirit.

Discernment, however, demands that we make distinctions. Power and wealth are not intrinsically bad, nor is poverty and weakness somehow virtuous. Wisdom teaches that it depends how the power or wealth was attained, how it is being used, and that men who have it must continually monitor themselves so as not to grow arrogant or indifferent in possessing it. By consigning wealth or power to some broad, non-virtuous category, those who have it are automatically forced to defend and justify their having it. It is as if we have no right to it unless we first irrefutably prove our innocence.

Nor should those unwealthy and less powerful be given a free pass as somehow being automatically virtuous. (In a later chapter, I will address the famous verse: "The meek shall inherit the earth.") No doubt, those raised on the model of the poor carpenter from Nazareth may see things differently than those raised on the model of "And God made Abraham wealthy with flocks of sheep, goats and servants" (Genesis 12:16). Ours is a free country and whoever wishes can divest themselves of their belongings and live the life of bare austerity.

Unlike the days of antiquity, wealth is not vested in the hands of the few. America has a vast middle class of 200,000,000 people. Unlike the days of old, none of us is consigned to a caste system or a permanent state of poverty. Our chance to own a home or car, eat healthy food, take vacations, have a personal doctor, have time for study and education for our children—*to me that represents wealth*—is in our own hands. And up until the last couple of years, so was upward mobility. By any standard of history, and in comparison to anywhere else in the world today, probably everybody we know is quite wealthy. Must we all have the wealth of Warren Buffet or Donald Trump? Long ago, just about the entire population (what today some like to call the 99%) had nothing. Today, in America, "the people" are the vast majority who, indeed, have wealth. Are we, therefore, not men of the spirit? Are we somehow bad? Most wealthy Americans do not live by cruelty or an overbearing haughtiness. Most came up the hard way and struggled. America is not Rome, aristocratic Europe, or something out of the "Lord of the Manor" medieval times.

Nor are strength and power things to be ashamed of and stigmatized when in the hands of such a magnanimous and moral country as the United States, which achieved its power by living in harmony with a Judeo-Christian ethos tailor-made to bring success, vigor, and blessing. Those who begrudge us our power are those who wish to undermine us for having the sense to follow the Judeo-Christian model.

Power is not only good when in the hands of countries such as America and Israel but is also the only mechanism available to protect us from the forces of evil salivating to conquer and enslave mankind. The use of power, under such circumstances, and the willingness to go to war to checkmate evil, is not only acceptable but virtuous and moral, for it is something that *ought* to be done. Our moral responsibility is not to wait until disaster hits and tens of thousands perish, but to strike beforehand so those thirty thousand never have to die. We did it when we fought Nazism and communism, and need to do so now against terrorism. These are the moral guidelines, and the knowledge of right vs. wrong that I mentioned in the previous chapter regarding America's standing out as a moral force, separate and distinct from most other nations.

★★★

Under dualism, the surest way for one side in a conflict to gain sympathy and immediately be labeled the higher moral side is to place itself in victim status. Whoever can claim he is the poor one, the weaker one, or the minority automatically is given moral standing. And that is because dualism deals in categories that are absolute: poor, weak, minority = good; wealthy, strong, majority = bad. Arabs can maim Israelis with rocks and rockets, and there is no outrage. Israelis build a wall to prevent infiltration by suicide bombers, and the world screams. Muslims kill hundreds of Christians and hang priests in Egypt and Iraq, and the world yawns. A soldier mishandles a Koran, and the world calls for his head. In the multitude of conflicts worldwide involving Muslims, they have been able to portray themselves as the powerless, despite the Arab oil with its trillions of dollars, and despite the fact that they, the supposedly weak, are taking over country after country. Israelis and Christians, on the other hand, find it almost impossible to get any political leader or media outlet to recognize their tragedies since they are considered strong and successful.

Because America and Israel are strong, they must act perfectly—there is no sympathy for them. An assumption of guilt regarding the successful exists, so anything short of perfection is grounds for indictment. It is as if they have no right to exist if not perfect. It must be said that those demanding impossible perfection from an entity are already telegraphing their wish for its demise.

Christians are a majority in the West, so there is no sympathy for them, even while Christians are being murdered by Muslims wholesale throughout Africa and the Middle East. Those clever enough to assign themselves the status as weak and a minority need not act perfectly, but can, in fact, act any way they want. But we must ask: What is weak about a movement that has the power to kill tens of thousands of Christians in Egypt, Sudan, Nigeria, Iraq, and Iran? Why is a group assigned the minority label when it has the tens of millions to outnumber and defeat Christians everywhere and bring Western governments to their knees? (In a later chapter we will answer this, the most baffling question of our age.)

Success has become the death knell of those wishing to have their side heard. And that is because in the collective conscience of mankind resides the ever alive paradigm of dualism wherein wealth and success are seen as something wrong and disqualifying. Discernment and the ability to make distinctions within these categories are becoming rare. But if the West continues to live by the absolutes of dualism, it will make itself impotent and a fish fry for an ever advancing Islam. That is why imams declare that, aside from Jews, their enemy is Christianity. It knows the battle against it will be waged only by those tied to Judeo-Christian morality and thinking.

If people of faith, and those wishing to be men and women of the spirit, sequester their lives into the spiritual realm only, they are leaving wide open the sure probability that men who wish to control the people will have free entree to do so. A religious philosophy that, in principle, limits itself to the spiritual only is theologically more willing to live side by side, and even under, totalitarian regimes. They do so under the peculiar notion that, "As long as I can take care of my soul and continue my weekly religious rituals, everything is fine and I and the Lord remain one." But freedom *is* a spiritual realm, especially since our rights to liberty derive from God. Failure to recognize this essential point is to make one's religious outlook puny and the God one worships as a God too small.

★★★

Those who divide the world into the spiritual vs. the physical, the temporal vs. the eternal, confidently cite "Render unto Caesar that which is Caesar's and to God that which is God's" as justification, indeed a celebration of their escape from responsibility. But Judeo-Christian morality understands it to mean: that which rightfully should be in the hands of the state should be left unchallenged, but that which does not belong rightfully to the state is not under the state's authority. Individual rights, as opposed to group rights, the rights given to us by the God of life, liberty, property, and freedom to choose—these do not belong to the state whether it is the communist state, the welfare state, or the envisioned worldwide caliphate. On the contrary, these rights belong to God, are of God, and given to us by God; and Caesar, the state, cannot be rendered them.

Perhaps it is philosophically easier to live under kings or accept an all powerful state above when one's own religious structure is top-down and where people must submit to a higher spiritual institution in order to have their spiritual needs fulfilled. To the enormous credit of the inimitable Pope John Paul II, he rose above the insular mindset of institutional survival and openly challenged communism in Poland and even in Cuba. The debate within some religious circles continues. Let us look at a recent example in Cuba. Father Rodriguez, a courageous critic of Fidel Castro, says: "The Church must liberate the people. Even the state must answer to divine law [the rights of man]." The current Pope Benedict has openly stated that "communism has not worked in Cuba." Like his predecessor, he is wary of what some call "liberation theology," which provides a religious stamp of approval to Marxism.

Many among the American Catholic clergy have been jolted by events in 2012 and have begun realizing that their ability to maintain their religious positions regarding abortion and traditional marriage cannot stand if capitalism and genuine free markets are replaced by a welfare state implemented from above. The Obama administration showed that it not only wants to level us economically through the welfare state, but also level our values, even our religious values. Many had been fans of National Obamacare, the cornerstone of the welfare state that placed us economically under one socially engineered and monolithic system. They now see that it is, really, Health Control, where the state can demand that public institutions, including Catholic hospitals, service abortion desires and that schools, including Catholic schools, conform to same-sex work rules. For what left-wing cultural Marxists want is not only redistribution of wealth but also a national sameness and monolithic distribution of abortion and same-sex rules as well.

I think a great number of people now realize they can't have their cake and eat it too. They cannot divide societal life and assert a national sameness for economic matters with no national conformity for religious matters. Religious freedom and economic freedom are inseparable. Both are based on the overarching principle that people be allowed independence, and non-harassment from government, regarding their pocketbook as well as the Good Book. The Judeo-Christian ethos does not divide the two. The God who gave us the right to religious liberty gave us the right to property. As we have seen, left-wingers in government today are not your father's old fashioned liberals, but hard-core cultural Marxists who want it all and intend to change *everything*.

Many clergy are now realizing that redistribution of wealth does not stop with distribution but negatively impacts the creation of wealth itself. Too many had erroneously assumed that with the compassionate welfare state, we would remain equally wealthy but distribute our wealth more widely. But our wealth and opportunity have severely contracted between 2009-2012. This should have been no surprise, since it has been proven every time that the controls of the welfare state halt ingenuity, productivity, and growth. Socialists place every one of their shibboleths and causes above job creation and see the purpose of industry not in making money but as pilot projects for their social or environmental goals. Wealth plummets. Those religious institutions looking for private charitable donations will find there is no wealth left from which to give charity. Former English Prime Minister Margaret Thatcher said it best: "After you have redistributed all the wealth, socialism leaves you without any more wealth to distribute."

★ ★ ★

Marxism attacks not only capitalism but also a nation's culture. The hard core Left, exemplified by White House operative Hilary Rosen, have, for example, gone after Mrs. Ann Romney because she, as a stay-at-home mom, is "not in sync with the needs of women." Rosen is wrong. I know more Mrs. Romney types than I do Ms. Rosen types. Hilary Rosen's attack on Mrs. Romney was not simply an attack for political purposes but an attempt by those on the Left to begin questioning the value of stay-at-home mothers, who do not square with what radical feminists have in mind for womanhood. The welfare state and cultural Marxists have as their goal the toppling of all traditional roles and models, be it family, marriage, motherhood, or masculinity. They have an all-encompassing ideological program designed to change human nature, which targets even our most simple liberties, including the right to love the traditions we love, the right to be wholesome, the right to think for yourself, and the right not to be continually pestered by radical iconoclasts.

Like Marx before, America's political Left is at war, out to defeat middle-class values, what Marx called the bourgeois. The last thing you and I need is for these Upper Westsiders to pester our space and invade our homes, marriages, and our children.

Many in the religious world talk of always being nice, as if nice is an absolute. But discernment teaches that distinctions must be made. Is it wise or prudent to be nice to someone plotting your downfall? Is it wise to be nice to those who see in your forever niceness an unwillingness to stand up and fight, thereby emboldening the aggressor to further aggression? This is *Barneyism* where we all love one another in a shallow sort of way. It is the religion of no courage, conviction, or fight. But religion did not come to keep us as perpetual children; for that we have television and Hollywood. The Bible came to make us strong adults so we would have the confidence and inner strength to do what we must do. The world is a serious place, and so must we be. Religion should make us strong not only in faith but also in human spirit. It came not only to nurture the soul but to supply muscle as well.

NINETEEN

Capitalism

[The blessings and morality of capitalism]

Nothing has provided hundreds of millions with more wealth and a dignified quality of life as has free market capitalism. That in itself makes it a moral paradigm and something which *ought* to be. And it has done so for the longest sustained period of time in human history. No system has given people more *choice* in how they feed themselves and in how they wish to make their living than has capitalism. This aspect of free choice makes it singularly moral.

In free market capitalism, people can choose to work for themselves, to gain income by exercising their talents, or to work for a company where one's weekly salary is pretty much guaranteed. Many of these companies are large and able to provide guaranteed salaries and upward economic mobility because thousands of people have invested their money into the company, which is what capitalism is all about. In fact, many people in America and countries all over the world make their living—and live with the dignity and comforts that come from having a living wage—from companies and corporations that exist only because people invested their money to make such companies possible—capitalism. Prior to the advent of capitalism, which means most of recorded history, people lived in squalor or in bare subsistence, without any savings, and could not live for even a day unless they worked that day. A system that has provided so many blessings for such large numbers of people over such a proven period of time —and continues to offer boundless opportunities—is one, I am sure, the Almighty finds pleasing.

It does not matter that some people have more than others. If one is able to feed and clothe himself and provide shelter and his needs of life, why should it matter to him that someone else is wealthier? That sentiment is called envy or jealousy. Such vices work against one's happiness. That is why God in the Ten Commandments warns us not to be envious of our neighbor's house, ox, and other possessions. Envy makes the individual unhappy, causes enmity toward the one who has more, and creates a society built on anger, resentment, and division. Envy plows the seed of mob destruction. Honorable people stay away from actions and rhetoric that create unnecessary discontent among individuals and within society. Those that engage in it lack personal character and usually have selfish motives. Simply read the stories in the Bible regarding Korah and Dathan, and you will see how overly ambitious and selfish men used envy and resentment in organizing the community toward mob anger. Those that exploit class warfare, as did Korah, Dathan, and Abiram, to stitch bitterness and anger in the bosom of men, are engaging in a sinful gesture. They come to incite, as Marx before, and make men transgress the Tenth Commandment ("Do not covet") and target not men's angels but his hidden demons. It might make good politics for Obamaites, but in the eyes of religion, it is sinful to purposely make men bitter and envious. Neither is it moral to purposely create acrimony between men based on who earns more.

If the 99 percent alluded to before or the 90 percent Mr. Obama speaks about had earned their money by stealing from everyone else, the upper 10% would be guilty. But they have not. More often than not, it is that upper 10% who have forged the opportunities and companies that have created the jobs employing most of us. Absent their new wealth creation through inventions, investment, risk, and their forming of new companies, we would be forced to find more difficult ways to earn our bread or limit ourselves to existing industries that slowly wither as cheaper foreign labor suck them out of the country. Soon the demagoguery will escalate by pushing the demonized to include the upper 5 percent, then upper 10 percent, with relief from stigmatization coming only by renouncing those in one's own earning bracket as cold and heartless capitalists. Wealth possessed by leftists and socialists is acceptable wealth because it is purified by getting on the anti-success bandwagon and speaking of "fairness."

Furthermore, in a dynamic economy, the income Mr. Jones makes does not come by making Mr. Smith poorer. It is not as if, as Jesse Jackson claims, there is a limited pie and you get *your* piece by taking *mine*. Economies are not finite but grow as goods and services expand. The Gross Domestic Product of this country is not stagnant as evidenced that the money in our economy today is thousands of times larger than it was at our birth because we have expanded our universe of goods and services. This expansion comes about only because men are free to invent, produce, service, and use their ingenuity and drive. That which allows potentiality in man is moral and good. When an economy's money supply accurately reflects the worth of the goods and services within the economy, stability ensues and we can be content. When, however, money is artificially pumped into an economy and exceeds the real worth of its goods and services, inflation sets in and the value of our money is diminished.

The only requirement to get a portion of the ever expanding pie is by participating in its expansion, by working and investing in it. One's share in the growing economy is not given out for free but is obtained when we, as *beings of action*, do what it takes to participate in that which is open to all of us. This is as it should be. There is no entitlement to wealth. Whatever we gain in this world should come because we made the effort to obtain it. That is the essence of being created as a free agent. God gave us eyes to see, legs to walk, a mouth to speak, and arms to fetch so that we could be active participants in life. We are not amoebas but humans; we are not here to be parasites but to be productive and useful. The creation of jobs by those in the business of job creation—the private sector—is the surest way for an economy to expand. The best thing government can do is to stand aside and allow individuals and groups in the free market to manufacture the new products and services that make for a healthy and growing economy.

The United States is the world's strongest power because it has been a sustained free market longer than any country in history. That power has given the American citizen a physical security known to hardly any other population on this planet. Safe and secure borders are a blessed thing, as mentioned in Exodus, Numbers, and Deuteronomy. Because of free markets, and the knowledge that one will be financially rewarded for one's research, work, manufacturing, and distribution of products, we have discovered wonder drugs and medicines that have allowed us to live longer and better than any time in history. We as individuals have reaped health benefits in every area of life that but fifty years ago would have been characterized as supernatural miracles from God. All this has happened only because of capitalism and free markets. In the Old Testament, God repeatedly declares health and abundance to be His desire for man.

★★★

With capitalism, people can undertake risky projects or the production of potential products because of investors providing the seed money needed to launch the research and production of a product or project. Investors are assured of financial reward—only if the product is successful—because we live in a free market, meaning that those who own the product are free to gain from its sale without undue coercion by government transferring it to others or unduly taxing it. The person is a freeman working for himself not the government.

I never see workers at union shops declaring they will work for free simply for the benefit of others. Why, then, do so many malcontents and complainers insist that corporations should act like charities and fork over their profits? Is not what they do called work? Profit is to risk takers what compensation and wages are to workers. When union shop workers have a surplus don't they, if they are prudent, put money into savings for a rainy day? Well, companies also have rainy years when their research does not pan out or their products do not sell. Investors have terrible years where they lose money and stay afloat only because of the profits they had previously made and saved. Companies need profits so as to continue future research, development, and production for those things that will give us a brighter tomorrow.

Take away capitalism, and the American dream of starting out modestly and steadily rising will be shattered as happened in socialist England. Is an ever dwindling standard of living, as is found in socialism, a religious goal? I think not. Is satisfying the class warfare claim of "fairness," which is but a justification for envy, worth lowering the standard of living of all men? The demand for contrived and feigned social justice cannot be a genuine desire of religion, since it has been shown to bring injustice to the vast majority who work, risk, and strive. Are we to live with guilt because we as a country or individuals have been successful, with expiation possible only by handing it all over, free of charge, to those less successful? Do we think that once having taken our wealth, the former gripers will be paragons of justice, kindness, and magnanimity, and live by their platitudes? No way!

I am often perplexed by those who live under the false assumption that owning a business is some type of cash cow where the owners simply live off the sweat of workers. My father was a partner with my uncles and grandfather in a small family business started by my grandfather and great grandfather in Cleveland. It was not a public company but privately held with the family being the limited shareholders. The company employed around fifty people. Let me tell you, each one of our family worked harder than any of the workers. The workers went home every day at 4:30 p.m., while the family stayed until 6:30 and most nights came back after dinner and worked until 9:30 p.m. We observed the Saturday *Shabbat*, so the family, not the workers, worked on Sunday.

There never was a guaranteed July 4th or Memorial Day holiday for the family, since inevitably a shipment would be arriving that day or a rush order had to get out quickly. The alarm went off (dozens of times, I remember) because of robberies, fires, and busted frozen pipes. As a kid, I worked there almost every vacation day, sweeping floors, loading trucks, cleaning wooden pallets, lugging boxes of screws and bolts, or collating glossy product sheets into the company's ever updated catalogue. Sometimes I did not get paid because we were all in it together.

My father often lent money, interest free, to workers needing a quick loan, and many, I remember, were given pay in advance when they were strapped for cash. But on the other hand, I remember countless times, my father coming home and telling my mother that this week there'd be no money for her because the family members had to cover company costs. Sometimes my father and uncles, and certainly my grandfather, went four to six weeks without getting paid so as to keep the company going. The workers, however, *never* missed a week's pay. Never. When needed, we would borrow from the bank to meet payroll.

It finally became a union shop, the worst mistake the company ever made. But this was, after all, Cleveland, Ohio—union central. Once inside, unions control the life of a business, while sharing not one iota of risk or one second beyond 4:30 p.m. As a kid, I was flabbergasted at how when the assembly line bell rang at 4:30 p.m., the foreman shut the line, and if a screw was only half way through the threading, it remained so until the next day. But it was all worth it. Owning your own business gives people two grand gifts—independence and pride.

★★★

The problem with socialists is that they do not judge free enterprise—like our family business—by its centuries of actual blessing to millions. Instead, they focus on the few who will not work or may have fallen through the cracks. On the other hand, they judge socialism not by its reality but by some concocted utopian dream. The English philosopher, John Stuart Mill, said: "The test of any ethical idea depends not on its theory but in its practice and actuality in the real world." Socialists ignore and defy actual facts that do not fit into their non-reality vision. They would rather most of us suffer if it leaves them with their morally superior perch. And as I have mentioned before, the socialist vanguard and clique rarely share the economic and social downward spiral the rest of us are forced to endure in the name of *their* socialism.

Beyond the economic disaster of socialism, it is simply wrong and undesirable even as theory. God placed man on this earth so as to produce and grow inwardly, to be greater at the end of his life than when he first entered this world. A society based on dependency, victimization, and entitlement is never one that engenders individual growth, which is based on challenge and individual productivity. American capitalism has been history's preeminent arrangement for man to realize the fullest glory of being created in God's image—robust and productive, getting up each day with *purpose* and goals. In a society based on opportunity, individuals create and businesses produce wonderful, life-enhancing products and services as great as any art, music, or literature. Mr. Obama does not appear to admire capitalism and endlessly speaks about and heralds victimization and entitlement. But man's self-interest in productivity, implanted in human nature, seems far more beneficial than the selfishness inherent in dependency and sense of entitlement. Man was not created to be passive but active—socialism atrophies man, whereas capitalism invigorates him.

Aristotle said: "How immeasurably greater is the pleasure when a man feels a thing to be his own; for the love of self is a feeling *implanted by nature* and *not given in vain*, although selfishness is rightly censured; this however is not the mere love of self, but the love of self in excess." He later wrote: "That which is common to the greatest number has the least care bestowed upon it." That which one owns brings to it a much greater sense of personal responsibility, and as God is a responsible Being so are we, created in His image, to be.

Beyond economic sharing, the socialist feels that society's children are, to a large degree, part of a collective, and the state's ruling elite should have inordinate say in directing our children's lives. For that reason, liberals seem to always be butting into our personal lives, telling us how we should raise our children, what we should eat, how our marriages should look, and what constitutes a "working mother."

In contrast, the Judeo-Christian belief in personal responsibility to those relationships freely chosen, one's own children, calls for parents to have an ultimate say in how their children are raised. They will also do a much better job. As Aristotle said: "In a collective society, each citizen will have a thousand sons not individually his, every son will be equally the son of everybody, and will therefore be neglected by all alike." Socialism, in every regard, is against that which is personal and that which is distinctive. Aristotle, a believer in family, found collectivism (socialism) to be detrimental to family. Perhaps that is why socialists and cultural Marxists seem too willing to malign the traditional family and, like putty in their hands, wish to reshape it.

***

Excessive ambition, greed, theft, and unscrupulousness—these are traits within human nature not as a result of any system. Do not think for one second that these vices vanish the moment one becomes a socialist. It is only because socialism squelches opportunity that the ability, on a grand scale, to reveal these vices is severely limited. But they are as equally visible, just on a smaller scale. In fact, those within the hierarchy of socialism live by and act with far greater corruption than those in free markets precisely because there is no competitive arrangement or free market to challenge them or make them pay for their corruption. Capitalism is a self-punishing mechanism; socialism is not. The idea of "socialist man" being "angel man" is a myth and political fabrication.

It is precisely in the broad life of flowing commerce that one has the opportunity to conduct oneself by the ethical business laws found in the Bible. God does not deny or criticize commercial life—not at all. He assumes it to be the norm. Indeed, it is commerce which, more than anything else, occupies our day-to-day living. It is precisely in this framework where God delineates most of His ethical laws, so that man can attain ethical awareness and live the honest life precisely in that realm where he is most occupied. One reaches ethical nobility not by separating from or decrying business but by conducting and doing business correctly. Majesty is not achieved in a renunciation of things but in an ethical engagement with things.

Capitalism as a paradigm probably began only around five hundred years ago. Up until then, if someone needed more money, he either produced more of what he made or, as the kings of Europe, sold what he already had. Capitalism taught another way: membership investment in a new project or product with the hope that your risked capital, your invested funds, would bring forth the creation of new wealth. Member investors became limited partners, shareholders in a concern or corporation constituting something greater than each individual stake in it, which was an entity independent of them personally. Capitalism, i.e., investment partnership in company shares, has accelerated the creation and production of new products and services to levels unimaginable to the generations that preceded it.

Simple and basic free enterprise, the ability and right to make something and sell it, however, has been around since time immemorial. Free enterprise is augmented, flowers, and reaches its full potential under the broad and exciting parameters of investment capitalism. Unlike socialism, free enterprise is not a "system." Socialism is contrived and requires a society socially engineered. Selling, buying, bartering, producing, and doing so at the level one wants for himself and his loved ones, is innate, like eating. The only obstacles to free enterprise were kings, thugs, or governments that either took goods for themselves, taxed profits into oblivion, or through edicts and regulation, made it impossible to do.

The Old Testament has always viewed free enterprise—the right of a man to make a living as he chooses and sell his products—as a moral undertaking. It prefers job creation and having a job over living off of charity. It lowers prices, increases choices, and narrows the extent to which we are but passive victims of circumstance and fate. It reduces absolute levels of poverty. It treats the environment neither as a god nor as a dish rag but as something to be cultivated and stewarded in service to human. Free enterprise is part of the Judeo-Christian ethos: without free enterprise, one of the great legs of the Judeo-Christian ethos is missing, and without the Judeo-Christian ethos, the *moral* foundation behind it is in jeopardy. For it to work and not degenerate into that which is ruthless or callous, men must be guided by a moral code that smoothes the edges and keeps us honest.

Free enterprise keeps us free politically and remains a moral enterprise when guided by the general themes of the Bible. We are not Japan, Inc., as some in the 1980s characterized her. Our free enterprise is part of something far grander. We conservatives are not libertarians but the last remaining advocates of the Judeo-Christian moral enterprise.

The Bible, as mentioned in a previous chapter, warns of keeping accurate measures and fair weights. It is part of the Commandment "Thou shalt not steal." One cannot withhold wages, nor demand any and every type of collateral. We cannot be excessive in pricing. There are other work rules, such as allowing workers to eat from the grapes they gather while picking, and the responsibility we have to animals not to overburden them, or muzzle them while plowing the fields. It is not that animals have rights, rather that we have obligations to them. These are not contradictions to free enterprise but guidelines to it and represent the contours of how it should operate. Every system, every arrangement, everything in life comes with guidelines. Guidelines are not to be seen as a challenge to something's legitimacy, rather the outline of how it should work. Marriage is an institution, but within marriage one cannot do anything he or she wants. Government has guidelines. Parenthood has guidelines. None of these guidelines constitute an affront to the concept but a formulation of it.

I am puzzled by those who claim that our need to make laws against unregulated capitalism prove there must be something inherently wrong with capitalism. The laws and regulations we make regarding business do not prove that in itself business is bad, no more than the laws our Constitution supplies in limiting government power implies that in itself government is somehow invalid. In fact, the laws that we have for capitalism are in capitalism's behalf. The Bible and we Americans finesse it so we can preserve it, for free enterprise is precious—our quality of life and dignity depend on it.

★★★

How, then, do we decide when regulations are of the preserving type and hence legitimate, or when regulations go beyond preservation into the realm of destroying it and become illegitimate? The answer has already been implied in the question. When regulations get so out of hand and unnecessary that they thwart free enterprise's ability to flourish, then we have moved beyond amelioration and into destruction. What is that benchmark? Job creation! When regulations, as we have seen recently, shut down private enterprise job creation, then we know it has moved into the area of destruction so as to usher in socialism. When government starts owning and controlling vast sections of the economy never before under its control, then we know the first steps toward socialism have already been taken.

When every ism—be it environmentalism, unionism, global warmingism, feminism, transnationalism, fairness-ism, class warfare-ism—takes center stage and becomes more important than job creation, energy independence, the ability to start and maintain a small business, and is more important than even people themselves, then it is obvious that those be-hind these regulations have come not to help but to conquer, not to induce but transform, not to strengthen but to replace. And all the words to the contrary are verbal clouds spoken to hide their real intentions.

As with everything else in life such as marriage and relationships, capi-talism has its peaks and valleys. But in our lifetime, capitalism has demon-strated a unique resilience. After every temporary valley, we have risen higher than before. Even during the valley periods, we here in this country live better than those who have no capitalism at all.

God created a world in need of periodic but constant rebirth. Rebirth comes only after an experience of decline. We rise and recoil. We are born again. But after the storm, the cleansed landscape emits a robust fragrance and regeneration. Capitalism too has its periods of creative destruction that bring in their wake something better than before. I live better than did my grandfather. Those who crave a socialism they imagine will always be level are fooling themselves. Socialism too has its valleys, but the valleys grow deeper each time they are experienced. Even during periods of stability, so-cialism offers but mediocrity and dispiritedness. Humans desire certainty and absolute predictability. But predictability brings with it inertia. It is not real living. Capitalism is real life, where no soothsayer or magic man can announce the future. "Do not put your trust in the soothsayer or sorcerer" (Deuteronomy 18:10-11). People of faith need not know the future and can accept periods of temporary setbacks because they are resilient.

★★★

Free enterprise is one of the centerpieces of the Judeo-Christian ethos. Those that come to replace free enterprise have as their ultimate goal the removal of the Judeo-Christian system itself: its laws, its morality, its defin-ition of justice, dignity, and equality. These people also come to wipe out our history (including our literature and documents), our form of politics, what we teach our children, and our sexual mores—in other words, our very identity and national soul. They are not simply economic Marxists but radical, cultural Marxists, who wish to change not a little but everything. Without a specific identity and soul, we Americans are lost, vulnerable to Islam that is marching forward to recast the identity of the lands it threatens. I question whether some of our left-wing leaders still retain loy-alty to the Judeo-Christian ethos and not a new transnationalism and part-nership with Islam.

175

No doubt America, like other countries, has seen its share of business scoundrels. There are scoundrels outside of the business and free enterprise world as well. Many media, Hollywood and government types, and artists, come to mind. Scoundrelism is part of human nature. Corruption is found, according to reports, to a greater degree in socialist and top-down systems. In America they are rooted out, while in socialist countries they remain entrenched. By and large, though, most of our successful and wealthy people in America have come to their money honestly, in great measure because of our Judeo-Christian moral and ethical demands and because we are a culture of honesty, openness, and transparency. American and biblical ethics demand transparency and honesty. Our system functions quite well on the premise of Numbers 32:23, "Be sure your sin will find you out." Furthermore it goes beyond the literal to include not acting deceitfully or obscuring the truth from those whose choice depends upon the information you give them. "Thou shalt not place a stumbling block in front of the blind man" (Leviticus 19:14). There is no need to *transform* our free enterprise system.

Nor has capitalism created more poor. It is much better to be among the statistical poor of America than any other place. Many are poor relative to others in our country, but the "poor index" in most cases here includes people with shelter, food, transportation, heat, basic medicine, and access to public institutions. The existence of poverty is a condition that will never disappear. The Bible in Deuteronomy 15:9 speaks of the "poor that will remain among you"—a condition that is here to stay. Socialism has never made the poor rich nor eradicated poverty, though it has made millions who were better off less so after its destructive implementation. But many people feel less piqued about economic disparity when more share a parity of mediocrity and misery.

To the poor, we must give charity. My grandfather's whole life revolved around business, home, prayer, and giving to charity. Growing up, I remember how every Sunday in Cleveland Heights the doorbell would ring every hour between noon and 8:00 p.m. with people requesting alms for the poor. Charity is not redistribution of wealth but a donation for some of us of around 10 percent of one's income—called a tithe. Society is not considered more charitable because it takes upon itself vows of collective, socialist downsizing. The Bible speaks to us directly regarding charity not government. Charity is to be voluntary and is to be done, as Father Robert

Sirico of the Acton Institute teaches, through the authority of the Bible (voluntary) and not the power of the state (mandatory). Authority and power are not the same.

Worse, left-wing governments use their power to make us donate by funneling our tax money to the charitable (and not so charitable!) endeavors and projects they prefer, those that match their vision of what in society is worthwhile. This country does a very good job of taking care of people's basic needs. Our problem is—the one that will lead to national bankruptcy—our overly generous supply for wants that go way beyond food, clothing, and shelter to enact parity. In charity, *wants* should *not* be characterized as *needs*.

Too many people erroneously assume that modernity, with all its conveniences and scientific and technological breakthroughs, are guaranteed since we live in modern times, as if once mankind passed the year 1620, modernity was etched in the calendar from that year forward. Modernity is not a permanent state of affairs but depends on continued living by the rules of modernity. The modernity we know today began with capitalism (America, and seventeenth and eighteenth century Holland) and free inquiry (most notably in England and Scotland during that same time period). Absent the continuation of capitalism and free inquiry, the rules of modernity are in jeopardy. Free inquiry is threatened by political and academic political correctness, where leftist indoctrination is preferred. Left-wingers don't want capitalism, seem very much against energy independence and cheap energy, and in the name of dubious environmentalist theories stifle industry and production. They have become Luddites, against increased industrialization or new technology.

Under such leadership, the entire West could enter a true postmodern age (not just in name only). Not all societies keep moving forward. In fact, many great powers and nations reverted to a darker age when they relinquished the principles that formerly had made them great and advanced. When a society regresses, poverty sets in. It doesn't simply stop moving forward; it can't even produce the parts needed to maintain what it has.

The war against socialism and stifling liberal political correctness is our battle to maintain modernity and our hope to keep moving forward. The irony of today's milieu is that left-wing progressivism will likely bring regressivism and the Enlightenment that began five hundred years ago could be snuffed out by leftists calling themselves enlightened. We have to stop them before they stop the quality of life we have all known and enjoyed.

TWENTY

Power to the People

[*Capitalism: an instrument for the human spirit and dignity*]

Capitalism offers the individual something more than making a living. It is not content with people only being laborers and holders of jobs, indistinguishable members of the masses punching in and out of mammoth factories of routine, or as service employees in government agencies. Nor is the Bible satisfied with solely offering such a stifling existence. Unlike socialism, mired as it is in the static reproduction of things already invented (the bricks and mortar jobs New Dealers speaks of), capitalism is dynamic and energetic, cheerfully fostering and encouraging creativity, unspoken possibilities, and the dreams of the individual. Because the Hebrew Bible sees us not simply as workers and members of the masses but, rather, as individuals, it heralds our creativity that endows us with specific individuality.

At the opening bell, Genesis announces: "Man is created in the image of God." In other words, we are like Him, with individuality and creative intelligence. Unlike animals, a human is not only a hunter and gatherer but also a creative dreamer with the potential of unlocking all the hidden treasures implanted by God in our universe. The mechanism of capitalism, as made real through investment and reasoned speculation, paves the way for our *partnership with God* by bringing to surface and disbursing that which the Almighty embedded in nature for our eventual extraction and activation.

Capitalism makes possible *entrepreneurship*, which is the on-the-ground realization of an idea birthed in human creativity. Whereas statism demands that we think small and bow to top-down conformity, capitalism—as has been practiced in the United States—maximizes human potential and benefits all those close to it. It provides a home for *aspiration*, referred to in the Bible as "the spirit of life" (Genesis 2:7). Capitalism and entrepreneurship are not simply ways to make money but vehicles for expressing the human spirit.

It is hubristic for those in power to think that among themselves, with their fancy pedigrees, they can decide what an economy needs tomorrow. Such elitists never take into account the human spirit and ingenuity bubbling within the tens of millions of individuals spread across this land. Spirit is not earned in the academy but placed in us by God and cultivated in an ethos. No one can plan an economy; it can't be anticipated. An economy is an open-ended living organism that becomes what its nation's individuals, with their expertise and ambition, make it become.

Why should government pay for command-and-controllers to plan what should be, when there already exists a hidden but vibrating economic force called Americans, who ask not to be paid by government but wait to be rewarded by the free market through profits? Entrepreneurs don't want a wage; they want profits. But elitists never see the people as innovators, only as recipients or tax payers. They do not see the people as equals but as inferior ones to be taken care of. They do not see clearly because they are blinded by so-called smartness. They think in terms of wages and jobs, not risk and reward capitalism.

The Bible speaks positively of payment and profit. "For why should a man so labor if not to receive profit?" Thomas Jefferson wrote: "Take not from he who has labored the bread he has earned." Morality includes reciprocity. The *Midrash* says: "He who plants the fig tree shall eat of its fruit." Again, Jefferson: "To take from one in order to spare to others, because it is thought that his own industry has acquired too much, is to violate the first principle that guarantees the free exercise of his industry and the fruits acquired by it."

Most innovators are first inspired by an idea and coming up with a solution to a challenge or problem facing them, not big money. Only later do these *products of the mind* transform into real money making ventures. Anyone who has come up with an idea knows how the concept itself, not future shares of stock, is his passion and what stirs his soul. When suddenly hit by a great idea, the human spirit is kindled and every moment after is intoxicated by making that idea come to life. Capitalism is what makes innovation and marketability possible. Inventions, ideas, solutions, and new services are our country's new frontier and manifest destiny, replacing what land west of the Appalachians was two centuries ago during those formative years of Manifest Destiny. Today, destiny is shaped in the ideas of the mind coupled with the passion of the heart. That is the real definition of *Power to the People*.

In days of old, men would have to solicit kings and queens to get their ideas launched, and artists and musicians needed to beseech noblemen and other patrons in the aristocracy to have their works presented to the world. Today we need only convince a group of investors—venture capitalists—of the workability of our idea. Some of us have even done it all on our own. Certainly, some communist countries had scientists working in universities or government laboratories, yet these countries remained stagnant. What the scientists did was a mere drop in the bucket compared to what individuals here in America—regular people—do in energizing, expanding, reshaping, modernizing, upgrading, and making more convenient American life. Scientists are not involved with coming up with a new service. A regular guy came up with the idea of fast-food hamburgers, coffee chains, cable TV, bulk retailing, popular software, and time saving computers. Reverting to an almost pre-capitalist, pre-modern era, Obamaites wanted the government to decide our industrial priorities and grant billions to friends from Green Industries, for example, who pled their case before him.

★★★

Our liberal academic institutions have long demonized capitalism. What else accounts for the hypocrisy of the "Occupy Wall Street" crowd who came to denounce capitalism while outfitted in their Nike shoes, Ralph Lauren jackets, speaking to each other on Verizon cell phones, while logging in to their Apple computers after a lunch break at McDonalds? There is an enormous disconnect between the reality of their lives and the blithe and comfortable way in which they attack the capitalism that provides all their amenities. They have been so schooled against capitalism by the socialists who wish to run our culture that they separate the capitalist reality that is their life from the theoretical thing they have been taught to demonize. And that brings us back to Karl Marx himself, that bitter and mean man who demonized the word capitalism in his *Das Kapital*.

Ever since *Das Kapital*, academics have continued to demonize capitalism even though they live comfortable and secure lives because of capitalism. Marx made it a dirty word, just as the Left demonizes and makes a dirty word out of everything and everyone not on their side.

The Frankfurt School that came here from Europe steadily and vigorously denounced capitalism. But long gone are the conditions that were part of those early years of the Industrial Revolution. Marx's theory was based on conditions that no longer exist. Marx did not know how science and technology would change the entire dynamic of industrial life, and how those at the bottom could rise to the top. In fact, most of America's wealthy people do not come from the aristocracy (bourgeois) of Marx's time but are the self-made wealthy. Many workers today (the so-called proletariat) live better than the bourgeois of the 1850s.

Marx hated capitalism because he hated Jews; it was his way of denouncing his ancestry, the people his father officially rejected when he formally left the Jewish people to become a member of European society. Jews were never from the landed gentry—they have always been lovers of business. For Marx, they epitomized energetic capitalism.

Those who subscribe to Marxism are living in a time warp, in a world of fixed theory. According to the erudite Professor Daniel N. Robinson of Oxford and Princeton, Marx's outlook was *deterministic*, meaning that it could not foresee possibilities beyond some type of permanent condition. He was bogged-down by the same determinism about man's fate found in some Eastern religions, namely that man cannot extricate himself from a preordained status or caste system. He did not see the wonderful possibilities that man himself could bring about to improve his condition. Marx was fatalistic and, as with all socialists, guided by pessimism. He never knew or understood the possibilities for man living by an optimistic Judeo-Christian ethos. For him, man had only one way out of his class boundaries—revolution. He totally misunderstood modern day capitalism and how, rather than wanting to keep men down, it prefers they obtain wealth and buying power for the goods of capitalism. Today everyone with an open mind can see the blessings and social mobility of American life. To retain Marxism in light of the blessings of American capitalism bespeaks an envy of those wealthier or, worse, an antipathy to economic freedom itself.

Among liberal American, English, and other European academics, it is a sign of intellectual superiority to denounce capitalism, for it is the essence of America; and, for many on the Left, a Jewish kind of thing. Most clergy come down against capitalism out of a nouveau *religious correctness*; though few even understand what it is except as a catchall phrase for "bad business behavior, greed, and economic inequity." Stand against capitalism and one is crowned with a halo of righteousness, concern, and compassion. Capitalism is an easy target in capitalist America.

If capitalism is not perfect, the Left says that it is somehow invalid, though people are willing to accept imperfection, far greater imperfection, in every other area of life. Why? I think it goes back to envy. Envy is the most powerful of negative human emotions. A lifetime of experiences has shown me that above all else, people envy the money and possessions of other people. Hundreds of times when I have talked to people and mentioned someone famous, the reply is always: "I wish I had his money!"—not his looks, his degree, his scholarship, his children—his money. Think about it, I'm sure you've heard it too. Capitalism is the engine of wealth, and wealth is what too many envy in others. My father, may he rest in peace, never envied someone for their money or possessions, but he was an exception.

Too many cannot abide what they call income disparity. But why should anyone care if someone else is vastly wealthier if his own *real* needs are met? Team Obama exploits (*capitalizes* on) the negative emotion of envy. But if we dismantle capitalism, we put in peril our economic future and prosperity as well as the military strength and protection that come from it. Nations fall because of a variety of sins, one of them being the sin of envy.

★★★

John Adams said: "Property is surely a right of mankind as real as liberty"; and "Property must be secured, or liberty cannot exist." Jefferson wrote: "The true foundation of republican government is the equal right of every citizen in his person and property and in their management." Alexander Hamilton said: "In the general course of human nature, a power over man's property amounts to a power over his will." Samuel Adams hit the mark when he asked: "Now what liberty can there be where property is taken without consent?"

When they spoke of property, they meant not simply one's real estate but one's earnings. "Take not from he who has labored the bread he has earned" (Jefferson). Chief Justice John Marshall said: "In a free government almost all other rights would become worthless if the government possessed power over the private fortune of every citizen."

There is no question that those in our society demanding the private property earnings of other people's labor would never agree to expend their own labor and energy—their property—to others for free. Their idea of shared property is a one-way street. For them, simply being who they are entitles them to someone else's energy and labor. However, it does not include reciprocating and sharing theirs with others. Abraham Lincoln said: "For some, liberty means for each man to do as he pleases with the product of his labor; while for others, it means for some men to do as they please with the product of other men's labor."

For Marx and all socialists who, if left unchecked, slide into actual Marxism, the obliteration of private property is the centerpiece of left-wing philosophy. Thus spoke Marx: "Communism [Marxism] can be summed up in the single sentence: Abolition of private property. Precisely so; that is just what we intend." He referred not to real estate only: "Regards the property question, no matter what its degree of development at the time," in other words, even while it is still cash. Redistribution of one's earnings and cash through heavy taxation, in the name of compassion, is today's clever formula for dissolving private property and handing it over to others. As Marx said, and as other community organizers know: "The proletariat [the working class] will use its political supremacy [its voting numbers] to wrest, *by degree*, all capital [money] from the bourgeoisie [the middle, upper middle and wealthy individuals]."

★★★

Let me conclude this segment with an illustration of unreasonable, bizarre anti-capitalism. I was friends with Norman Mailer, a highly re-garded novelist and writer. Among his books was *The Naked and the Dead*, his favorite, he told me. We met at a dinner function in 1996 when he was seated to my right and a former Miss America on my left. He was covering this event and writing a piece about it for *Esquire*. On a personal man-to-man level he, unlike others in left-wing literary circles, was not haughty. I enjoyed his company. He was actually a tough guy and manly, quite dif-ferent from so many of the effete trendsetters who make up New York City's left-wing artsy circle.

But Norman hated capitalism, and our relationship evaporated when, after a conversation about Microsoft, he realized I was a capitalist. I men-tioned how private property is the essence of capitalism and how the Old Testament believes very much in private property: "And each man shall sit under *his* fig tree and under *his* vine" (Micah 4:4); "Each in *his* camp and each under *his* own flag" (Numbers 1:52); how the Ten Commandments and other parts of the Torah speak of a "man's home, his ox and cattle, and all that is *his*."

I mentioned to him that ownership is so vital to a man's sense of self-identity that the Torah in Deuteronomy 20:5-9 exempted a man who had just bought a field so that "he not die in war and his fields go into the hand of another man." The other military exemption included a newly married man, who while in battle would be forced to ponder that his death would result in "another man taking her as a wife." The Torah understood that part of human nature craves what is his to remain his. Though very literate and born Jewish, Norman told me had he no real acquaintance with the Torah or Old Testament.

The funny thing is that Norman Mailer was an owner of very outstanding private properties. One was a townhouse in Brooklyn Heights, one of the most tony and expensive neighborhoods in New York City, right on the No. 4 subway line leading directly to Wall Street. His other home was on Cape Cod in very expensive Provincetown. Furthermore, like all novelists and people in the arts, he made his wealth precisely due to copyrights on the books he wrote. He and others in the world of arts and entertainment guard their intellectual property rights and negotiate the best deals they can get. Their royalties come from publishing companies that are part of publicly traded companies listed on the New York Stock Exchange, the home of daily capitalism. Like so many on the Left, it seems to them that their work is so important they must be excluded from the very rules and propaganda they espouse. After all, their work is dedicated to showing the ills of capitalism and America.

In the end, our friendship could not last. I loved America too much. Norman's hate, or envy, for capitalism produced in later years a hate for America so much so that he ignobly wrote after 9/11 that the rubble of the Twin Towers, the World Financial Center in Lower Manhattan, looked better than the formerly erect towers themselves. It was cruel to America and, for me, personal, since I woke up every morning in 1989 and 1990 looking straight into the glistening towers themselves. You see, my apartment on West Street was the closest residential building to the North and South Towers. Norman became what my wife and I call *"American-lasters."*

★★★ TWENTY-ONE ★★★

Courage and Conviction

[*Lessons from the Bible for everyday life*]

In 2012, when I published an Op-Ed article about capitalism in *The Wall Street Journal*, I was amazed by the many hateful responses of people who disdain capitalism and see it as the root of all evil and the source of many of our problems. I am told that left-wingers coordinate people to go onto conservative websites and inundate them with liberal propaganda. It is all part of the Left's attempt to monopolize every inch of cultural, political, and media territory they can. Their motto is: *Live and do not let others live.* Much of what I have just written should answer their erroneous and, I must say, ignorant understanding of capitalism. Too many have been schooled to think capitalism is a green light for robber barons and that businessmen live by the creed of Jay Gould and James Fisk and burn dollar bills at dinner parties in vacation homes in Newport, Rhode Island. Their view of capitalism is informed by Marx and caricatures from 125 years ago. They seem unaware that by owning stocks, they are capitalists and that capitalists are not some faraway Astor or Vanderbilt, but their neighbors, friends, and relatives.

Many who commented about the article claimed the Bible was an advocate of socialism because religion is, they said, compassionate and nice. It is true that many people look at the Bible as some warm and fuzzy book telling us that happiness, inner peace, and sharing is what religion is all about. After all, socialism today is being marketed to fit our touchy-feely cultural attitude and our unexamined mantras regarding fairness and tolerance. We like platitudes that make us feel good about ourselves and do not require the hard work of discernment or a need for responsible judgment, or an ability to say no. For many liberals, themselves not very religious, the Bible can be summed up as: *Let's all just get along and give everybody what they want.* But such is not the case.

185

What is religion? Religion is man's attempt to ascertain from Scripture God's guidance as to what brings about individual growth and maturity and what, in the end, preserves and protects society. Religion has standards and involves a lifelong, ongoing struggle to demarcate between right and wrong. It provides moral clarity so that we can act and react with principle. It is certainly not a knee-jerk capitulation to feel-good, unexamined clichés. It is reality based. Ultimately it leads to cognitive growth and maturity and provides us with the inner strength and fortitude to live by principles. The Bible hopes for strong, sovereign individuals imbued with self-responsibility who can make tough decisions.

The Bible is not a manual on economic structures but a divine document explaining our relationship to God and His expectations of us, as well as a blueprint for an active, moral, and religious life grounded in human nature. It could not address modern day capitalism per se inasmuch as the paradigm of corporate and investment instruments had not yet been devised. But it did favor the natural rhythm of commercial freedom. Nothing in the Bible seems to advocate communal living. Twelve hundred years after Sinai, a tiny group called the Essenes tried communal living, but they died out since they did not reproduce. If the Bible preferred communist type living as an ideal, it would have basically done away with its dozens of laws regarding ethical business conduct and simply said: to each according to his needs from each according to his ability.

Based on its language toward the individual, its guidelines regarding private business practices, and its telegraphed assumption that commercial life consisted of buying and selling, it is obvious the Bible considered commerce part and parcel of normal life. Furthermore, its stated hope that mankind live with physical blessings, that he cultivate and subdue his environment for his own welfare, and that individuals become emotionally strong, leaves no doubt regarding its preference for a free enterprise society inherently most suitable for producing these outcomes.

Nature and man's environment were created to help men survive. Environmentalism that takes precedence over men being able to work and be supplied with energy for their hospitals, homes, transportation, and food is a worship of nature and the original brand of paganism. In the Bible God showed us a hierarchy in nature, with man at the top. God, out of love for mankind, embedded into our earth all that man needs to survive and flourish. He buried copper, ore, diamonds, oil, gas, and coal within earth's plates so we could responsibly extract them for mankind's welfare.

The Judeo-Christian belief system follows the Bible's gift of understanding and does not subscribe to Princeton's Professor Peter Singer, who posits the possibility of killing a disabled child up to twenty-eight days after birth while at the same time insists that animals should be accorded the same value as humans and should not be discriminated against. Singer is a tenured Professor of Bioethics—but it is pagan ethics, reminiscent of ancient pagan societies that allowed the killing of newborns within the first few days. Absent the Bible's basic mindset, pagan man begins valuing almost everything as more important than man. It is a form of nature worship. Too many clergy, agents of religious correctness and fearful of having religion deliver a message, which counters what the trendy beautiful people call good and nice, have endowed this form of nature worship and radical environmentalism with a religious imprimatur.

★★★

The Bible addresses the practical aspects of charity. It requires direct charity, something beneficial not only for the receiver but good for the giver as well. It speaks of a 10 percent tithing and additional (below 1 percent) giving to those impoverished or the completely stranded widow and orphan. There were offerings of thanksgiving to God from first fruits, and bountiful harvests and herds that were shared with Temple workers such as priests and Levites in compensation for the public ceremonial work they did. Due to the nature of their work, they could not get a job or own property. This arrangement between the people and the priests and Levites is rooted in the moral paradigm of reciprocity, wherein between parties trade, so to speak, on behalf of mutually beneficial partnerships.

The Bible also speaks of leaving the *gleanings* from the corners of already harvested fields for the poor. These people could harvest the grains left behind after the cutting of the crops. In Hebrew this is called *le'ket*, *shik'chah*, and *pe'ah*. But it was hardly redistribution and constituted no real loss for the owner. Leaving but corners in the lower forty and strands here and there are certainly not an indication for welfare statism. This arrangement sent the more symbolic message that one gives thanks to God and does so by remembering others of God's creatures, that we need not deplenish ourselves in our giving, and that no man is an island.

Three fundamental principles were sent by this arrangement. The first is that those wishing to partake of gleanings had to get up and do it themselves. It was not delivered to them. It constituted a type of workfair, not a check in the mail. And they needed to get up early, for failure to do so meant that others in the locality would have beaten them to the field. In other words, the Torah recognizes that in life there is competition. The owner did not have to plant more fields or work harder so as to take care of and satisfy everyone in need.

Second, we wish all citizens to be part of societal life and, for example, pray and look forward to a nation's successful bounty and other outcomes. But to do so requires *active* participation in it. Sitting back and receiving without any effort is not being actively engaged. Nor is the belief that everything is society's fault, and we need to make some type of full restitution to everybody. The Torah understood that blaming society is the tool of those who want a free ride.

Nor does the Bible say owner/producers are indifferent and bad, and that non-owners/receivers are the epitome of unblemished good. It does not operate by those dualistic categories. Nor does it subscribe to an absolutism that sees full-fledged entitlement even to those who are worthy of society's generosity.

Third, what we do is called *giving*, not sharing. Sharing implies some sort of communal ownership. Once we call what we do sharing, there is no limit to how much we, in the name of shared ownership, will be required to share. But there is *no* entitlement to that which we give others. Instead, we give with an understanding that what we give comes from the individual and is out of that which belonged to *him*. The party that gives is the benefactor, and the one who receives is a recipient. Socialists hate calling this a benefactor-recipient relationship since, in their mind, mere citizenship entitles one to that which belongs to others, making us all part of a collective. They believe that what we have belongs to the government, and we should have only what government decides should remain in our hands. In other words, they do not look at what we have as ours and tax us, at say, 30 percent; rather, they believe the government is entitled to 100 percent but lets us keep 70 percent.

At this very moment, liberals extend this belief in citizenship as a stake in collective ownership and entitlement to include every member on the globe, so that transnationalists, through the U.N., are ready to impose a global tax on us American citizens. European elites espouse the same rationale when they state that the world's citizens are entitled to share in the economic wealth of Europe and should immigrate to it and be provided welfare benefits from the earnings of its citizens. It also figures in the mentality of elites here in America who do not believe in borders.

In the Bible, every fifty years at *Jubilee*, some lands were returned to original owners. Some say this indicates redistribution of wealth. In fact, it demonstrates the opposite. Under redistribution schemes these lands would have been redistributed nationally to whomever was considered poor, as was done in certain south African countries when land was summarily expropriated from white owners and given to blacks. But during Jubilee, the lands did not get publicly redistributed to citizens in general but returned back to original owners and remained private for them. Nor were earnings and general wealth suddenly divided among all the citizens.

So as to retain the character and integrity of each of the twelve tribes of Israel—something very important to the idea of local control desired by the Bible—lands that over years were disbursed through marriage, for example, ended up back in the hands of the tribe and its families. This return was limited to land and not money. There was no Jubilee redistribution tax policy on anyone. If anything, this is a repudiation of national economic egalitarianism.

Besides keeping each of the twelve tribes intact, the Jubilee served the purpose of giving families a chance to reboot since after all, ancient Israel was an agrarian society. Our economies today are not agrarian but manufacturing and service centered. We earn our living in an actual job market. That being the case, the real opportunity for a second chance lies in jobs, jobs, jobs, and job creation is best done by the private sector, the welfare state being the nemesis of real job creation.

★★★

The prophet Micah said: "Do justice and walk humbly with your God." But the justice that Micah had in mind is not the political and sexual social justice schemes that liberals speak of for the purpose of ushering in the welfare state and socialism. Micah had in mind real justice, the type we spoke of in our chapter on social justice. Indeed, I would remind those on the Left of the "walk humbly" part, a characteristic and attitude severely lacking in their attacks on the rest of us.

Quite often, redistributionists cite the very famous verse: "And you shall love your neighbor as yourself." Let us examine this in real terms. If love means giving to him as you would give to yourself, then why are we not required to give our neighbor our house, our car, children and all our earnings? Shouldn't we, out of love, give to him what we have for ourselves? Evidently it does not mean giving to him what we have or distributing much of our earnings to him. Rather it means, as understood by wise men who pondered the implications of this passage, "Do unto others that which you want done to yourself." The love here is not in materially giving but in relational treatment. Treat others well, with dignity, respect, concern, and friendliness—until, of course, they abuse the relationship and pose a threat to life, property, and liberty. We are all entitled to equal justice under the law, access to public institutions, and respect as human beings—all part of our national Judeo-Christian American ethos. Attaining dignity comes not only by treating others with dignity, but by the receiver himself acting in a dignified manner and engaging in that which inculcates dignity—work.

★★★

"The meek shall inherit the earth" refers to those who are *humble*. Meek here does not mean poor, though quite often the poor have been made humble by their condition. Poverty is not a biblical ideal to which we strive. If it were, we should simply shed ourselves of possessions and most comforts. None of us do. Nor is it logical or right to say that the wealthy, the opposite of poor, will not inherit the earth. Many wealthy people are wonderful and came to their wealth through God-given talents and by precisely following the religious model of the Judeo-Christian ethic: hard work, frugality, sacrifice, and removal from destructive vices. It would be ludicrous and religiously inconsistent to deny them earth's inheritance because they lived by the rules.

No, inheriting the earth has nothing to do with how much one earned or owned during his lifetime. It has to do with conduct, specifically humble conduct. That meek means humble can be seen from the origin of this verse, which is the passage in Psalms 37:11: "But the humble shall inherit the land," i.e., those who have smarted under the oppression of the sinful. We have probably all known humble wealthy people as well as demanding and overbearing poorer people. Generosity of spirit or stinginess is not tied, respectively, to being either poor or rich. Let us, once and for all, disabuse ourselves of this preposterous notion that if but wealthy, no poor person would be anything but generous; and if poor, no wealthy person would be anything but noble.

Nothing more offends the biblical spirit than those who lord it over others with cruelty, forcing those beneath them to be powerless. Judeans were unduly humbled by the Romans and made meek and frightened because of them. What recourse did the meek have? Two recourses were theirs. The first was God, who said: "Vengeance is mine, sayeth the Lord." When man is powerless to fight evil, God will ultimately do battle on his behalf. And while the humbled may not in this world always see daylight, the future belongs to them, for "the meek shall inherit the earth." (Socialists involved in the politics of compassion need to become more humble themselves and stop using their governmental power to frighten people into submission, purge political enemies, and prevent people from speaking their minds. When in power, socialists overuse such terms as "hate speech" or "hate crimes" to frighten and criminalize those below whom they do not approve.)

When there is no recourse left to man, he must rely on "Vengeance is mine sayeth the Lord," but up until that capitulating moment, man is obligated to defend himself, his family, and his country from the forces of evil. Nothing is nobler than fighting evil on behalf of something far better and transcendent. "Turning the other cheek," I imagine, had to do with situations involving neighbors, friends, and family. Often, it is better in these domestic situations where no great and abiding principle is involved, to let bygones be bygones and let things pass; though it should not be done if such turning will be seen as weakness and induce the aggressor to slap once again. But when our lives and those of our children are at stake, we need to take up the cudgels of battle. Nations must do so as a matter of executing their first responsibility of protecting citizens. It seems unreasonable to me that God would demand from us a suicide pact, a formula that says the pagan may fight you, but if you are to be My follower, you cannot fight. God is not that cruel or inconsistent. Besides, He reminds us, "Therefore choose life," not suicide.

One can turn the other cheek when it comes to his own pride, but never as an excuse for allowing others to be harmed. On the one hand, if there is a chance for victory, we must do battle. On the other hand, I imagine that when the terrible time comes when all is lost, as during the period of Roman occupation of ancient Israel and Judea, it may have well been better to turn the other cheek than fight a losing battle and have untold numbers killed for no gain. When the final messianic era arrives, "Nation shall not raise sword against other nations, and men will no longer learn the ways of war" (Micah 4:3). But until such messianic time, though we do not engage in war, as did pagans before us solely for the sake of sport or to take the lands of others, it is our duty to learn the ways of war and take up arms when necessary. Anything short of that is foolish and dangerous disarmament. Liberal theologians think the messianic era will come only when we first disarm and then hope others do as well. I am not willing to sacrifice all that I love, including America, to such pie-in-the-sky notions born of escapism under a veneer of morality. My first loyalty is to people, not imaginings of man-made utopias.

I am also from those who do not believe that we can create the messianic era but see it as something that will come in its appointed time, a time God has ordained but unknown to us. Until then, I remain with the belief that, as the verse says, "*He* shall make peace" (Psalms 29:11). Ultimate peace resides in Him.

I am from those who believe that while prayer is efficacious, it is a partner to action and, by itself, not always enough. We consult with doctors, we perform our jobs, and similarly, we must be prepared to fight. As the old saying from a World War II film goes: "Praise the Lord and pass the ammunition." We pray that what we do will be supported by God. We pray that God answers our actions.

At His crucifixion Jesus said, "Forgive them for they know not what they do." The Romans knew they were killing Him but did not know *who* they were actually crucifying. They knew not what they did. Today's jihadists, however, know exactly who they are killing and what they are doing. They want to kill or at least assume power over those who are indeed known to them—Christians and Jews.

The Bible tells us, indeed inspires us to be "a light unto the nations." If the Bible said so, then what constitutes light must be the guidelines found in it, not in the Koran, not in communism, and not in socialism. These came, after all, to replace the Bible, which preceded them. They therefore cannot be the light of which the Bible speaks. Light is moral clarity to see evil and fight it. It is up to us to act by kindling that light.

To fight evil, one must first possess an appropriate moral code and perspective. United States Supreme Court Justice Potter Stewart once said: "I may not be able to define obscenity, but I know it when I see it." Without Judeo-Christian moral clarity, we are unable to apprehend and identify evil even when it is right before our eyes. One must have courage. Absent the courage to see it, speak of it, and act on it, we are left with but wisps of words, beautiful but non-supportive clouds.

Religion never came to provide ease but purpose and standards, not passivity but action: we work, we produce children, we choose, and we do. The Judeo-Christian ethos makes us strong and helps us overcome the squeamishness we feel when having to do the tough things of life. It makes us into adults who accept the gravity of responsibility. This ethos requires hard work and the ability to overcome sentimentality in favor of enduring and sometimes uncomfortable principles. Therein lies our nobility—the nobility of principle. It is not good to be nice to those who wish to rob you of your liberty, your children's future, and your nationhood. Religion tells us to arise from our childhood and take on the adult responsibility of facing a tough world. Our resolve is made easier because we know our cognition and duty are biblical. Indeed, the Bible calls us soldiers, people of strength and valor. Let not niceness be an excuse for escapism. Religion says: *Be a man*, and *be a woman*.

Being a light unto the nations does not mean leading from behind, nor does it mean conforming to a world of nations run by corruption, communism, and Islamism, which all bring darkness. It is being that *singular beacon of moral clarity* that looks at the evil ensconced in transnational moral relativism and says: No! Never!

TWENTY-TWO

Burying America

[*They come to bury America, not to praise her.*]

Many people find it difficult to believe there are Americans who dislike their own country, even though they live by its blessings. Our unwillingness to grasp this reality has contributed to our incremental capitulation to them. We keep thinking that if we just give in one more time, they will stop agitating. Wrong! They have long-term goals and longstanding prejudices.

Anti-Americanism is not new in this country. On New York's West Side from Canal Street all the way up to 179th Street, and on the East Side, from East Broadway to 23rd Street, there are enough America-haters to fill ten stadiums. I'll never forget how only two months after 9/11, *The New School for Social Research* in Greenwich Village held a lecture-symposium blaming America for the attack by Islamists. The old, grey haired communists with their new crop of *we-hate-America-firsters* couldn't wait to latch onto the anti-American Islamic cause. It made me realize that we have Americans who are anti-American, and I began writing about it in a series of articles for *Human Events*. Their dislike for America is not only political but *personal.*

Being in their unpleasant company, as I have for years, is a trying experience, requiring that you endlessly defend America from every conceivable accusation. Then, it hits you. Anyone who never gives America any slack but requires that America first prove itself regarding just about every matter is unbalanced and deluded. This is especially so since they have nothing bad to say about China, Cuba, Russia, and the PLO. We who love and respect America should pay those national hate mongers no heed and not waste our time on them. America does not need to prove itself to them; they need to prove to us why they should even live here and not emigrate to a socialist paradise they admire. They stay, unfortunately, because nowhere else is it better!

They hate America for they cannot accept the religiosity of our people and how this country was founded upon Judeo-Christian religious principles. They do not like our distinctiveness, for they are universalists. It is difficult for them to accept that the farmer in Postville, Iowa, and the businessman in Joplin, Missouri, have as much right in determining the direction of this country as do they, the "smarter" and more "enlightened." Yes, I have heard this!

They see in Islamism, as they did in communism, a movement whose goal is to replace the Judeo-Christian system and bring America to its knees. They like that. They want a top-down system under which Americans will be forced to live with the cradle-to-grave benefits they think will come to them. While they want freedom for themselves, they do not wish that freedom for everybody. It is not just a bad brand of politics, but a bad brand of character, a capitulation to the demons in human nature instead of the angels in our nature.

Many hate America because they hate regular Americans. They have a very low opinion of their fellow countrymen outside New York City, Los Angeles, or San Francisco. After a while, one begins to realize their constant reference to Americans as racists and Islamophobes—despite how Americans have turned themselves inside-out and upside-down to be fair—simply proves their own bigotry. They were raised with it. It's their problem not ours.

Others may not be viscerally anti-American but have had it too easy and have not been forced to pass through the time-tested rituals that take one from adolescence to adulthood: the hard work, the worry, the survival fears. Their bodies grow but they remain adolescents, relishing the adolescent excitement that comes from being part of a revolutionary mob. The Talmud tells us, "the proposed constructs of the immature are sandcastles and do not build up but tear down."

★★★

Let us also be mindful of the liberal ruling class. Nothing cements a ruling class status like having most citizens look to it for sustenance. This ruling class comes from the ranks of politicians, academicians, media, socialites, NGOs and other organizations, and left-wing moneyed people who not only crave power but see themselves as part of an elite internationalist set. They want "United Nations-ism" to replace Americanism. "There is nothing new under the sun," Solomon tells us. How right he was: men live still by self-worship and an inflated sense of being better than those they wish to control.

They are huge proponents of multiculturalism that will balkanize and internally weaken America, leaving no powerful constituency to stand in its way. Some, such as Ben and Jerry of ice cream fame, speak of distributing over $2 million in grants to *Occupiers* for the express purpose of agitating in the streets. Not to worry—they and their businesses will be protected by the very system that the mobs and the violence were designed to overthrow. The moneyed socialist string-pullers will make sure their wealth is secure and never have to live by the utopian formulas they envision for the rest of us. In fact, years ago in *National Review*, I published an article showing that while the Left demonizes the profits of certain companies, such as oil, mining, and timber, it approves profits in entertainment, media, and software: the former are not their businesses, while the latter are predominantly owned by them. In other words, *their* money is OK.

The very wealthy on the Left often spout socialism and speak of the unfairness of the capitalist system as a way to inoculate themselves from the charge of being from the oppressive and indifferent class. Hollywood types are notorious for doing precisely this. It is as if they say: "I am from the 'good' wealthy, and I wish I didn't have all this evil money, but I use my money for 'good causes' only." Once they establish their partnership with the "cause," they are free to continue with their lavish lifestyles and indulge in liberally using fossil fuels and other extravagances beyond the reach of most. It is one of the biggest cons of our time.

Leonard Bernstein, the *New York Philharmonic's* outstanding and dynamic conductor for many years, epitomized, and perhaps began, the phenomenon the great novelist, Tom Wolfe, was to later label *radical chic*. Bernstein spoke against wealth and privilege, yet he lived a most privileged and glamorous lifestyle—and he wanted it. He spoke against white discrimination on behalf of black power, yet he lived in a rarified and exclusive world, lily-white in its orientation and as far removed from the ghetto one could imagine. He was the embodiment of New York's upper class, protected social world. So what did he do? He invited the Black Panthers, a militant and dangerous group who spoke of bringing down whites, to his swanky New York City apartment for a fundraiser and to meet some of its most powerful socialites. He was now part of the "cause," so he had no more guilt and no more concern about living the privileged life, let alone living with huge inconsistencies and hypocrisy. After the fundraiser, he could go back to his door-manned, protected life, and not worry over his promotion of a movement that could be harmful to the rest of us who didn't have his protections and insulation. "Lenny," as called by New York's "in" social group, could get away with this because he was the most accomplished and brilliant musician of our time.

One detects among this crowd a sense of being better, which they believe gives them the authority to pontificate to those below. Inevitably this sense of being morally superior leads to a self-righteous selfishness. It is very easy to sit in one's fancy urban domicile in San Francisco, New York City, or Los Angeles, and in the name of environmentalism, shut down enterprises that provide jobs and self-reliant dignity to those in the timber and logging industries in Oregon, to fisherman and oil drillers in Louisiana, or to miners in West Virginia. Their big city livelihood is not at all affected and they can continue buying and consuming the upscale products that derive from the very elements they, the supposedly concerned environmentalists, denounced.

★★★

Like everything in liberalism, the use of lofty terms, such as multiculturalism, hides the Left's real end-game. They see how compliant too many of us Americans have become, and how we can be trusted to act with never-ending good will, even at our own cultural and economic expense. A talk show host friend of mine once remarked to me how the American people are goodwilled and constitute the most civilized, gracious, and humble people the world has ever known. We have idealism and grit. But we should not allow others to exploit our good will to our own detriment and cultural demise. Let us not be patsies.

The liberal ruling elite are the new oligarchy, and some even see themselves in the mold of Plato's "philosopher kings." Two centuries ago the aristocracy and oligarchs ruled from the Right, today they rule from the Left. They are the most dangerous to America's historic civilization and ethos, since they are the opinion shapers who daily bombard us with the incantations of liberalism. They are deft at redefining those terms precious to Americans to conform to the liberal gospel.

Mr. Obama's goal is the disintegration of the middle class. He does not desire their robust economic independence but will slowly sweet-talk them into becoming wards of the state, dependent on ever more government programs. For it is the middle class that stands in the way of the Left's complete takeover and political and social hegemony. I began writing about this subject three years ago in the *American Thinker*. America is distinguished from other countries by its robust, prosperous, and independent middle class.

Many of our middle class have already fallen for the easy money from government and have become addicted, and will vote for the liberal program lords who will feed their addictions. Many women, especially those not married or unmarried with children, see in the Bill Clintons or Barack Obamas men who will take care of them, surrogate fathers and husbands. They will vote for the presidential sugar daddies. Their choices in life will be limited to what the programs allow, and their children will be penalized by the constricted opportunities of socialism, but they are thinking of now. Unfortunately, without significant change sooner or later, the fire of self-reliance and independence will be squelched. Without the continuation of this middle class, America will become what the ruling liberal elites desire—Europe and Latin America.

★★★

Unless we reteach Americans the language and words of our moral history, the Left will shape the minds and attitudes of Americans and with it our future. One such example is their redefinition of patriotism. As mentioned earlier, I consider patriotism a moral imperative. Patriotism is loyalty and gratitude to America. America not only protects its citizens but gives them something found in greater proportion here than anywhere else in the world—freedom, the freedom to live your life according to your conscience.

America owes no one a living; it needs only to provide freedom. For this one thing alone, one should offer his loyalty and gratitude—patriotism. The Hebrew prophets delivered God's message about ingratitude: "Even the ox knows his master as does the donkey, yet the people know me not" (Isaiah 1:3).

Liberals now define patriotism as "dissent." Why? Because extreme American liberals dissent against the government when in Republican hands and dissent against America itself, both here and abroad. The late Jeane Kirkpatrick referred to them as the "blame America crowd."

In their twisted linguistics, blaming America has been morphed into "loving" America. But we all know we usually criticize and blame that and whom we detest while holding back from criticizing that and whom we love. Sure, from time to time we criticize those we love, but the Left's carping of America is constant and vitriolic, and they criticize in her that which they overlook somewhere else. Can there be any doubt, then, they find in America something so personally dislikeable that they cannot refrain from finding fault? It is America—not something else—that has been the butt of their never-ending fault-finding.

When growing up in the 1950s and 1960s, I knew many hard-core liberals who smirked at the notion of patriotism and ridiculed friends who displayed American flags on holidays. But after the U.S. hockey team victory in the 1980 Olympics (*U.S.A., U.S.A., U.S.A.!*) and the election of Ronald Reagan, it became obvious that disparaging patriotism would not fly at that time. But what does one do when he doesn't feel patriotic but must assert patriotism if he wishes to be part of the national political discussion? Redefine it to cover what you do. So in Orwellian fashion, dissent against the country has now become a sign of love of country.

But how? By asserting that dissent represents one's loyalty to the First Amendment's right to free speech. However, speaking one's mind is no more an act of patriotism than eating dinner or speaking on the phone. It is simply exercising a right one has. It is not service to one's country but service to one's own appetite or need to be heard. Serving in the military is service to one's country. Standing by your country when it is being assailed from all sides is service and patriotism to one's country.

We conservatives, in contrast to the liberal left, believe in a certain set of impartial standards that define who we are and our hopes for society. What class warfare is for liberals, honesty and fair play are for conservatives. What predetermined social justice is for liberals, impartial justice is for conservatives. What power and control are for liberals, liberty and religious conscience are for conservatives. We would never imperil our soldiers with lawsuits as does the Left. We do not believe the end justifies the means; the liberal left does and firmly believes you need to "break a lot of eggs to make an omelet." For liberals the definition of tolerance is tolerating only what liberals prefer.

Our dilemma is how to maintain or regain our freedom against those who will use any coercive power to gain power. Do we continue our nice guy standards if by so doing we deny ourselves the tools needed to fight an opposition ready to take everything from us? In other words, are we supposed to fight this ongoing battle with one hand always tied behind us? I think we no longer can. It is now crystal clear what the Left intends to do to the country—which means us. The stakes are too high.

The Left outnumbers us in full-time activists because many of these activists do not have spouses and children or attend churches or involve themselves in non-political, wholesome community life. Radical politics *is* their life and the length of their days. But more on that subject in our final chapter, "Let's Roll."

As with so many of the terms discussed, Leftist definitions are not exercises in honest description but have become acts of brainwashing. Beyond redefining words to affect domestic and foreign policy and remake the country, liberalism wishes to transform the personality of the American individual, especially the American male. In everything, they wish to make us more European, more pliant. The less Americans appreciate rugged individualism, the more easily they will submit to control from above. By disparaging the virtues we historically admired—physical bravery, self-reliance, robust families, independent thought, readiness to do battle— and loading them with negative connotations, the more likely will Americans eschew conservatism.

Even notions of self-esteem have been broadened to include antipathy to any school competition with winners and losers. Now, I am not a believer in heavy competition between youngsters when playing at home, in the backyard, or at recess. But some school activities were historically designed precisely to instill and prepare students for competition. By not preparing youngsters for competition, as adults they will need to rely more on government to fill their daily needs, because it will diminish our historic free-market system based on an ability to compete. The assault from the Left on the automobile is designed to wean us away from the notion of independence and instill in us a sense of belonging to the masses because of the resultant need to use mass transportation. Similarly, the now-fashionable criticism of home ownership, as opposed to renting, is designed to lessen our yearning for taking care of ourselves.

Many East Coast liberals, both women and men, have never been comfortable with the persona and swagger of the American male. His independence, self-confidence, and rugged nature frighten them. They like European men—not self-sufficient "cowboys." By changing the American personality, liberals can forever change the politics of America leftward.

★ ★ ★

We are at a stage now in America where the Left is telling us what we can and cannot say. We are being told what is proper thought and expected to renounce our own common sense, judgment, standards, historical awareness, and need for reciprocity. It is a power play through words as we saw in chapter 3, demanding nothing less than our intellectual surrender. We are being played for fools. We should never allow the liberal left to determine for us what is open for discussion and what is not. Who do they think they are? And who are we, if we capitulate to such control?

Worse, too often conservatives have to worry about liberals or left-wing prosecutors charging them with "hate speech." Liberals never have to worry about that. One of the big union bosses spoke of breaking the bones of Republicans. Nothing happened. But daily we see conservatives afraid to speak their mind under the ever expanding threat of being brought up on hate speech or discrimination charges. When one looks at the inconsistency and deliberate selectivity in this whole charade of hate speech, it is apparent that it is based not on a neutral test but as a tool to silence those whom liberals hate. It seems that chargeable hate speech is only that which comes out of the mouth of those whom liberals feel they have a right to hate.

In contrast, I am reminded of the incidents of Islamic speakers at public rallies shouting over microphones to cheering public crowds of their intention to "bring shariah law over America" and of their goal of "overthrowing our detestable democracy and free speech and live under submission to Islam." The views of the preannounced speakers were well known beforehand to public officials. They were nonetheless allowed to speak; nothing happened before or even after to them. They were never charged with hate speech, although their words dripped with hate.

These speakers speak with the confidence of those who know that left-wingers in power, specifically the U.S. Attorney General, will never bring them up on hate speech charges, nor will the media challenge their views. But what can be more hateful than threatening Americans—you and I—with taking away our freedom and rights and enslaving us to a forced doctrine demanding our absolute submission? To me, threatening to overthrow our country's political system and have "the American flag above the White House replaced with the flag of the Islamic Caliphate" constitutes an act of sedition itself. Yet Islam, unlike religious conservatives, is a favored minority among left-wingers, so they are allowed much latitude that prosecutors would never give conservative groups they hate.

Hate speech was a nice sounding piece of legislation that all "concerned and sensitive people" supported. I never did, even though I am Jewish, because I understood that the ultimate goal of most legislation proposed by liberals is for: (1) the purpose of social engineering, and (2) as a future tool for the strong arm of government to club conservatives. It should also be noted that many black-on-white crimes are unquestionably motivated by bias against the white victim but are never charged as hate crimes. Again, to be considered a hate crime, it must be perpetrated by those that liberals feel they have a right to hate.

In late April 2012, a few weeks after the Trayvon Martin case, a white man in Mobile, Alabama, Matthew Owen, was beaten up by a gang of twenty black people (mostly adults) with brass buckles and other items because he had asked a group of youngsters early that evening to stop playing basketball in the street and let it be quiet. I bet most of the readers have not heard about this case. Of course, not! The mainstream media today does not see its role as delivering the news but in pushing forward those news stories that bolster its view of a racist America and other liberal axioms. After leaving him in critical condition, one of the assailants yelled: "Now, that's justice for Trayvon!" Beyond doubt, this has the elements of a hate crime. We have yet to hear from Attorney General Eric Holder on the subject. Are civil rights a one-way street? Why do we sit idly by while these double standards and injustices prevail? It seems that individual rights rooted in the Constitution are no match for those called group rights, especially now that group rights are part of the United Nations international agenda, something for liberals that is far more significant and transcendent than the parochial thing called the American Constitution.

This assumption among *smugsters* of assigning automatic guilt to mainstream groups and innocence to minorities or any group within the liberal coalition is epitomized by President Obama's selective use of the term "soul-searching." The Moralizer-in-Chief exhorted Americans to do some "needed soul-searching" after an incident where police in Cambridge, Massachusetts, came to the house of Professor Skip Gates in response to a possible break-in. Although the police were trying to protect his house, President Obama assumed the police, and by implication all of us, were guilty of racism.

Similarly in the Trayvon Martin case, President Obama called upon us to "search our souls" when, in fact, it may well be that George Zimmerman was acting in self-defense and was not motivated by a dislike of blacks. We have not, on the other hand, heard from the President regarding a need for members of the black community to do some soul-searching when obvious black-on-white crime takes place or when black leaders spew venom against whites. Nor has Mr. Obama ever asked the Muslim community to search its soul after the dozens of deliberate acts of terrorism coming from its community against non-Muslims.

Obama speaks the language of morality but, in fact, reveals a value system that does not view right and wrong through a neutral lens. It is a left-wing, agenda driven value system that uses the language of morality to demarcate our society into the bad groups vs. the good groups, and it reflects a deep seated, emotional attitude of reverse racism. It is designed to condition our thinking leftward. We are wrong to assume the left-wing shares our moral value system. Their definition of morality is from a different planet—Rousseau and Marx's. We are talking into the wind.

One more example: Though the Israelis have spent the last thirty years relinquishing land to Arab states and have made and offered self-harming concessions to the PLO, President Obama asks the Israelis to "engage in soul-searching" and make even more concessions. He does not ask that of Arabs who continue rocketing Israel, refuse to recognize it as a Jewish State, and want to steal Jerusalem from her. He, as with so many liberals, lives by a mindset where well-run and productive states and communities are automatically at fault for the problems and pathologies of revolutionary societies for whom the Left automatically proffers innocence. All this soul-searching rhetoric is simply a display of President Obama's personal preference for particular groups, in this case Mideast Muslims. It is his attempt to emotionally condition us to live by a new, one-sided value system where we decide laws and reactions according to whom leftists favor. It is using the language of morality for the purpose of leftist indoctrination and ownership of our soul.

So much of this indoctrination is, I fear, geared to pave the way for a political culture where our laws will no longer be evenly applied, akin to two sets of laws. Free speech will be offered without condition to groups within the left-wing coalition, whereas conservatives and religious conservatives will have their speech curtailed by a ruling political elite determining their allowable parameters. The same for hate crimes, hate speech, and public protests. Liberal groups and individuals will be given carte blanche, whereas conservatives will be under strict scrutiny, and their basic right to public protest or self-defense will need to first pass a deliberately restrictive litmus test.

Rush Limbaugh has spoken about it and I have seen for myself the self-censorship by countless conservatives knowing that Liberal Big Brother is listening and watching. I do not ever remember a period when so many Americans were afraid to simply give a conservative opinion. Making people live in fear may come natural to left-wing leaders, but wouldn't you agree that in the last four years there is something in the air utterly censorious and un-American? You and I hear on a daily basis of some left-wing politician or activist, be it Nancy Pelosi or Al Sharpton, threatening to shut down a conservative talk show host or calling for the removal of conservative commentators—threatening their jobs and livelihoods. Left-wing organizations monitor whatever anyone says. School principals and students, office managers and coworkers are afraid to talk like regular human beings used to talk prior to the reign of liberal political correctness, Eric Holder, and soul-searching.

★★★

Liberals need not fear that Republicans in office will subject them to the same scrutiny that liberals demand of conservatives, for in the area of political power, Republicans have shown far less willingness to exercise power as do liberals. It is either out of fear of how the press and media will portray Republicans or due to the license given to liberals to do anything they want so as to help the people and combat racism, a template not granted Republicans.

In politics, which touches all of life, power goes to those who are willing to use it, and society gradually accepts the demands of those who exercise it. The Obama years are proving exactly this. Similarly the aggressiveness of Islam to exercise power is what is bringing so many societies under its heel, reshaping societies worldwide to accept demands it would never accept absent the use of Islam's power, intimidation, and plain old in-your-face assertiveness.

We are reaching what Senator Ron Johnson (R-Wisconsin) called a national Stockholm Syndrome, where so as to be spared further harassment from our liberal captors, we begin accepting what is presently demanded just so we can hopefully be left alone. But we know we won't be left alone. My question is: Why don't Republicans use these overreaches and intrusions as *opportunities* to alert the public to the authoritarian nature of Mr. Obama and left-wing Congressional leaders?

The Achilles heel of America has always been our good nature and desire to be fair. But we can't allow ourselves to become suckers or indoctrinated. Some street smarts and discernment are in order. We cannot allow deliberately false definitions of fairness to be the tool to bring about our serfdom and self-abasement.

As worrisome as this is, nothing is as reprehensible and dangerous as what we are now seeing, which is frothing into an uncontrollable nightmare: *the liberal justification to hate*. It begins with demonizing those mainstream groups that liberalism considers guilty and ends with a permission to hate them. It appeals to the dark side of human nature. That is why I say today's Left is not so much theory-based as it is emotion-based, giving the emotional license to hate, which under normal circumstances is ignoble, but with the stamp of approval of political liberalism is given credence.

We conservatives fervently disagree with the liberal agenda and find many of its spokespeople rude and obnoxious, but when we confront them, one does not see hate on our faces. In contrast, just look at the faces on TV of so many from the left-wing community and listen to their voices on the radio. Listen carefully to their extremely angry talk and the dreadful things they say. When George Zimmerman's father was basically placed under house arrest by the Black Panthers, he remarked how "he had never in his lifetime seen such hate."

Just look at the hate-filled faces of *La Raza,* the Hispanic group protesting our immigration laws, when threatening Americans. Look here in New York City at the faces of radical feminists when mockingly speaking about men, or members of *Queer Nation* when speaking about the Catholic Church. Look at MSNBC hosts when speaking about Evangelical Christians, and left-wingers when speaking about conservatives. Listen to the calls into WLIB in New York City, a black station, where callers have spoken of doing horrific things to white people. Then there are the faces of hate and the vile speech coming from Islamists when speaking of Jews and Christians and America. What is even worse to behold is the accepted hate on the faces of those arrayed against Israel who seek her destruction, the Middle East's only democracy and only humane society.

All these haters have one thing in common: assigning themselves victim status or labeling the groups they oppose as being oppressive and therefore worthy of being hated, making the age-old demon within us as something *proper*. In other words, we have permission to hate as long as we hate the right group. In the name of racism, Islam, black power, feminism, Hispanic power, secularism, gay rights, colonialism, the poor against the rich, and liberalism, we can hate all who fit into the categories they deem hate worthy. And we can feel good about our hate. We vent all the pent-up demons in our nature and, in the name of progressiveness, submit to Satan's spell.

In the new left-wing morality, the good that people do will not count if they are a member of the wrong group. The Judeo-Christian ethos judges the individual by what he does while the leftist morality evaluates according to group identification. Therefore all the merciful, humanitarian, and medical treatment Israel provides Muslims and others are negated by the Left, as are all the herculean efforts by whites to be fair and kind overlooked by the race hucksters. For left-wingers, no redemption is possible among the groups it considers outliers, while no effort or fairness are required for those groups assigned victim status. No good deed is allowed to stand in the way of the pleasure that comes through self-righteous hatred.

Left-wing morality is a complete repudiation of Judeo-Christian morality. The phenomenon of self-righteous hatred is not new. What is new is that while up until World War II it was the province of those on the extreme European Right, today it is the province of the universalist Left.

What is it that the Left abhors the most? *Distinctiveness!* Universalism, which is leftism, despises anything distinct. America and Israel are distinct in their fidelity to liberty, the Bible, and their special relationship, as well as in the energy and entrepreneurship of their people of action. Both represent a specific Western heritage. Evangelicals are not simply Christians, but distinct Christians religiously attached to Americanism and sexual morality. Manhood is, in universalist liberal circles, something too distinct, as is Americanism itself.

For secularists, religion is too distinct. For radical egalitarianists, the division of men and women, boys and girls as separate biological and emotional beings is too distinct. For radical environmentalists, man himself is too distinct and guilty of speciesism. While each left-wing group specializes in its particular hostility, they are all joined and branded by a victimhood they claim comes from groups living in distinctiveness.

Liberal Christians are generally spared the wrath directed at distinctly Christian Evangelicals. After 1960 and the election of a Catholic

Democratic president, Catholics were spared wrath, but with the advance of the pro-abortion and homosexual movements, Catholicism has become a target of left-wing activists once again due to their pronounced condemnation of abortion and homosexuality. In this area they, like Evangelicals, are distinct in their opposition to our culture's sexual permissiveness.

Israel is distinct, and so as not to be accused of anti-Semitism, closet Jew haters (and those Jews who hate their own Jewish distinctiveness) accuse her of colonialism, though Israel is the tiniest of countries and is simply trying to hold on to the little territory it has. The false charge of colonialism is being used by Israel's enemies as a left-wing tool to steal from Israel its tiny land simply because the Muslims want it for themselves. In contrast, actual Islamic colonialism all over Africa, Asia, and Lebanon in the Middle East is overlooked and seen as an entitlement.

★★★

The greatest machine for hate today is emanating from the Muslim leadership. Like the Left, it rationalizes and sanctifies its hate by pretending to be a victim. I say pretend, since an aggressive, conquering Islam is the last thing one would characterize as a victim. But its fraternity with the Left is that it justifies its hate under the banner of victimhood. Thus, it is allowed to hate.

Islam is also part of the Left because it subscribes to top-down rule from a supreme leadership, submission of its population to "authorities who know best," and because, in typical left-wing fashion, it espouses a welfare state system where the productive (infidels) will take care of the people (Muslims). It chooses to side with the Left because it and the Left are motivated by a singular emotion—anti-Americanism.

Aside from the anti-Americanism they have in common, why has the Left chosen to partner with Islam? Because at the root of leftism today is permission to hate those it considers hateable. Left-liberalism is part of the global fraternity of hate, and the leader of that fraternity is Islamism; Islamism has become the flagship of hate. The Left practices hate but is still reluctant to admit it, while Islam, with Tehran as is its headquarters, proudly and unabashedly proclaims it.

People of good will, bereft of excessive anger, usually end up being conservatives. People filled with gratitude usually end up conservatives. Many people, however, with deep-seated latent anger and resentment gravitate to left liberalism.

No people are as distinct as the Jewish people, and thus no people will be a greater target of left-wing hate as will be the Jewish people. For whatever reason, it is viewed as a separate identity. The Bible in Numbers 23:9 declares: "It is a nation that will dwell alone." I thank God for our Christian friends, who have been the single exception, showing that while the Jewish people are alone, they need not be *totally alone.*

Anti-Semitism is an immovable force that forever has been around. Up until ten years ago, I thought that maybe things had finally changed. But looking at the worldwide obsession of dismantling Israel while ignoring all the genocide in Africa and Asia, has brought me back to the belief we all felt after the Holocaust. Anti-Semitism is an inexplicable emotion forever growing in the bosom of mankind, with the exception of the few noble spirits among us.

Jew hatred was a driving force in pre-World War II right-wing politics out of its sense of being superior to the stateless and non-powerful Jew. Today it comes from the Left for precisely the opposite reason: because Jews have a distinct and successful state and because Jews stand out as a people that excel. Left-wing politics is based on group resentment and jealousy of successes achieved by other groups. The jealousy is papered over by claiming the success of such an outside group has come through oppressing the grievance group. America is, similarly, hated because of its success.

Jewish distinctiveness is a matter beyond the purview of this book. Many Jews have run from it and embraced its opposite—universalism, which is a false messiah. We Jews did not historically engage in proselytization when we defined ourselves mostly in religious terms. But there does seem among Jews on the Left, and those who subscribe to universalism, a pronounced effort to proselytize on behalf of left-wing causes.

My concern is not regarding right-wing anti-Semitism, but with left-wing anti-Semitism, since today's Western world operates (except for conservatives in America and pockets in Australia and Canada) by a decidedly left-wing cultural and political ethos. The glorification of leftism is the message of worldwide entertainment, media, universities, books, politics, and international agencies. It is not conservatives who target Israel; rather, it is the global liberal and socialist fraternity that reserves a specific and mind-boggling animus for Israel.

The justification of and free pass for hate provided by today's left liberalism is not limited to the object of hatred but extends to all those who identify with the object of left-wing hatred. Thus, not only are Israelis targeted for hatred but all Jews who identify with Israel. Islamists have declared that any Jew in the world is a justifiable target since it is assumed that he identifies with the Zionists. Furthermore, he who identifies with a victim is given license to hate, so now Irishmen and Norwegians can hate Israel and try to smash her because these northern Europeans are doing so on behalf of Muslim victims in Gaza.

Indeed, anti-Semitism will soon be openly acceptable to a degree stronger than the racism we saw against blacks and others because it will be coming not from the Right but the worldwide Left. What the Left does is always acceptable because it is done on behalf of the people. Nor, I fear, will the establishment Jewish organizations tackle the anti-Semitism as is done when coming from the Right inasmuch as these organizations find it difficult to denounce the left-wingers to whom they are so tied. In 1991, none of the establishment Jewish organizations did anything during the pogroms against Hasidic Jews in Crown Heights, Brooklyn, because the attacks were coming from blacks, their co-partners in the left-wing coalition.

As has been shown, many Jews are hard-core leftists. So as to spare themselves left-wing criticism, or because their loyalty is, in principle, to leftist causes and not Israel or Judaism, they have abandoned Israel. I will never abandon her. Not only because I am, like David of Zion, a Zionist; not only because of the indisputable justice of her cause; but because the battle today between Right and Left revolves around support for Israel and love of America.

As I will explain in the next chapter, political liberalism is the cancer that has disproportionately affected post World War II Jewry. So strong is its grip that, in loyalty to leftism, thousands of Jews have traded in their birthright and become part of the anti-Israel movement. Evidently being born Jewish is no guarantee of nobility, though nobility still resides in the peoplehood itself, which transcends those puffed-up, individual scoundrels within.

The historic and monumental irony in all this is that the very Left that is a political god and personal identification for so many American Jews is turning out to be the single greatest vehicle for anti-Semitism, a nightmare that is taking over socialist-Islamic Europe, otherwise known as Eurabia. Wherever Leftism grows, so will anti-Semitism. Wherever leftism takes hold, so will anti-Israelism, including the Democratic Party.

Our country is heir to definitions and concepts that represent the accumulated wisdom and faith of great thinkers and forbearers. It took thousands of years to reach these understandings, beginning as far back as the epoch of the Bible. It represents our heritage. Conservatism wishes to conserve this wisdom and attitude. Moral conservatism is more than a political ideology but represents an approach to life itself. We dare not allow the high priests of political correctness and the modern-day leftists intent on destroying this heritage, to redefine who we are, what we believe, and tell us black is white, and canards are truth. For what is at stake is Americanism. What is at risk is—everything!

★★★ TWENTY-THREE ★★★

The Tower of Babel

[*Multiculturalism, transnationalism, and universalism*]

We understand the advantage of socialism to those who do not wish to work and would rather be supported by fellow citizens through government's redistribution of wealth. But why are so many wealthy people and elites in government and academia pushing for the welfare state and socialism? People on the Left are not casual about their positions but zealously and unremittingly push them to a degree that exceeds anything found among conservatives. And they do so with anger, arrogance, and self-righteousness. There must be something at play here that goes beyond the politics of the day and represents something fundamental that reaches back even to the days of man's antiquity. What is it?

As we have seen, leftism is rooted in a personal abhorrence for that which is distinctive and that which represents specific identity. Socialism as a political ideology gives outward body to an inner, emotional disdain found in many people throughout history for that which is distinctive and identity specific. The Old Testament came specifically to uproot this pernicious disease, for what it represents, as we will soon show, is paganism itself. Socialism desires sameness and rejects the hierarchy of values and judgment regarding activities that the Bible enunciates.

Cultural Marxism, introduced by Antonio Gramsci, is the ultimate goal of socialism. It reduces and levels every activity to equal value, and unlike the Bible, does not distinguish between the sacred and profane, the holy and the vulgar, the pure and impure, the wholesome and the unwholesome. It blurs light from darkness and diminishes the dignity and majesty by which men are to live.

The Bible came to battle the moral relativism of paganism and release men from its enticing but vulgar grip. Political socialism is paganism's modern day version, a *neo-paganism* arraying its forces to undercut and vanquish the biblical God and His prescriptions and standards for whole-some and blessed life.

The battle is not new, rather the oldest battle of mankind. It is the battle within and among humans regarding which spirit is to be their guide and god. It is the most titanic and enduring of all human struggles. It is the battle that never ends. Just as we religious people do not take lightly the *call* of the Bible, neo-pagans, the socialists, and cultural Marxists, drive forward in zeal on behalf of their god. It is no accident that Marx, Lenin, Mao, Castro, and so many movers-and-shakers in yesterday's and today's Left were and are secular, indeed anti-religious and disdainful of the Old Testament. They came not simply to promote a philosophy but, as Amalek, battle God Himself.

What else but human arrogance accounts for a battle against God Himself? What else but self-righteousness instead of God's righteousness? And what else but anger motivates those livid at a God who limits our lusts and demands obedience? The battle eternal and within nations is always—on a deep, unconscious level—a battle over values and morality—God's or Apollo's.

Thus for socialists, the first order of business is to strip America of its godly Judeo-Christian ethos and slowly dissolve the distinctiveness and special identity of America to its creed of sameness. President Obama, for example, cannot bring himself to admit *exceptionalism* to America nor even a special identity. Elitists tear down our Founding Fathers by calling them Dead White Males and, like Mr. Obama, criticize our Constitution as a flawed document. Are we to accept socialism's economic sameness for all, and its ultimate goal of social, cultural, and sexual sameness? Remember, the elites, like Lenin and friends before, will exclude themselves from forced economic parity. If they have their way, we will no longer be allowed to demarcate; we will become a judgment-free and values-free nation; and will have cast away the individuality and standards befitting those whom God created in His image.

The battle over which spirit will prevail—the secular or majestic, the pagan or distinctive—is playing out on dry land in our physical realm. The battle line has been drawn: Will America be allowed to continue to exist as a Judeo-Christian country and will Israel be allowed to even exist? Undermining capitalism, which is part and parcel of the Judeo-Christian heritage, is but a first step in socialism's march.

The Tower of Babel

It was almost three years ago when I first heard President Obama and some in his administration speak of *freedom of worship*. It sounded strange to me, an American, raised on the idea of *freedom of religion*. Immediately I knew this was no accident but a casual and sly way of convincing Americans that our religious freedoms are limited to houses of worship, performed at particular moments in private buildings. Only someone raised as a child outside America could be so alien in his thinking as to what America is. He may have studied *about* America but evidently never adopted its spirit. "Okay, little doggie, you can go out now for a few moments and do your religion."

It is a brazen attempt to change America's historic understanding and thinking regarding its public Judeo-Christian face, an outlook where God is not confined within someone's four private walls but remains our public backbone and touchstone. It is an affront to a nation that shapes and recognizes its distinctiveness precisely by the values and morality of our Bible. Without it, we have no special identity, and Obama knows it. "We are no longer a Christian nation," he tries convincing us. Like all socialists and cultural Marxists, he seeks to neutralize and rob us of our public religious values, since they continue to inform and guide our culture. Public Judeo-Christian expression is the single greatest and most effective obstacle to cultural Marxism and economic socialism.

★★★

What is this paganism that the Bible came to overturn? Paganism is the belief in many gods—pantheism. Ancient paganism did not make judgments over which god was better; each nation could serve its own gods, though it had to acquiesce to the supremacy of the ruler's god. At first blush, it seems like a very inclusive arrangement, except that gods were not simply objects to be worshiped but represented values, moralities, and lifestyles. Though God created man in His image, pagan men created gods in their image to reflect their personal preferences. It seemed as if they were worshiping gods, but what they were worshiping was themselves.

Let us return for a moment to the Bible. We read of people worshiping the stars, the moon, the *Ashera* trees, and a host of other deities. Let us not think the Canaanites, or the Israelites who sometimes departed from God and worshiped the Canaanite gods, actually believed that a stone, or tree, or animal was able to deliver blessings. No, these gods were fashioned to express particular human desires and lusts, and by worshiping them as gods, men were giving themselves permission to satisfy their lusts and desires and sanctify it under a spiritual template. Their obscenities became sanctified; a hedonistic lifestyle became acceptable. They venerated moral relativism, in other words, all gods and the moralities they represent are equal and the same. This is the seductive, universal appeal of paganism.

Along came the Almighty, the One true God and Creator of man, and declared *No*. Not all values are equal; some are dangerous. Not all so-called moralities are valid; in fact, moral relativism—sameness—confuses and blurs the difference between light and darkness. What seems benign or is characterized as simply an alternative is actually deadly. Not all pleasures of the flesh are acceptable, nor is tolerance for everything healthy. While it feeds man's appetite, unbridled tolerance lowers the standards of mankind.

God in the Torah called paganism, *avodah zarah*, which means a strange and alien ideology. God admonished over paganism's casual values and its system of moral relativism that rejected what was distinct and pure. God did not want man to be lured by a value system that harmed man's soul and body—his outlook. While paganism can appear beautiful and self-fulfilling, it ultimately infects the individual and corrodes society.

The nations surrounding Israel did not depart from paganism, and the Book of Judges and the Prophets is an historical record illustrating Israel's slide into and out of *avodah zarah*—the value system of paganism. As it was then the battle of the ages, so is it the same battle today, except that the gods of paganism have been given different names, such as tolerance, openness, love, understanding, socialism, worldliness, Marxism, and *multiculturalism*.

God told ancient Israel and then later the Christians that morality and values come from a singular, distinct God. God's morality should apply to all men, since God, who announced these values and morality, created all men. Men created by One God should abide by His singular system of morality. As God is distinct so is His morality distinct. God chose the seed of Abraham, Isaac, and Jacob to live by and carry forth this message: "For you shall be for me a holy nation" (Exodus 19:6). Being "a light unto the nations," as spoken by the later prophets, was God's reiteration that light, blessing, and health come from living according to biblical morality.

It is not enough to simply worship one entity—there are other nations that worship one; it is living by His values and morality. Not all religions are the same simply because they share a noun called religion. We know the distinct God by the biblical dictates He has taught. We are Jehovah's servants only when conforming to His distinct morality—a morality that says not everything is equal, the same, or as good.

After the destruction of ancient Judea, no nation committed itself to live by this distinct morality until the creation of the United States, a society founded in and dedicated to the Judeo-Christian ethos. We are not Africa, Europe, or Saudi Arabia.

"Religion and *morality* establish the principles upon which freedom can securely stand," John Adams said when talking about the Old and New Testament. We are not a pagan nation of moral relativism and our religion is from the one, biblical God. George Washington said: "It is impossible to govern rightly without God and the Bible." America, like Israel, is the most distinct of modern day nations. It has a specific identity, one that sits in the craw of the neo-paganists, socialists, and all the other ists of moral relativism. In their mind, now is the moment, in the name of sameness, to finally smash the Ten Commandments on the altar of Baal.

★★★

Each era and epoch in mankind's history speaks with a different terminology. The ongoing conceptual battle continues but is titled according to the language and cultural idioms of the day. Secularists today do not speak in terms of pantheism. It is not the idiom of the day. Being secular, they do not justify their beliefs and what they do by referring to the many gods. Today we speak in terms of culture or race. But self-worship, moral relativism, hedonism, and emotional distaste for that which is distinct or not wishing to judge remain very much alive. As we have seen, the word used today to express the paganistic value system of old and lure people to it as something transcendent is *multiculturalism*.

For liberal secularists, multiculturalism is transcendent, for it is the ultimate virtue above everything else, more important than nation, common sense, and even family life. But we need to judge so we can maintain and uphold standards. Not being allowed to judge means we are but animals, instead of humans with brains given by God precisely because of our need to demarcate, discern, and judge.

Secularists and elites in Europe worship multiculturalism as a type of social messianism and liberals and cultural elites here in America have, for the last twenty years, inundated us with it. But it is not the harmless theme they pretend it to be. It preaches that all values, cultures, moralities, and religions are the same and "relative"; that what the United States has lived by is not better, not even for here. Lately, it has been used to assign not simply equal validity of other cultures to ours, but diminish and cancel out our historic culture in favor of foreign cultures and religions. In terms of values, *multiculturalism is today's version of multigods*, and open-ended *tolerance* is today's version for allowing *hedonism* or accepting the *intolerable*, especially regarding whatever Islam wants or does.

Multiculturalism is the sociological tool by those in the West wishing to shove aside Western values and, in the United States specifically, to announce that we have no distinct culture and no specific identity. It denies and mocks not only our religious roots but also our cultural ethos, our value system, and even our mainstream population. It believes that, like 2012 Europe, our identity should be *No Identity*, indistinguishable from others, simply one landmass among the many landmasses. It says our identity should be decided by those who have come here of late, legally or illegally. It is universalism. It demonizes those who believe in language, culture, sovereignty, borders, and Americanism.

The English language is essential for teaching an American culture rooted in common and specific values. Literature conveys the values of the country in whose language the literature is written. If one wants to know the values of America and the Judeo-Christian ethos, one needs to read the authors and literature written in the language wherein these values are singularly embodied—*English*. Sticking to Arabic or Spanish simply reinforces the outlook and value system of those cultures.

★★★

The multiculturalists do not like our culture, and multiculturalism is the god behind which they are changing it without our knowing it. They have waited a long time for this opportunity and in finding *the* hallowed term under which to transform America, so that while the land, the shell, seems the same, the spirit, our inside and content, is no longer. A bottle that on the outside is labeled Coke, but on the inside is filled with dark-looking root beer is not Coke.

Diversity is enriching; multiculturalism is deadly. Diversity allows other cultures to introduce us to various foods, music, and language, but is done under an overarching American culture and value system by those who identify as American. In contrast, multiculturalism comes to erase any overarching historic American culture and value system and wants its adherents to remain separate entities.

A multiculturalism that began as an effort on behalf of inclusion of others has ended in exclusion—exclusion of us. Multiculturalism wishes to disenfranchise us because it knows that we are the last and only thing standing in the way of its transformation of America into the Land of No Identity. The term *racist* is being harnessed and exploited to silence those who see multiculturalism for what it is, understand its end goal, and have the honor and conviction to oppose it.

Referring to what people do as being pagan sounds so harsh and something that only a religious nut would suggest. Certainly so when those engaged in cultural paganism call themselves Christian or Jewish. So what is paganism? Paganism is not defined as worshiping Zeus. If that were the case, the world today would have not one pagan—yet, we have many. Paganism is *moral relativism*, making the vile seem as good as the sacred; *hedonism*, claiming all values are the same or equally valid and a rejection of certain biblical fundamentals regarding sexual conduct; and the worship of one's many trendy gods. It exists even within those who, out of convenience, call themselves Christian or Jewish. Some are Jewish not by faith but simply biology, while others have transformed the Jewish faith to match and reflect popular, easy, and all-permissive values.

Liberal Jews fear that if anything and everything is not assigned equal sameness, that if one demarcates, then Jews will be singled out as a minority. They have this fear of what they call "majorityism": unless proven otherwise, one may assume someone from the majority is inherently racist. That is why so many of its major organizations are so quick to call people racist; and that is why, as a safety valve, so many push for social engineering. This need for safety in sameness leads many to promote the concept of "nothing is distinguishable" to far-fetched levels which belie reality. But I maintain that goodwilled people can make distinctions, have standards, and acknowledge differences between groups without it leading to prejudice. Among the conservative groups to whom I speak, I have received warmth and a feeling of brotherhood. They love my being Jewish.

Pagans need not appear like Attila the Hun, but are very often charming, well educated, cultured people with manners, who attend the theatre and fine restaurants. The Greeks, Romans, and Persians did. Many powerful people advocate, or at least mouth, all the trendy and fashionable slogans of permissiveness and universal sameness; and that is because in many of today's upper echelons, one needs to spout the left-wing creed if one is to be part of the glamorous social life, get invited to the sought-after dinner parties, obtain awards and recognition, and move up in much of Wall Street. Liberalism is one's ticket into the elitist club—and money. It bestows one with instant *I am good*-hood and the important people will, therefore, not feel uncomfortable around him. Many people simply cannot resist the lure and temptations. No one ever said it is easy to remain a person of principle.

★★★

Nothing more suits those who have made tolerance their new god than tolerating and accommodating Islam, for Islam represents the ultimate test for tolerating that which is radically different. One proves his bona fides as a worshiper of tolerance by tolerating that which is most contrary to his own national ethos and background. Islam has misogynist views regarding women, censors speech under blasphemy laws, controls every aspect of human life, imposes its ethnic will over others, believes in submission, excludes those called infidels, and lives by cruel "honor" codes. Its outlook is more at odds with Western and America values than any culture and religion ever brought into our midst.

For the tolerance-worshipers, Islam is the ultimate verification of their tolerance, by *tolerating the intolerable*. No one in America gets tolerance points for tolerating things Christian, and that is why the tolerance industry rarely cares to show a tolerance of things Christian. But so much of what Islam advocates cannot be tolerated by us people of enlightenment, standards, and basic humaneness.

The multiculturalist mongers among us have been pushing Islam at breakneck speed, for nothing serves as a more useful tool to transform our culture than does Islam. For Western and American multiculturalists intent on dismantling our specific culture, Islam is a godsend. On behalf of fairness to Islam, multiculturalism is making us accommodate and change to Islam's preferences. In England, schools no longer plan to teach about the Holocaust because it is offensive to Islam. Certain Islamic leaders say the Holocaust never happened, though I am a personal eyewitness of Holocaust survivors with concentration camp numbers branded into their skin. Like in Europe, certain Islamic neighborhoods here want to live under Islamic shariah law. Each time the multiculturalists are successful in forcing these things on us in the name of accommodation, our society gets a bit more transformed.

The ACLU and other groups are allowing school curricula to teach portions of the Koran, celebrate aspects of Ramadan, produce school plays with stories and themes directly from the Koran, and set aside rooms in public schools for Islamic prayer. This is 100 percent opposite of how during the last fifty years the ACLU has tried to outlaw any public or educational expression of Christianity. The ACLU says none of this poses a problem regarding separation of Church and State, for it is "not religion but simply cultural." This is humbug; and it demonstrates how, all along, the ACLU and other multiculturalists were not bothered by religion per se but only Christian religion. The more the ACLU and multiculturalists can push the religious aspects of Islam into public life, the sooner it reaches its goal of America no longer being a Judeo-Christian society. We will become members of what President Obama calls the "Abrahamic Code," because Islam claims lineage from Abraham.

Islam is a very willing partner to multiculturalism, for they have come, unlike other groups, not to integrate but to push their faith and culture—*to change us*. We are the new frontier for creating *dar al islam*, territory for Islam. No group has so vigorously and rapidly pushed and forced us to bend to it as has Islam. Many in our society are unaware how almost hardly a week goes by without C.A.I.R (Council on American Islamic Relations) instigating a complaint or lawsuit to have its ways forced on American society. Everything is couched as a civil rights issue, but its unrelenting aggressiveness indicates it is about making us submit. (Islam is Arabic for submission.) America has had a multitude of groups come here, but none have used the legal system in such short time (ten years) or intimidation process to change society as has Islam—not the Italians, Chinese, Vietnamese, or even the Hispanics. There is no Hispanic theology or political mandate to take over on behalf of Cortezism. But the multiculturalists require us to capitulate to Islam in order to prove our innocence and lack of racism. But shouldn't it be the other way around? I don't think we need to prove a thing; rather, they need to prove it to us!

So as to allow Islam to play its part in transforming America into the multiculturalist dream, we are being forced to be blind to what we see and suspend our commonsense judgment. Unwillingness to be part of the lie and opt for truth, brings immediate condemnation and demonization as one who is intolerant, phobic, bigoted, old-fashioned, or non-multicultural, a cardinal sin. The multiculturalists' agenda will not abide the American people getting in its way.

Because multiculturalists do not like our specific historic culture and wish to denude us of it, they prefer *transnationalism* to nationalism. They are much happier with an America that is no longer distinct and makes her needs secondary to the needs of the world. This is the overriding principle of Obamaism. It is transnational and, as shown in the previous chapter, makes our national interests submissive to the socialist world. One is either a nationalist or transnationalist.

★★★

This dislike for one's own distinctiveness was the source of ancient Judea's two destructions—the destruction by Babylonia in 586 BC and by Rome in 70 AD. Toward the end of each Commonwealth, the cultural and political elites succumbed to cynicism, boredom, and embarrassment regarding their own national Jewish distinctiveness. They preferred outside powers and cultures to their own. Many collaborated with the enemy by endorsing a national cultural suicide. They became all caught up in universalism, and their loyalties were not to Israel but Israel's would-be conquerors; after all, the would-be conquerors represented the world at large. So they did the enemy's work for them. They made it easy for the enemy. As I will show later in the chapter, there are those in today's current cabal of "Jewishness as Universalism" who are in similar fashion trying to weaken and bring down the Third Commonwealth, today's State of Israel. *Avodah Zara* refuses to die and remains the most potent challenge to our identifiable existence. It constitutes the *Fight of the Ages*.

Similarly toward its end, Rome's cultural elites became cynical about Rome itself. Cynicism about one's own nation is at first considered sophisticated and worldly, but it always leads to national weakness. Rome's borders became porous, and invaders entered and settled. In the end, Rome payed tribute money to those invaders and new settlers to protect them from *them*. As history has shown, "sophistication" is not necessarily a sign of maturity or of practical responsibility. Elitist cynicism is often rooted in a sneering disbelief in the sincerity and integrity of the common man who puts his country first. Cynicism and pessimism regarding human nature is at the core of Marxism and all left-wing ideologies.

Nations that engage in the sins of hedonism, cynicism, and moral relativism do not get punished in some type of divine tit-for-tat immediate way. No, God warns of how the consequences of sin lead to weakened and confused societies, cultures preoccupied with foolishness and indifference

220

to that which constitutes genuine valor. It becomes so internally weak that enemies from without can just march in and simply take over.

Universalism is a by-product of the disdain one feels toward one's own cultural and religious distinctiveness. Universalism is a rejection of specific personal and national identity. A nation that rejects its religious distinctiveness rejects the moral and sexual codes, and limitations, set by its religion. Let's go back to the Bible for some insight, since the Bible chose to write only those stories of ongoing, timeless importance. This is exactly what happened during the time of King Ahab and his foreign Queen Jezebel. As a foreigner, Jezebel did not subscribe to Israel's distinct religious code. She had inordinate influence over her husband and, together, they changed the national culture of ancient Israel to a permissive and hedonistic one, similar to the paganism and pantheism of surrounding nations. They reintroduced the alien and strange ideology referred to before as *avodah zarah*. Only one man, Elijah, stood in their way and defended the distinctive religious code of Israel and fought their ideology of universalism and pleasure.

There were hundreds of other prophets. Where were they when it came time to defend the faith? The answer is that they were but false prophets, clergy, who, instead of doing their job, endorsed the multiculturalism and template of open-ended tolerance. They became advocates of moral relativism. They chose fashion and reformed the religion to reflect the popular values of Jezebel's reign. But why didn't the people throw the bums, the false prophets, out? Because outwardly, the false prophets observed all the rituals and religious practices. They did not condemn the God of Israel, but simply felt that He should live along with the other gods. God, they felt, needed to be a little more open and inclusive.

I can only imagine the loneliness Elijah felt, ridiculed by society and his religious peers in the clergy. Like many in the clergy today, the false prophets of old co-opted the religion they were entrusted to guard and made rights the cornerstone of the religion, even though those sexual rights and sacrifices of babies to Molech were a negation of the biblical Word and Judaism itself. Fortunately for history, monotheism, and religious distinctiveness, Elijah prevailed and the pantheism and universalism of Jezebel and her false clergy were vanquished. But not forever, since pantheism and its gods of alternative values keeps resurfacing among all mankind.

In the case of the Jewish people, after the Nineteenth Century Emancipation, many Russian Jews turned to universalism. They no longer wanted the old religion and felt no need for a different one. But as with all human beings, they wanted something transcendent in their lives. It became universalism. Universalism was a way to be tied to all of humanity instead of to one's own distinctive people. Besides, they probably reasoned, if all of mankind were universalists, they would not see Jews as members of a specific race or religion.

Their children who came to America latched on to political liberalism. Liberalism became for them a substitute religion, indeed liberalism became their primary religion, intermingled with some of the homey and cozy Jewish rituals and holidays they yearly reinterpreted to conform to, and reflect, whatever was the liberal agenda or slogan of the day: civil rights, disarmament, environmentalism, choice, multiculturalism, or feminism. I call it *pop religion* or *bubble-gum religion*, where every ancient ritual is morphed into a symbol expressing the trend of the day. Unlike Christianity, Judaism is not strictly faith-based, but comes to one automatically through the biology of having been born into it. Many remain Jewish, though their real faith lies in utopian liberalism. Their *particularism lies in universalism*. For a vast amount of secular and liberal American Jewry, the only remaining identification with being Jewish is voting for the Democratic Party. It constitutes their observance of Judaism.

The problem with universalism is that it always makes primary the interests of the world over those of its own people. Every idea and ideal becomes secondary and is in service to universalism: thus, their discomfort with patriotism. In fact, among very secular Jews, the purpose of Judaism and Jews is to do everything on behalf of everybody but Jews—universalism *uber alles*. For them, the needs of Israel are secondary to those making demands of Israel. For them, nothing could be more Jewish than making Israel sacrifice itself on behalf of those who wish to cancel it as a Jewish state. Because of their universalism, they are in the forefront of the campaign to discredit Israel and are claiming to do it in the name of "Jewishness"! For them, Israel represents national Jewish distinctiveness, something which makes the "Jews-as-universalists" crowd quite uncomfortable. Unfortunately for Israel, the Arabs seem to be aware of this self-destructive quirk among liberal, universalistic Jews and are milking it to their advantage.

★★★

Transnationalism is a route to personal power. For hard-core socialist and cultural Marxists what is as important as ideology is the power they get from instituting their ideology. Power and control is at the heart of leftism, and the more power and control, the better. People who have an inordinate need for power and control become leftist-socialist leaders precisely because socialism is the ideology of the few exercising power over the many, in the name of "the people." Simply because someone lives in America does not mean he abhors grandiose power or believes in limited human control. The demon of power-and-control does not fly with a GPS that automatically passes over the houses of those who, for example, come from Chicago or San Francisco.

The first step toward reaching that power is to remove the one thing standing in the way of the socialist takeover—the core Americans who believe in a distinct Americanism and who will never vote for a multicultural socialist. But by hammering away and demonizing conservatives and those who believe in Judeo-Christian American exceptionalism, the Left hopes to shrink the number of Americans who will continue identifying America with distinctiveness.

There is something else in the brew that is turning out to be even more effective; and that is, the erasing in each Western country of any national and cultural distinctiveness—*transnationalism*—so that populations in particular countries that are continuing to subscribe to nationalism will feel more and more isolated. If the entire Western world rejects nationalism, then each leader within the socialist fraternity can remind his citizens of the worldwide move away from nationalism and specific culture. In each Western country, multiculturalists have been able to marginalize nationalists as aberrant, extreme, or xenophobic. However, nationalism is uplifting and terrific if one's nation is America.

Socialism is being augmented through the stealth power of what are called NGOs—transnational, non-government organizations of unelected officials who set the tone—be it in policy, attitude, law, or in support of homogenized culture as to how Western societies should operate. The unelected officials of the NGOs are often wielding greater power than elected congressional officials, especially since so much can be effectuated through executive fiat and courts without worrying what Congress says. It is effective because the left-wing media delivers the internationalist, socialist message and labels those who assert nationalism as Neanderthals out of step with international law and norms. International law, as the higher form of law by which all countries should live, is being used by our own domestic internationalists to weaken American sovereignty. America's internationalist set would much rather identify with NGO peers in Geneva and The Hague than as mere Americans tied to those "hicks" in Boise, Idaho.

One of the most influential NGOs is the *Alliance for Civilizations*, which endeavors to make a homogenized, new Western civilization denuded of any particular conservative, indigenous distinctiveness. In a way, it is proposing a New Global Order. It is largely funded by oil rich sheiks from the Muslim world. They see it as Islam's way to take over the West without having to use force. They fund it just as they fund so many departments in our U.S. colleges and universities for propaganda purposes. They have learned they can radically change our civilization simply by buying it.

The *Alliance* talks of multiculturalism, openness, and inclusion for all things Islamic and how much more enriched our societies will become by learning the "beautiful lessons" of Islam. Forget what they do back home in Saudi Arabia. The face they present to a gullible Western world and to those eager to change their own home culture is democracy, peace, understanding, and religious rights. NGOs of this sort have tremendous influence in shaping State Department policy among the political glitterati, who are wined and dined and receive honors, rewards, and high-level access for attending and later promoting the agenda.

Liberal Western leaders do not have the stomach to battle a forward-marching Islam, while the internationalists, like Mr. Obama, see Islam as a powerful ally in diminishing the Judeo-Christian distinctiveness of America. Both, therefore, whitewash all of Islam's horrors. Liberals have created a romantic, figment Islam, an ideology that simply wants to sip coffee at a café on Manhattan's Upper Westside while discussing Schopenhauer and the latest *New York Times* Sunday magazine. After all, *we are all the same.* They have little fear of an Islamized West, since those of the Islamic world they come in contact with are not peasants from Kabul but wealthy sheiks or academicians who vacation in Monte Carlo and shop at Harrods's in London. Mr. Obama is the poster child for the new transnationalism—a cocktail of economic socialism and cultural Marxism, mixed with bitterness against colonialism, flavored by a deep empathy and adoration of things Islamic. He is the official spokesperson with a broad outward smile that masks the authoritarianism and seething anger within.

The Tower of Babel is an episode in Genesis that speaks of the transnational mindset similar to that of the left-wing leaders we are now witnessing.

It is from the smallest of chapters but one of the most illuminating and important in Genesis 11:1-9. So as to consolidate their power, leaders came together and did away with distinctiveness, separate languages, and separate sovereignties: "And the land was of one language and one speech" or attitude. There was no ethos of individualism. National distinctiveness was removed. Men were governed in a post-flood world under a closed fraternity of leaders sharing authority and ideology.

Only one thing stood in the way of their hegemony—God. Each nation living according to God engenders a specificity and religious identification that challenges universalism and sameness. And so they came to build a tower to vanquish God Almighty who stood in their way of hegemony in sameness. They wished to be secular, unbound to God and His codes. "Let us build a tower...toward the heaven...and let us make us a name." They wished to be called by that which was their goal—secularism.

But "God confounded them and their single language." No longer would they live by a single language and attitude, but as individuals, and in different lands with different languages. After the fall of the Tower, men returned to their lands and reinstituted distinct cultures: "And the Lord scattered them all across the earth." No more hegemonies or transnationalism. No more international sameness. The fraternity of leaders controlling humanity was dissolved as men moved on and created new societies across the earth, free of globalism and far away from each other so that nations and peoples would no longer be forcibly united under one set of international laws and mores.

The next historical episode in the Bible is: "And God called to Abraham..." (Genesis: 12:1). Man finds God and God finds man when lands are separate and cultures are distinct. God speaks to the individual, a singular man named Abraham.

★★★

Many people by nature dislike *national identity and distinctiveness*. They do not like having to make judgments; it is easier not to. They can do whatever they like or whatever fits their pleasure without worrying about a moral or sexual code that requires demarcations. Subscribing to a world where we are all the same gives them a sense of belonging to something global and makes them feel worldly and is, for them, a badge of sophistication. It is much easier to blend into worldliness than have to defend a specific identity. It is much easier to simply accept the world's constant criticism of America and Israel and not be considered separate by defending it. People unwilling to be separate from the global crowd are emotionally weak people. They are globalists. By fooling themselves that we are all the same and everything is the same, the globalists need not fear what may be coming over the horizon, since everything is benign and harmless, simply an alternative view or alternative lifestyle posing no threat or danger. This is the comforting appeal of *moral relativism.*

They need not fear Islam despite what they daily see around the world, for moral relativism lulls them into the false consolation that everything, including Islam, is the same and what we see are simply aberrations, controllable if we but provide the proper conditions and understanding. It is a "religion of peace," they say, and its aggression must be our fault, requiring that we tolerate more, understand more, and accommodate and appease more. People are no different today than during the time of Jeremiah, who cried out but was thrown in jail because he warned about that which the people did not want to hear. His words upset the comfortable lifestyle and parties they were convinced would go on forever.

★ ★ ★

We may be witnessing the first time in history that a civilization is *volunteering* to surrender itself, and as a culture be overrun. Fifty years of demonizing America has concluded in too many elites no longer wanting America. Too many liberals no longer even want it to exist as a distinct culture. Does anyone actually think that Mr. Obama, who has spent his life criticizing the Founders and our Constitution, sought the Presidency so as to affirm the Founding Fathers? He came not to praise and fortify it, but to transform it.

Smugsters deride the whole notion of a unique and *historic American civilization*; and when forced to confront the fact of America having had one, scandalize it, call it racist and oppressive, and find fault with every single American Founding Father or Mother. Those who disdain distinctiveness ironically have no qualms with the distinctiveness of other cultures or religions; in fact, they laud them. It makes them multicultural, in their mind the highest virtue. At the very moment they deride their own culture, they romanticize other cultures or our religious opposites. They attribute all their personal obstacles to having been a victim of their own culture, while see the alien culture as their salvation if they could just have been born into it.

This is at the core of today's leftism and why it views Islam, our culture's opposite, as some sort of glorious panacea, just as it did before with communism. Ah, they say: "If only we would allow Islam to be real Islam and not, through our colonialism, force it to be what it certainly does not want to be, what a wonderful world this would be." They said the same thing about communism: "If only America would stop its aggression and allow Russia to be what it could really be, what a glorious world this would be." For today's multiculturalists, Islam has become the imagined utopia, the romanticized dream. As Michael Savage, the author and talk-show host, correctly said: "*Liberalism is a mental disorder*," a personal mental disorder, reflecting a very troubled person.

The cultural and economic battle we are in now between liberalism and conservatism is the battle over *national identity* and *distinctiveness*. No nation can survive as itself without a distinct and special national identity. Identity is tied to religion, culture, and nationalism. Socialism and liberalism have come to uproot that identity. It hates nationalism, is uncomfortable with distinctive religion, and lukewarm regarding national culture. Secularists think religion is inconsequential to identity. Many of our clergy treat religion with casualness and as something in service to popular liberal isms, even those that undermine traditional values and family life. They are wrong. Unfortunately, Islam does understand how important serious religion is. We will either fall into socialism and permanent cultural Marxism or overcome it. *This is a fight to the finish!*

The choice is between nationalism and self-interest vs. transnationalism with our interest way behind. The fight is whether we are a nation defined by a distinctive national character, the Judeo-Christian. We must be willing to say *Judeo-Christian*. We are not simply a democracy and capitalist. I believe that in order to win this fight we must be willing to assert an *identity*, something that makes some of our country clubbers a little uneasy: *Judeo-Christian*. The other side is fighting hard and viciously every minute. They do not rest. It is up to us to fight harder and longer. We cannot allow them to silence or demoralize us. To allow that is unbecoming and contrary to the American personality and the spirit of liberty and independence. As for me, I am honored and proud to be part of this battle. It is not only a battle for the soul of America, but the classic and on-going battle for the soul of man and the morality and values of God.

TWENTY-FOUR

Let's Roll!

[It's your country—fight for it!]

Aside from voting, what can each of us do to help America save its historic identity so that the blessings and opportunities we had will be available to our children? How do we stop the Left's path of destruction? One thing is for sure: they will not stop on their own. No matter how many legislative victories they win and changes are made, they will never cease from their obsessive need for social engineering and redistributing. For them, there is no point of satisfaction until they have total control.

We are fortunate that our Founders built a country based on local control. While exciting debates take place in our nation's capital, the events that impact our daily lives and communities most directly occur in decision centers close to home. Unfortunately, the Left also knows this, which is why they are pouring money out to the states and sending in activists to transform the local institutions that directly impact American life and the attitudes and values that will shape our children. Those wishing to impose Islam know this as well.

Winning this battle requires, on our part, face to face verbal confrontation. We must be *assertive*. It is emotionally hard to do that, and not all stomachs are so inclined, but we have no choice. We can no longer simply coast and think everything will turn out right just because this, after all, is America. Nor can watching Sean Hannity, a great American, substitute for what we need to actively do the next morning.

We tend to think that all decisions in America are made by votes in the legislatures or by judges in court. It is not so. The one thing the Left has taught us since 1964 is that most legislative and institutional decisions are made after decision makers look at what the people in the street are saying and doing. Just about every cultural and societal shift that has taken place in our lifetime has been a consequence of what happened, first, in the streets or at gatherings of citizens. Be it ending the Vietnam War, the women's movement, Black power, capitulations at City Hall, or bringing to trial George Zimmerman after the police lacked enough evidence to arrest him—everything took place because of what was happening on the ground. The Left has shaped and changed this country because, unlike us conservatives, they had the guts to go into the streets or raise their voices at public meetings.

When we think of most of the major public activist figures of the last fifty years, they have come from the Left and made their name and causes known from being *on the ground*. When the Left holds rallies and protests, tens of thousands come. Perhaps too many conservatives think that it is unreligious to be outspoken, assertive, and demand their rights. I hope I have satisfactorily made the case that being nice is no excuse for allowing others to take your liberty or rob you of what is yours, especially when we are talking about a heritage and a country's very identity. Haven't we read of Jesus going into the market in the Temple and overthrowing the tables of money exchangers?

Each of us has to muster the inner fortitude to face off, one-on-one, personally, against those on the school and library board who are proposing a change we know is part of cultural Marxism and socialist leveling. Yes, we will have to go face to face against other citizens who want to force Koran readings on our children at school, who demand special prayer rooms there that we know no Christian would ever be given, and who ask that our children participate in Ramadan activities.

We must have the courage to go eyeball to eyeball and not blink when superintendents decide to introduce obscene sexual learning programs into the curriculum. Everyone seems so preoccupied with environmental pollution, but what about the pollution of our children's minds and souls? When someone says we cannot mention the name of God or that a nativity scene must be taken down—fight back, raise Cain, and find lawyers. Don't just accept it as a done deal. Often these threats come from people who do not even live in the district but disrespect us and our ways so much they self-righteously feel they can uproot local traditions and monuments that have been part of the community for 150 years. There is rarely, for them, a monetary cost for their invasions for, too often, we give in and so they have no court costs or organizing costs.

No, we do not have to tolerate the intolerable. Why? Because we say so! We don't lose our right to citizenship and free speech the moment we leave the confines of our house. And we don't lose our authority and final decisions for the welfare of our children the moment they leave the house.

This war cannot be fought by our soldiers outside our borders because the multiculturalists and those intent on destroying what we hold dear are operating inside our borders. There are groups aligned with the multiculturalists who cynically exploit and speak in the name of democracy, free speech, religious freedom, and brotherhood, but we all know that if, God forbid, they ever got power they would stop democracy and forbid our free speech and our freedom of religion. We would become *dhimmis*, second-class citizens in our own land. This battle, as we see in Europe, takes place school board to street to neighborhood to entire sections of cities. Those who thought that capitulation was acceptable for just one school, one street, just one…have lost entire sections of their cities, their safety, and their freedom.

Many conservatives think that articles, books, blogs, talk radio, and *FOX News* can win the battle for us. They cannot. These things merely verify our beliefs, which is certainly good. But only action on the ground, in the streets, at meeting halls, in protests, at school boards, local community councils, zoning boards, state houses, and in the offices of congressmen will win the battle. It is action that we need, action from us, we the people. After all, we are the people too. If we don't fight for our way of life ourselves, we will lose it. Each world belongs to those who fight for it. In Goethe's *Faust* there is a wonderful line which says: "Freedom is everything, but it must be reclaimed every day." We need to relearn what we have forgotten due to the unprecedented ease of American life. The preservation of that which is necessary for survival is an everyday battle. We freedom loving Americans will not be spared this dictum of life.

The other side will not back down if they are not challenged face to face. They are on a mission. But they are not giants, geniuses, or miracle men. If strongly confronted by people who show determination, conviction, and no sign of backing down, most of them will yield. Look at the success of the Tea Party that took to the streets, the town halls, who raised voices, and who spoke back. The decision makers knew they would be there wherever they went. Look what happened when New Yorkers, and the nation, protested against building a Mosque of Triumph on the very site of the ashes of those who were killed in the name of Islam. Look what happened when New Yorkers protested in the streets against holding a civilian court trial in their city, instead of a military tribunal, for the mastermind behind 9/11, with Federal authorities labeling him a criminal instead of an enemy-combatant. We have not won enough because we have not personally faced off enough against them or been in the streets as we must be if we are to win.

Yes, we can raise our voices—and loudly. They do; we can. There is nothing wrong with them knowing we mean business. Expect them to call you all sorts of names: racist, bigot, mean-spirited, uncompassionate. It is their modus operandi and has worked for them...up till now.

★ ★ ★

Did you ever ask yourself, why the Left is able to rev itself up in righteous indignation? It is because they feel robbed of a certain right or feel mistreated. I see through their feigned victimhood, but it does show the power innate in righteous anger. Such anger on the Left convinces, sways, and frightens people.

Well, shouldn't we have some righteous anger after being told for fifty years we have no right to the rights given to us by God and the Founding Fathers? Shouldn't we have some righteous anger knowing people are deliberately working to steal our heritage, weaken us, and jeopardize our physical security? Shouldn't we display some righteous indignation after fifty years of being called racist, bigoted, and phobic by people who mock our religious values and family life and who, themselves, are bigoted and phobic against us. They never make a decision based on what is good for *us*, rather for themselves and their preferred groups. Yes, we should be angry! Most conservative Americans are humble by nature. It is an endearing quality. But being humble cannot translate into forfeiting our self-respect. Besides, as I have shown, we hold the moral high ground, not those on the Left who are pushing moral relativism.

We cannot give up our civic heritage simply because Barack Obama and his associates do not like it. My family fought in wars on behalf of this country while his family was still in Kenya. We cannot give up our liberty and greatness simply because Bill Ayers, a 1960s radical student bomber, tells college audiences "America is in decline." If America is in decline, it is not because of the American people and spirit, but because President Obama, a protégé of Mr. Ayers, is governing in a way to bring us to decline. The aging Mr. Ayers hopes, with words of defeatism, to demoralize and bring America down as he did when he was younger and bombs were thought more effective than words—same goal, different ammunition.

★★★

We should be inspired by the individual person of action. It is remarkable what one person can do when he stands proud and pushes back. Look at Jan Brewer, Governor of Arizona, but one lady alone, fighting against the immense power of an Obama administration that refuses to let her perform her duty of protecting her citizens from pillagers coming from Mexico into the yards and streets of innocent citizens. Look at Sheriff Joe Arpaio who, alone, is protecting his people from rape and assault despite all the terrible names and concocted legal action, the witch hunt, coming from Obama's Attorney General against him. And consider the solitary judge who told the Obama administration they have no Constitutional authority to bypass Congress and the will of the people and make laws by fiat.

Look at Congressman Peter King who is called all sorts of names by CAIR because he insists on finding out who the dangerous elements are in the American Muslim community intimidating citizens. King does not back down. Look at those in Dade County, Florida, who knew their votes were being stolen by liberal lawyers from New York City who had come down to use "hanging chad" legal tricks to disqualify or change votes the Cubans knew were for George Bush and not Al Gore. They rushed through the doors where the lawyers were doing their trickery and said, "*Stop. This is fraud.*" Articles didn't do it. Prayer didn't do it. Appeals to good will didn't do it. Bold face to face action did it! And because of that we had a President and Vice President who fought the war on terror and classified it as such, instead of a President who would have looked at it as a mere criminal matter as did his predecessor after the first World Trade Center bombing in 1993. Real action by a few saves lives!

The Left is pro-active and on offense all the time, in fact, engaging in property damaging action. In Dade County, a few brave citizens simply showed resolve and a willingness to place one's body in action, something Republicans and conservatives seldom do on the local front. Politics is not a house of worship, and the streets are not pews. We act one way in worship and must act a different way when responsible confrontation is required. Each is necessary and each is appropriate in its realm. As Ecclesiastes says, *A time to…and a time to…*

We cannot rely solely on members of Congress to do our job. So much of American life takes place beyond their purview and jurisdiction, and they have only so many hours and, like all of us, limited energy. Moreover, they will only be as strong as the *vocal* support from back home and what they see on the streets of their district. The Left knows this and that is why they have tens of thousands of activists planted all over this country.

No one can do everything, but each of us can choose one or two projects and make them our own. Janet Folger from Faith 2 Action is a splendid example of an energetic, powerhouse individual who spearheads activist projects, as do many in the Tea Party. In fact, any person can make their own organization, and any person can stand up and speak.

Preservation of what we have needs activism from regular people. The country will no longer be preserved automatically. Those days are gone. It seems to me that people will need to reconfigure their lives a little to make room for a little bit of conservative political action. We can all start out small, but we need to start out. While it is virtuous to be gentle with your family and genteel with your friends and associates, boldness is needed when up against those hell bent on getting their political way no matter what. A left-wing tornado is sweeping through the land, uprooting everything in its path. It cannot be sweet-talked away: "I cannot keep silent, for I have heard the sound of the trumpet. I have heard the battle cry" (Jeremiah 4:19).

The first thing we need to change is *attitude*. For too long we have accepted the media propaganda that those who verbally tear down our country do so out of a heightened sense of concern and morality. They do not. It comes from an unsavory desire to mock and destroy. The Talmud, long ago, had their number: "What they call building is, really, destruction." They are motivated by the active demons of destruction and envy still lurking in the hearts of many men. Knowing they do not hold the moral high ground but are spurred by a desire to throw us into the burial ground should bolster us toward active defense of what we hold dear. They despise what we love. They do not deserve our respect. Let us resolve to publicly discuss every issue and subject the Left declares we are not allowed to talk about! We should question, openly, everything regarding Barack Obama and the people he appoints and those surrounding him. We now go into this conflict with an attitude of valor.

★★★

Pastor friends remark to me of their exasperation over parishioners not wishing to get involved even in voting. They quote: "Render unto Caesar that which is Caesar's and unto God that which is His." I cannot accept that because in this country Caesar is not imposed but elected by us, and the same with all the little Caesars down the line. Furthermore, there is a religious component to this battle, since religious rights and activities are under assault. President Obama, as mentioned, speaks of freedom of worship as opposed to freedom of religion. Believe me when I say that this is a war against biblical Judaism and Christianity.

The secular Left has been more active in politics than us because that is where their energy and activism is directed. We, on the other hand, have poured our energy and activism into church or religious life. If we are to match them, we will need to channel more of our energies into politically conservative projects. To feel good about such redirection of energy, we need to understand that these activities are indeed needed to preserve our religious freedoms and, yes, constitute a religious undertaking.

Beyond that, as I have shown throughout this book, our rights to speech, property, self-defense, and to make choices out of our free will are granted not by government but God Himself. These are, therefore, religious tenets. "The God who gave us life gave us liberty." This is the crux and animating principle of the Judeo-Christian ethos our Founding Father's believed in. For that principle they were willing to give their lives and sacred honor. These rights are already being reduced by the Left and Obamaites, and this is just the beginning. Denying me *real* free speech is akin to denying me hearing the shofar blast on Rosh Hashanah. Denying the right to self-defense is akin to denying participation of Christians in Communion.

Obama's proposals for radical disarmament put all of us and those we love at great risk. Protecting life and loved ones is a *religious* issue. We have been placed here on this earth not simply to save souls but people as well. It is not only about the Kingdom Come but, when it comes to people, the earthly kingdom here. Individual faith is not enough; it should be intertwined with a sense of peoplehood among the faithful. Self-defense is a biblical mandate, written in Scripture, not only for ourselves but in defending others' right to live, and live in liberty. We learn that from: "Thou shalt not stand idly by while the blood of thy neighbor is shed" (Leviticus 19:16), which is expanded to include his liberty, without which one has no chance to live with dignity. Those of us who are not soldiers engage in self-defense by voting and actively asserting. Hands so pure as to eschew involvement are not pure but *antiseptic*, devoid of life.

Beyond continued opportunities for children and loved ones, I want America to survive simply because it is America; because it has been the single greatest beacon of liberty, moral clarity, and goodness the world has ever known—more outstanding than Rome, Greece, or the Kingdoms of David and Solomon in ancient Israel. I could not go to my deathbed fulfilled and happy knowing that a few decades after my death, the unique and historic America would have ceased to exist as a vibrant expression of its Judeo-Christian self. A world without a strong and free America is unthinkable to me. Make no mistake, the only thing keeping this world safe from the sword of the crescent is America. If America were to weaken, the world, I believe, could enter the Dark Ages once again. So let us reclaim America's Judeo-Christian spirit. "Blow the trumpets in Zion. Sound the alarm on my holy hill" (Joel 2:1).

If left to themselves, without the heavy hand of left-wing elitists, Americans can handle every challenge, vanquish every foe, and solve every problem. It has been a sweet land of liberty because of its dedicated, hard working, and civilized people. It is a profoundly remarkable place and idea. It has been my greatest privilege to have been born and raised here, and an honor to be called an American.

So...let's roll! Let's do the job. Fight, fight! Let's take our country back. It's our country, fight for it! It belongs to those who love it, not those who want to transform it. It belongs to those who, without qualification, say: *I'm proud to be an American*. It belongs to those who work for it and give, not those who deride it or simply sponge off it.

There should be no more guilt, only pride. Stand proud! Push back. We can do it. I know we can. After all, we are today's Minute Men. We are Americans. Americans!

Contact information:

To contact Rabbi Spero, go to his website at:

caucusforamerica.com

To contact the publisher, go to the *Push Back* website:

PushBackAmerica.com